520 TINY
– BUT TERRIFIC –
'HOW TO' TIPS
FOR JOB SEARCHES AND
CAREER
IMPROVEMENT

(United States; English Version)

a compilation of the series of e-books

Dawn D. Boyer, Ph.D.
Resume Rewriter &
Job Search Advisor

COPYRIGHT 2019

FOREWARD

I have been providing job search advice as well as rewriting resumes, for over 20 years now. Each time I get a new client, I teach them something new about the job search process. There are so many 'lessons learned' from being on this side of job search efforts – including lessons I learned personally as a job candidate – as well as being on the receiving end of resumes.

I have rattled my brain shaking my head at the mistakes some job seekers make.

I wrote 'Ask The Expert' column stories for the *Virginian Pilot's Inside Business* (a weekly publication). I produced about 60 stories (to date, as of September 2019), and well as shared the stories with other career websites and businesses. About 2012, I stumbled across HARO – the organization that assisted reporters connecting to experts in their Help A Reporter Out service. When I see a request for information about job searches and resume writing, I respond with subject matter expert (SME) tips and advice to reporters' questions. In the last six years I have been cited as a SME advisor in about 40 articles in books, newspapers, and online websites.

For each piece of advice I offered to news reporters and writers, I logged the original question, as well as the answers I provided. In most cases, the reporter culled out just the most important pieces (the 'sound bite'). They didn't use the more extensive explanations.

My log grew to over 150 pages. I decided it's time to share my wealth of knowledge with job seekers who are just trying to grab a quick piece of advice to better their job search activities.

I compiled a series of short e-books to make it less painful and more useful, topics that provide quick reads. Each e-book focuses on modern, easy to digest explanations about the 'who' or 'how to' use the tips and suggestions wisely.

The series provided some 'how to' guidance on how to write resumes, prepare for job searches and interviews, and other topics of 'need to know' information, with job search tools that truly showcase the job seeker's capabilities.

I hope you enjoy this compilation of the series of e-books – all in one – and use this information to improve and accelerate your job search to a successful conclusion of receipt of a letter of an offer of employment!

NEED YOUR RESUME REWRITTEN?

Visit this website to review what Dr. Boyer can do to help you revise and upgrade your current resume and review her levels of services and current pricing.

http://dboyerconsulting.com/resume-writing/

http://dboyerconsulting.com/resume-writing/stage-one/

TABLE OF CONTENTS

Career Change 9
How to Change Careers 11
Resignation - Giving Notice 17
Education & Capability...............................25
Education, Training, and Certifications to
Enhance Your Job Capabilities to Land that
Next Job..27
Experience Building 35
Job Seeker Business Portfolios 37
Must Have Job Skills 43
How To Get Job Experience...........................51
Equating Volunteering to Work Experience on
Your Resume...59
Job Search 65
Avoiding Age Bias in the Job Search..............67
Creating Job Alerts 75
First Steps After Losing A Job 87
How to Determine the Best Asking Salary for
the Job 95
How to Look for a Job on the 'Down Low' 107
Job Fair Advantages......................................115
Job Overqualification, Age Discrimination, and
the Law 125
Job Search Steps and Resources 133
Passive Job Search Activities And Preparation
....139
Reading and Interpreting Job Descriptions...147
Researching Your Future Employer and the Job

Posting..155
Researching Your Next 'Employer of Choice'
....163
Resume Farming for Job Seekers................169
Reviewing the Job Announcement 175
Scam Job Announcements............................185
Using Linkedin To Turn on a Job Search 195

References 205
Obtaining References 207
Resume Writing 213
Leadership Wording In Resumes 215
Degrees Vs On The Job Training – Resume
Description...223
Listing Technical Skills in a Resume 233
What Not to Include in a Resume 245
Resume Gaps – Addressing the Workforce
Absence...253
Resume Key Words and Language..............263
Making a Resume 'Automatic Tracking System'
(ATS) Friendly...271
How Far Back and How Much Job History ...279
How to Write a Cover Letter 287
Formatting A Professional Resume 291
How and Why to Avoid Lying On Your Resume
....303
Avoiding Filler and Passive Words in Your
Resume by Substituting Action Verbs 309
Metrics to Build Capability Believability 315
Beating the Automated Tracking System (ATS)
– Getting Past the Firewall............................323
Keep Your Resume Updated and Dynamic..331
Bio, Resume, CV, GS: What's the Difference?
....339
Elements of a Perfect Cover Letter...............347
Creating Your First Resume – Elements to
Include 353

Why Recruiters Will Not Call You Back 361
Converting an Objective Statement to a 'Years of Experience' Listing....................................371

Interviews 379
Filler (Killer) Words in Interviews 381
Background Checks for Job Searches 387
Speculation Work & Skills Testing 395
Avoiding Answering 'Illegal to Ask' Interview Questions..403
Interviews – What To Know Before You Go .413

Compensation...419
Benefits & Compensation Questions And Considerations..421
Salary Negotiations......................................429

Lessons Learned 435
Job Search Lessons-Learned for Government Contracting Positions....................................437

About The Author 447
Hire the Author for Publishing Your Work 450
Connect with the Author...........................451
About The Book 452

CAREER CHANGE

HOW TO CHANGE CAREERS

Nothing is more frustrating than to have a full career behind you and you decide – hmmm – "I would rather spend the rest of my working career working as a …" (for example, dog groomer). Unfortunately, no one will look at or consider your career resume full of juicy metrics and achievement as a Fortune 500 corporate CEO. (I can hear them now "… they are overqualified.") What is a job seeker to do? The mindset is essentially to 'rebrand' oneself.

1.   Start off by studying what job skills are necessary for the job, field, or industry in which you are targeting your next job search. What are those skills that are minimally required? Do you have those or need to take classes or go back to school? Make your list and start working on learning or polishing those job specific skills towards your new career.

2.   Get computer software savvy – and I mean *really* computer savvy. Too many folks think they are 'tech savvy' if they can turn on a computer. When employers seek hires today, they want a candidate able to turn on the computer, but to operate the software. There are working class folks who can't set

margins or indented spaces in a word document or don't know how to enter formulas to a spreadsheet. Employers demand workers who have embraced technology, but continually learn how to improve knowledge on specific software and hardware (which showcases analytical skills). While learning computers – get tool and technology savvy, too. If you have been stuck in the office all your career, but want start working on cars, learn how to change the tire and oil and transmission fluid. Look for opportunities to start as the dealership 'yard jockey' (moving cars around for repairs and maintenance) and work yourself up to assisting certified mechanics; ask the dealership to send you to manufacturer's training.

3. Obtaining training doesn't have to be expensive. If you are serious about becoming a dog groomer (or whatever your desired career job), then start watching Internet videos. You don't need a prime account to YouTube to watch dozens, if not hundreds of 'how-to' videos on just about any topic or subject.

4. Adult-Learning classes in your local city are usually available for free or very low cost. Search online for the name of your local city and "Adult Learning" in the search. You may find some inexpensive courses related to business, education, or hobbies. You may find some business-related classes: Microsoft Office Word, Excel, and

PowerPoint, QuickBooks accounting
software, Adobe Creative Cloud suite, as
well as hobby-related classes such as
painting, pottery, and home-buying for first
time buyers classes.

5. Look for apprenticeships – even if you are in
    your forties or fifties – local businesses may
    be interested in hiring on an 'old-timer' as a
    mutual symbiosis arrangement. The mature
    worker can provide subject matter expertise
    on finance, accounting, buying a business,
    and the business owner or manager can
    provide hands-on training for the new skill
    (of dog grooming) from calming an animal,
    shampooing, and then grooming.
    Understand these are not your typical
    'internships' like a college graduate would
    look for.   Ask for the training in lieu of a
    paycheck as an option. (You may have to
    sign a non-compete document, so you don't
    take business away from your trainer
    afterwards!)

6. Non-profit organizations often beg for
    volunteers, as well as low-to-no pay
    assistance. Trying to become an event
    planner – go knocking on doors and offer
    your services to plan any of their fundraising
    events, even if you have to work for free or
    a commission on the 'donations' at the end
    of the event.   Your goal is to (a) get more
    experience under your belt, (b) get known
    as the planner in the community (including
    your name or business name on the
    marketing materials that go out about the

event, (c) get exposure to those folks more likely to hire others to plan events, and (d)

7.   Join the Peace Corps. Yes, they are still around! One you join you will receive 'pre-service' training, including: Technical (agriculture to community development), Language (based on the geographic community in which you may be assigned), Cross-cultural (behaviors, cultural practices, protocol, resiliency), Health (for self and to teach others), Safety and Security (including transportation, gender issues, bystander intervention, avoiding unwanted attention, and emergency action planning).

8.   Join trade organization and take advantage of their available training. The organization that used to be known as the American Society for Training & Development (ASTD) changed their name to Association of Talent Development (ATD) in 2014. Once you have the capability to training others, that often provides you the perfect opportunity learn something yourself! Many a teacher has had to learn the lesson plan for the next day to teach it to students as a new topic.

9.   Search for local business incubators / accelerators which provide mentors who may have networking contacts they can introduce you to potential businesses and entrepreneurs who can use the mature worker's knowledge and skills sets as a Director, Manager, Supervisor, Team or Project Lead or a Subject Matter Expert in a

one field where the knowledge or skills parallel or can easily be transferred to another field. (Accounting skills in corporate finance transfer just fine over to a dog grooming business.)

10. Look for a new health care or vocational career. There are some health organizations that offer free tuition and training in exchange for the learner working for the organization for a set number of years after graduation. Shipyards often are short on qualified welders, so they offer welding programs (and sometimes an accompanying Associates degree!) for graduates with a guaranteed minimum salary and compensation. Usually the payback period is about two years (24 months). Some organizations will pay the graduate just a little less than what others in the same job are being paid to 'recoup' the cost of the training over a long period of time.

RESIGNATION - GIVING NOTICE

Resignation (noun): an act of retiring or giving up a position. "he announced his resignation"; *synonyms:* departure, leaving, standing down, stepping down, retirement; giving up, vacating, relinquishment, renunciation, surrender, abdication; *informal* - quitting; "his resignation from his government post" (dictionary.com)

A formal letter of resignation provides a current employer with the notification that you are going to part company and employment with them and are providing them with an appropriate amount of notice, so the current employer has sufficient time to recruit for and replace you with an equally-qualified candidate.

There is excitement, worry, and possibly anxiety and stress when you decide it's time to move on from a current employer to the next in your career progression. It's best to plan way in advance for what steps need to be taken to ensure your departure works well for all parties involved, as well as preparing for unforeseen circumstances. Planning to move on to a better and more upwardly mobile or better paying position also includes planning those steps just as carefully as you rewrite your resume for that next job.

1)   Ensure you have updated your resume (if
       you think your resume is not that good, it's
       probably sucks royally). Find and hire a
       professional resume writer to help you
       showcase your KSAs (Knowledge, Skills,
       and Abilities) as well as your achievements
       and accomplishments for current and past
       employers. Collect all your past
       performance evaluations and print them for
       your records – or – email them to yourself to
       have at home or stored to the cloud for
       reference.

2)   Prepare for the possibility that if you quit
       one job, it could take weeks or months to
       find another job if you don't already have
       one lined up. Understand that quitting a job
       without having another one waiting could
       spell financial disaster. If you have health
       insurance with the current company, and
       your future employer's benefits won't start
       for 90 days after hire, then you will have to
       convert your health insurance policy to
       COBRA, and may be responsible for paying
       the full monthly benefits premium, plus a
       processing or administrative fee.

3)   Ensure your LinkedIn profile is updated and
       loaded for everything you can possibly input
       to the profile. Concentrate on the 'skills'
       words and phrases as that section is the
       'search engine brain' in LinkedIn for
       recruiters and headhunters to search for
       your skills in your profile. Concentrate on
       connecting with past employers, co-
       workers, supervisors (ask them for

references / recommendations specifically in the LinkedIn platform), peers, and other connections in the industry, as well as joining industry or trade groups to increase your potential job search and networking scope. The optimal (and 'vital') number of recommendations and referrals on LinkedIn to ensure more attention from future recruiters and headhunters is 10 (minimally). Revisit your LinkedIn profile (daily, if not every 2-3 days). Interact with connections, comment on posts inside groups, provide recommendations to others, and communicate via LinkedIn with others to drive up your visibility.

4) Ensure your resume is posted on as many job boards as possible (e.g., CareerBuilder, Monster, Indeed, and your state's employment commission online job boards). If worried that your company's recruiting department has access to resumes (via the big resume databases via a contract license to conduct resume searches), post your resume on job boards using an 'anonymous' name and note that is it anonymous on the resume (e.g., instead of noting Suzy Smith (your real name), put 'Anonymous Jobseeker' in the name place at the top). In the 'current employer' place, instead of putting the current company name, put ("company name available after initial phone contact"). Recruiters will understand you are searching for a job 'under the radar' of your current employer.

5) Collect your list of referrals and references –
written letters are great, but nowadays can
be forged. Future employers and human
resources departments will want full names,
job titles, companies the referrals work for,
phone numbers and email addresses to
contact those references. Job seekers
should have at least three professional
(work-related) references, and at least one
personal reference.

6) Ensure you have all the phone numbers,
addresses, and points of contact you need
from your current employer if you need
those POC for referrals, references, and/or
potential networking resources. If you have
a list of clients (not for poaching in the next
job – that would be unethical, but used
instead for job search purposes), ensure
you have that contact list stored safely. If
you store those contacts in your personal
phone (or business phone) ensure your
contact list is backed up on your personal
computer (or to the cloud) for access later.

7) Ensure 'how-to' lists and job task
instructions are written up and available for
anyone who will be filling your empty seat (if
they are replacing you with another
employee). You want to leave a good
impression behind and to ensure your
departure is as painless as possible for your
current employer. Don't make the company
you're your ex-boss) go through a painful
and time-consuming period to train the new
person. Leave clear step-by-step

instructions behind for how to perform job tasks. If you are in an IT position, especially if heavily involved in software coding and programming, make sure everything is not only documented, but peers and supervisors know where to look for that documentation. If your supervisor has not gotten on the 'cross-training' train, then put a bug in their ear to start cross-training peers and co-workers in each other's jobs. This not only allows the company to have back-up when co-workers are absent, it lessens the burden of training others after you leave. This also provides the company or your supervisor more incentive to provide a great referral for you when you move to your next job.

8)   After giving notice, ensure you have been and continue to be politically correct in your communications and interactions with all your co-workers, peers and supervisors. Do NOT send a massive email to all your co-workers dumping angry comments about your discontent with the company or alternatively 'sappy-happy sorry to leave you' and I will miss you communications. These are potential firing offenses and not a good use of the company's assets. Ask your supervisor if company policy would allow them to write a letter of reference for you on company letterhead (some companies allow this practice, others do not). Ensure your financial ties with the company are clean (all travel or other reimbursements submitted, company

equipment returned, 401(k) plans auto-debits are cancelled, and credit cards or company vehicles handed back to accounting).

9)   If you don't already have a new job waiting - start your 'alternative,' new, full-time job - start applying to other companies for work. Rarely, but it does happen, a company will provide an offer letter of employment to a candidate, the candidate provides a resignation letter to their current employer, then the offering company may renege or change their mind for a dozen reasons. If the current company won't allow you to remain in the position, then you need to start a new job search immediately. Job searches can take a lot of time so go into the tasks as if it were your new full-time job. Start the job search process – part-time at night for 1-4 hours nightly while still with current employer, and/or 7-8 hours daily applying for jobs during the day – when you are no longer working for your 'current' company.

10)   If you have a new job waiting, ensure you conduct yourself as professional as possible the final two weeks of your current employment tenure. Be transparent, be visible to everyone so they can see what you are doing or not doing. Wrap up tasks that need to be completed. If your current company has hired a replacement, ensure the replacement is well-trained in every aspect of the position and knows the ropes

before you leave. In some cases, a company will decide to forego the two-weeks' notice and terminate same day. For some companies, a same-day release from employment may be a necessity based on the type of job (security, access to company proprietary assets, or other reasons). If you have a future employer's offer in hand, ask about the possibility of starting employment with them earlier during the interview process, as a potential option, if your current employer decides to let you go early. If the future employer is accepting of that condition, you can start earlier. If they are unable to accommodate you, then take the time over the next two weeks to go on a trip you would not have time for otherwise or start/finish a project you have been neglecting for a while!

EDUCATION & CAPABILITY

EDUCATION, TRAINING, AND CERTIFICATIONS TO ENHANCE YOUR JOB CAPABILITIES TO LAND THAT NEXT JOB

When companies are reviewing applicants' resumes for matching experience, knowledge, education, and skill sets against the open job requisition, they want to see what parallels the minimum requirements to the job description. Recruiters look for additional knowledge, education, and skill sets 'above' the minimum requirements that may offer the company an advantage against the market for reaching company organizational goals. Additionally, the job seekers can showcase competitive knowledge, education, and skill sets this is competitive and above those offered by other job seekers.

What types of job skills are 'hot' as a modern job seeker? Math skills, writing and English skills, computer skills including word processing, spreadsheets, and presentations, Internet of Things (IOT), and industry related software (e.g., customer relationship management (CRM) databases and applications; QuickBooks or Peachtree software for accounting and bookkeeping). Additionally, if the job seeker has taken – or has the ability to teach co-workers and peers, any of these topics, they become more valuable in the eye of the future employer: leadership and management, customer and client communications, workplace ethics and anti-harassment, industry safety and emergency procedures (catastrophe recovery), cyber-security protocols (password encryption and avoiding email phishing).

Where does one get those job skills?   If one is lucky, the job seeker may nab an internship when they are young to get hands on skills in a working environment. Many middle- and high-school students are exposed to word processing (MS Word) and presentations (MS PowerPoint) at an early age while they are being trained in keyboarding skills. While modern technology has advanced to the point of being able to convert verbal conversation to text content, it's not perfect. So the human user needs to know how to 'clean up' text content via typing on their computer or hand-held device. Getting clean and accurate typing skills up to speed (over 50 words per minute is ideal for business professionals) is vital for being able to write business documents, memos, e-mails, and other written documents (including contracts) in a timely manner.

The following are venues that job seekers can research and analyze for the best access to training to increase new skills or polish current skills for maintaining or obtaining an advantage against job competitors.   The list starts with the lowest cost training venues and work up to the more costly training options.

1.   YouTube videos are free to watch (after costs of Internet connection are covered) and usually is the best source for most initial

training or 'how-to' do something informal training in the world. For instance, searching on the site using the keywords "How to Format a Word Document" (with timing under four minutes) brought back hundreds of videos discussing formatting, but also saving, inserting, converting to PDF, setting up thesis or dissertation documents, and adding Headers and Footers.

2. Google (search browsers) can be used to search for local classes on just about anything. Using the key search words "Free Training Classes" in the search box, one can click on over half a million results from programming, healthcare, Massive Open Online Courses (MOOCs; offered by prestigious schools – for non-credit-classes), as well as free training classes that also offer certifications. Most of these will be 'online' training (which drastically lowers overheads costs for the providers, as well as increases the number of folks who can take the classes, regardless of their own location).

3. Adult-Learning (local city) classes. Search online for your local city and "Adult Learning" in the key search words, and you may find some free or relatively inexpensive courses related to business, education, or hobbies. These may be government funded, non-profit supported, or economic-development related to increase the available skilled-worker population for local

businesses. While the author lived in Virginia Beach, Virginia, the local city offered adult education classes in a location near the main library that offered some of the following classes: Microsoft Office Word, Excel, and PowerPoint, QuickBooks accounting software, Adobe Creative Cloud suite, as well as painting, pottery, and home-buying for first time buyers classes.

4. Non-Profit Organizations provide some free or subsidized job training. Goodwill (find out more at: https://www.goodwill.org/jobs-training/) provides online learning classes at no cost to participants, as well as customized career services for those seeking jobs, but need specialized assistance (e.g., People with Disabilities, Veterans and Military Families, Older Workers, Youth and Young Adults, Returning Citizens and English (as second) Language Learners. The AARP provides a Senior Community Service Employment Program (find out more about locations and services at: https://www.aarp.org/aarp-foundation/our-work/income/scsep/info-2014/aarp-foundation-scsep-locations.html) which helps older (over 55 years of age) low-income workers find employment (find out more via https://www.aarp.org/aarp-foundation/our-work/income/scsep/). The Small Business Administration, via SCORE, has city and state chapters that offer free or low-fee courses on entrepreneurial 'how-to' classes that are either online or offered in a face-to-face environment to a group of

interested learners (contact the local city chapter for scheduled courses). Find out more via: https://www.score.org/content/take-workshop.

5.   Uncle Sam offers training via Internships and Apprenticeship classes (check out https://www.apprenticeship.gov/become-apprentice for more information). On this website, the government posts apprenticeship positions as well as offer a search engine to research specific geographic areas for potential apprenticeship openings (see more at: https://www.apprenticeship.gov/apprentices hip-finder).

6.   Some large corporations may have apprenticeship programs for skill sets where they can't find enough local talent, so they have to 'home-grow' the skills. One example is the Apprentice School via Newport News Shipbuilding, providing the student welding and other ship-building and ship-repair skills with an entry-level job at the shipyard upon schooling completion.

7.   Training companies offer courses on a pay-by-the-class catalog via individual seminars or webinars, or online, self-paced courses. Udemy, Ed2Go, and Teachable are a few training companies. LinkedIn purchased Lynda.com and now offers access to the training catalog for free to LinkedIn profile owners with a paid subscription. Courses

include: Photography, Adobe Design, Human Resources, Business Strategies, Writing, Business Financials, Marketing, SharePoint, and Speaking.

8. For profit schools – ranging from technical schools (Practical Nursing and other health care jobs such as radiology technicians) to art institutions provide accredited certifications and Associate Degrees in Arts and Sciences (some provide accredited Bachelor's, Master's, and Doctorate degrees). These schools can often provide 'fast-track' learning and classes enable job seekers to train quickly to a trade in as little as 18 months versus a four-year degree with semester or summer breaks. Many for-profit schools offer online courses, while others have brick-and-mortar classes to be attended in person.

9. State Community Colleges and Universities. The trick to finding funding for schooling is if your current income is below a specific maximum level. Apply to the FAFSA government student loan program to attempt to qualify for Pell Grant for tuition, books, and educational expenses (depending upon household income, funding could range between 25%-120% of school and living expenses.

    Apply for the Pell Grant *before* April in each year (income taxes must be filled already to use data in the application). The reason for applying early … once the Pell Grant funding is expended, there is no more free money for the year. After the Pell Grant funding is exhausted, most schools will work with the student to identify and apply for student loans.

Knowing one must pay back these loans, it is prudent to start at the public, lower-cost-tuition, and accredited community colleges. Complete as many transferable classes as possible, then transfer the credits (most four-year universities usually only accept "C" grades or above), into the four-year school to complete the degree-centric courses of the discipline.

10.   LinkedIn has an online skills assessment tool that job seekers can test themselves to showcase their skills through the testing platform. Once your LinkedIn profile is completed, and you have added up to 50 skills (words or phrases) in the Skills Section of your profile, you can take assessment quizzes. LinkedIn provides a badge for that skill (if the assessment minimum test score is 70% or above), which provides job seekers documentation of a mastered skill.[1]

---

[1] Jersin J. (2019, Sep. 17). Announcing Skill Assessments to Help you Showcase Your Skills. Retrieved from:
https://blog.linkedin.com/2019/september/17/announcing-skill-assessments-to-help-you-showcase-your-skills

EXPERIENCE BUILDING

JOB SEEKER BUSINESS PORTFOLIOS

It may be hard to 'show' your work if a business-person, but there are ways of showcasing what you have done in examples, especially in work-related projects (as long as proprietary company secrets aren't released). Different industries have different platforms to share work-based portfolios. Find the best platform to publicly showcase the best work you can demonstrate – this acts as a 'self-referred' recommendation for your capabilities.

1.   A freelance writer can upload a sample of work on their personal (business) website to provide samples to others for what can be done by the freelancer. Or, they can showcase a list of completed work in the form of their customer's referrals – e.g., if the writer has edited content for websites (URL), books for authors (the book link on Amazon or Barnes & Nobel website), or college papers for students (paper posted by student on Google Scholar), the writer can provide a list of URLs where the finished work can be found.

2.   LinkedIn purchased SlideShare in 2012, which allows business professionals to share their presentations of projects, programs, research, or white papers

publicly as a professional business portfolio. LinkedIn purchased the training system, Lynda.com (2015). If the job seeker is a teacher, professor, or instructor, they can post a slide presentation of some of their classroom lectures. If the job seeker has presented a TED-talk, they can provide the slides used in the presentation. SlideShare is part of the LinkedIn learning applications, so someone who is in training, teaching, instruction, or academics can use this to store and share their training modules.

3. LinkedIn connected with the Behance platform (now owned by Adobe (2012). If the LinkedIn profile owner is in Fine Art, then link to Behance to showcase their portfolio of art or videos of their dance or music. The Behance platform allows profile owners to create a portfolio of their work (especially in the creative arts). It would be productive to upload samples of one's artwork and connect it to one's LinkedIn profile.

4. Another platform to showcase art and design work is https://www.artstation.com. This is a primary platform to demonstrate graphic artwork by those in the design industry to showcase their digital artistry.

5. If the fine artist wants to potentially earn while they showcase their art, they can load their best work onto Fine Art America, where they can create a store for selling their artwork printed on products such as

canvases, towels, phone cases, or more.

6.   If the job seeker is in the computer and
     technology industry, as a computer
     scientist, website developer, or information
     technologist, and creates software
     programming, GitHub is perfect for posting,
     storing, and showcasing IT-related work,
     work on team projects, and programming
     and coding strings while different versions
     are worked on and updated. If the
     freelancer is a website builder, they should
     link 2-3 URLs inside their LinkedIn profile to
     those websites so recruiters can view their
     work.

7.   Students may have a hard time with
     showing more professional work, but there
     are ways to demonstrate their progress for
     school-work as a 'fresher' (straight out of
     high school or college).

     a)   Create a LinkedIn profile with a
          professional headshot and a list of
          school or job related activities, as
          well as volunteer experience.

     b)   If the student is in the 'fine arts' -
          create a portfolio of videos,
          photographs, or audio recordings of
          their sample work as an online
          portfolio.

     c)   If the student is in sports, then
          perhaps create a social media
          (Facebook?) page that showcases

the entire team and their participation in the team achievements, including leadership (e.g., team Captain) .

d) Post essays, books, or successful school projects descriptions or information on the LinkedIn "Projects" section.

8. Patents are going to be a unique method of showcasing skills or experience. On the resume, the patent-owner can list the approved patent-identification number, then a short description of the invention and its purpose.

9. Copyrights for publications or creative works indicate the writer or artist has extended a lot of effort into not only creating a work, but also took the time and trouble to register it with their country's copyright office (in the USA, the Library of Congress in in charge of this function).

When a job seeker lists their publications on their resumes, they should provide a publicly accessible website link to the published work so hiring managers can link to the book profile (if on a marketing page) or directly to the publication if open market sharing. Ensure that the publication listing is in the writer's style guide for the industry (in the sample case below, the author uses APA 6th Ed.). While in this case the links to the publications are not 'hot,' in a resume or online portfolio, you DO want the links to be 'clickable' to take the viewer straight to the article to prove it was professionally published.

Sample of Publications listing:

Boyer, D. (2019, Aug. 8.). Recruiter Nightmares: The Copy and Paste Resume. *News + Advice. Inside the Net. ClearedJobs.net.* Retrieved from https://blog.clearedjobs.net/recruiter-nightmares-the-copy-and-paste-resume/

Boyer, D. (2019, Jul. 4). Best practices for a job seeker's cover letter. Ask the Expert Column. Inside Business: The Hampton Roads Business Journal. Retrieved from pilotonline.com/inside-business/news/columns/article_ce3dd85c-9e6c-11e9-a845-27edae5f26e9.html

Boyer, D. (2019, May 3). Do you need a business plan or a marketing plan? *Inside Business, The Hampton Roads Business Journal, 25*, 17. Norfolk, VA. Retrieved from: https://pilotonline.com/inside-business/news/columns/article_0c23aa3c-6db9-11e9-ab3f-eb8caeea0c78.html

10. Business owners can provide portfolio of their work using their own business website. When one purchases a URL domain name, it's best to purchase it for a 10-year history, because search engines will target those

with the longer history in existence, as well as the longer purchase plan (yeah, they have a way of seeing that somehow).   If you are in business, your purpose is to sell a product or service to your target market. So use this business website to explain what you do, what you sell, why it is helpful to your clients, and why can can't live without it. If you can't convince your business target market, you won't be able to convince a hiring manager of your talents.

MUST HAVE JOB SKILLS

The author taught a 200-level class at a large university and was flabbergasted at students (ages ranging between 17 to 24 years old) that claimed to know how to use technology, but really didn't. They knew how to use their 'smart phones' and access their email and some social media accounts, and in their minds, that was the equivalent to being technology savvy. The students had learned to keyboard in high school, how to type content for class papers, and had a little presentation background for presenting projects via slides. Some students didn't know how to use the spell and grammar check in their word-processing software! In a previous life as a recruiter, the author was amazed at how many mid- or executive-level job applicants did not know how to type or used the one-finger-peck typing method. Generations ago, management had 'secretaries' to whom they dictated letters for typing and signatures. Today, that is unacceptable. Everyone has to answer emails, texts, and other correspondence personally.

The following is a list of basic skills expected of any professional that adds to the value of the job seeker's assets to future employers:

1. **Math Skills** - ability to compute - add, subtract, multiply, and divide; so many

companies have huge losses because the employee may not know how to do simple math and the money walks out the door. How many times have you paid cash for a purchase and the cashier couldn't count change back or handed you back more change than was warranted? (Hopefully, you pointed out the clerk's error to avoid 'stealing' from the business?).

2. **Writing / English Skills** - the ability to write clear and concise (short) memos, communications, letters, respond to texts and emails, as well as be able to write policies and procedures or training manuals using word processing tools. The ability to use and format Levels (A, (a), 1, (1)), and the ability to spell correctly and formulate correct grammar and punctuation.

3. **Basic Computer Skills** is the ability to use computers, cellphones, iPads, Tablets, and portable electronics tools. Even low-level positions use technology nowadays. Amazon, Federal Express, and the UPS delivery drivers use electronic tools to follow routes, record deliveries, and even take a pic of the delivered item on the door stoop. Warehouse workers use RFID (radio frequency identification) tools to audit inventory, find merchandise, and record storage moves. Financial analysts on Wall Street keep up with their client's funds, purchases, and sales with a bank of computer monitors and software applications. Authors of books need to

know what software to use to compile their books for print-on-demand publishing, but also how to access ISBN numbers (purchase), registering their books via Library of Congress' Copyright Office, and how to load their files online for funneling books for sale to Amazon.

4. **Internet of Things (IOT)** is the ability to use software, applications, and technology, and operate cloud-based applications, store documents for posterity or sharing and editing with teams, and back-up files, documents, and photos on servers (in house or cloud-based). Recruiters use Automatic Tracking Systems (ATS) stored in the cloud on the vendor's server, and simply access the program via the Internet, a user-name, and password to post job openings, review applicants, and send out messages to potential candidates to schedule interviews. Human resources information systems now are 100% cloud-based, which eliminates users from 'accidentally' deleting files on the company server (which may or may not have been backed up).

5. **MS Office: Word** and **Outlook Mail** - including Formatting for paragraphs (We are talking about 'not' using single spaces or tabs to create a paragraph indent, but honest-to-goodness knowledge of how to format an indented paragraph (styles)). Know how to use the Grammar and Spell Check on your word processing software.

Know how to write a business letter with all the required elements. Know how to use the fewest words possible to respond to email inquiries. Know when NOT to use the CC to reply to an original mass email and when to NOT reply at all (if initial email is simply a FYI, there is no vital need to reply).

6. **MS Office: Excel** - being able to compile, and plug in formulas (add, sum, subtract) and the ability to set up formatting so spreadsheets are centered on the page with headers and footers (it's amazing how many folks have no clue or have never opened up a spreadsheet program!). The importance of being able to use a spreadsheet was spelled out when a young job seeker told his story of being hired. "I showed up at a job interview and there were about 20-30 others standing in line to be interviewed – all about my age – some a little older. The interviewing manager came out and asked, 'Anyone know how to use Excel?" and I was the only one that raised my hand. The hiring manager told everyone else to go home, and had me in for the interview. While I was not an expert on the spreadsheet program, I had the basic knowledge, and that got me hired, and they trained me to speed on the software to their basic needs."

7. **MS Office: PowerPoint** - has become a powerful presentation tool, including the ability to turn the presentation into movies with timing, animations, and transitions.

These can be amazing sales tools for private clients, or public YouTube 'home-made' advertising with professional quality looks. In the I last decade PowerPoint presentations have gained the ability to be transformed into Videos (MP4) files and uploaded to websites and social media. Learn to add public domain music from the personal computer or use the playlists available on the social media editing management software.

8. **Industry-related Software**: If you are in a particular industry and that industry has specifically related software applications (e.g., Accounting = QuickBooks; Professors - Blackboard Student Management System; Graphic Artists = Photoshop), it would be vital for skills sets to shop for new jobs to have at least beginner knowledge of the industry-related software. Many cities have adult education classes at low prices offered to public for job / workforce training. Some software companies offer online for the training of the use of the software to current users (and potentially future users). LinkedIn now connects paying users with Lynda.com for online training in just about anything for no additional cost - use it!

9. **Soft Skills**: people, diplomacy, ethics, political correctness, and customer service (patience and ability to deal with rude customers). While the previous bullets more 'hard' skills in which job seekers should be skilled, there is the 'soft' skill

element of the business world.

a)   Get along with other people, peers, team-members, and supervisors. Practice simple etiquette – exchange (morning) greetings, say thank you and please, and "I appreciate what you have done", as well as compliments on work-related topics – all go a long way towards getting along with co-workers. Don't send an email to a co-worker across the room when you can get up and visit their desk for the answer in a face-to-face (unless they are on the phone and the email is not an immediate knowledge requirement).

b)   If there is contention or conflicts in the office or workplace, figure out how each party is viewing the issues or debate, look at the pros and cons of each viewpoint, and work towards diplomatically getting each of the parties to see the other's view, and offer suggestions that are a win-win for all parties involved.

c)   Ensure that everyone involved in a project gets the credit – don't steal all the limelight from other team-members or co-workers.

d)   Ethics is a required training topic in some companies, especially in the government contracting industry and federal level workplaces. Simply put – don't steal from, lie to, or harass co-workers and customers or the company. Respect whomever you are dealing with at the moment as another human being and do unto them what you would expect yourself. Behave appropriately. Don't yell at your co-workers.

e) Steer away from discussions of politics, religion, and personal health or medical issues in the workplace. If you want to discuss the topic, leave the workplace and go to a neutral territory, and only steer towards the topics for discussion if all parties present are agreeable AND if the discussion does not later strain working relationships (e.g., if out to lunch with your boss, a dyed in the wool Democrat, and you are a rabid Republican, don't bring the opinions discussed back into the workplace, such as affecting performance evaluations).

10. **Personal presentation** – dress, cleanliness, hair styles, and hygiene. You would think this doesn't even need to be mentioned, but these are vital skills to look good and professional in the business world. Dress appropriately, bathe often, don't drench yourself in perfumes, colognes, and aftershave (many folks have allergies; others just don't like your favorite scent). Don't wear ethnic-based hair styles to work if your job is to present yourself professionally as the 'face' of the business and a member of the salesforce to clients.

The best judge for appropriate style of dress and hairstyles can easily be judged outside of what the company may dictate as policy … what are the general professional dress and hairstyles of your clients and customers? Those are what you should be emulating.

HOW TO GET JOB EXPERIENCE

1. Internships

Internship (noun), plural noun: internships:
the position of a student or trainee who works in an
organization, sometimes without pay, in order to
gain work experience or satisfy requirements for a
qualification. "they encouraged students to apply
for newspaper internships." (dictionary.com)

While the traditional method of obtaining
work experience of any type while still in one's last
year of high school or college is with obtaining an
internship, more experienced workers looking to
transition into another, or new, career should also
keep this type of learning work experience in mind.
How does one obtain an internship? There are two
types of internships when you search for new work
experience: (a) paid internships and (b) unpaid
internships. There is a human resources aspect to
these types of internships for taxes and federal
employment law purposes.

The paid internship means the company for
which the worker in performing the internship can
be assigned any work or tasks the company
requires of the worker - meaning you could be
running out for coffee and filing paperwork in
folders – work that is not at all what you wanted to
be learning new skills at performing. The company

is paying hourly wages for you to earn the right to put the company's name on your resume, regardless of your tasks, duties, and responsibilities as an intern. It is up to the intern to look around for some interesting projects, tasks, or assignments that can be indicative of a higher-level of work experience during this period.

The unpaid internship is normally reserved for companies possibly looking for a new 'permanent'[2] employee after they 'test' the worker's capabilities, ability to perform assignments, tasks, and work on projects, and feel out how they work within a team of co-workers and peers. The unpaid internship is subject to state and federal laws, and the Fair Labor Standards Act (FLSA) governs how interns must be compensated under federal law. Unpaid internship programs must meet six federal legal criteria and participants are *considered* 'employees' under the Fair Labor Standards Act (FLSA). The training is for the benefit of the interns, not the employer.

- Training resembles learning curriculum in an academic setting or a vocational school, albeit the internship takes place in a working business facility.
- The training is for the benefit of the interns, not the employer (profit or revenue).
- Internships are not used to displace regular employees; interns work in partnership with and

---

[2] *Human resources should not use the word 'permanent,' because it implies employment for the life of the worker; the better word would be a 'regular, full-time' employee, but the author uses this word to imply 'other than' intern, part-time, or temporary worker.*

under supervision of regular employees.

- Employers receive no immediate benefit from interns' activities, and may impede business operations or take away hours from regular program or workers' productivity.
- Interns are not entitled to a regular position once they have completed the internship; there are no promises or guaranteed of an offer for regular employment.
- Employers and interns have a mutual understanding the internship will not be paid before the internship begins, in exchange for training and learning environment to hone their education and add to their work experience.

2. Apprenticeships

Apprenticeship (noun): the position of an apprentice. "the company once offered apprenticeships" synonyms: traineeship, training period, studentship, novitiate. (dictionary.com)

From the beginning of time, fathers passed on survival skills to their offspring (flaking arrow heads, hunting, fishing). As trades grew, the fathers taught their sons to the trades of brick masonry, carpentry, carpet weaving, and trading in the marketplace. Apprenticeships grew from a family affair to taking non-family members under the mentorship of a master-tradesperson to learn the fine art of the craft.

Apprenticeships differ from internship as the mutual partnership is normally long-term – sometimes as long as five to seven years. Apprentices are paid a sustenance wage (in the colonial era, food, shelter, clothing) or minimum wages as they performed the 'menial' chores related to the trade. Silversmith apprentices may have gathered firewood to fuel the smelter and worked the bellows to keep the fire hot enough while they observed their master silver smith pour the metal into molds, then clean the final product to the finish. It would potentially take years to reach the level where the Master was comfortable enough in the learned skills levels to allow an apprentice to create a piece from start to finish.

3. Volunteer for a Cause, Non-Profit, or For-profit Company. ...

Volunteer (noun): a person who freely offers to take part in an enterprise or undertake a task. synonyms: subject, participant, case, client, patient; informal guinea pig; "during the investigation, each volunteer was studied three times." (dictionary.com)

Volunteer activities are not often thought of as work experience because the labor is unpaid. But, volunteer activities are a great source of learning teamwork, supervising others, and project work that requires regular work environment skills. Scheduling other volunteers is like herding cats and showcasing the ability to do so on a resume, and documenting the results of volunteer efforts with metrics can emphasize good business habits. For example: "Lead a team of 10 volunteers in fundraising activities selling candy door-to-door in an identified target market neighborhood, resulting in over $600 in funding raised to benefit the Girl Scout Troop #123 for FY20."

4. Job Shadowing

Job shadowing provides a worker an opportunity to observe or "shadow" someone doing their job. You observe someone actually doing a job with all the relative and associated tasks, procedures, and steps. Because the learner is at the place of work, you also get to see what goes on inside the workplace. This is a great opportunity for those already in a company to learn co-worker's job functions. This enables the shadower to learn how to perform a task from someone who has already mastered it.

5. Train-the-Trainer

Nothing gets you up to speed on how to perform a job faster than having to train another person to do that job. The author once had to teach a Grammar class at a for-profit school and had to study and learn the intimate details of grammar, and how to showcase samples, the night before the class was taught.   Studying a job and how it's done will enable the training to learn it from the basic level. For example: If you have to learn to sail, then read books, watch YouTube videos, talk to others who have sailed, and ask for advice on how to sail to get the knowledge under your belt.

6. Temp Agencies

If a worker has no hard-skills to shop around, then they can focus on providing their 'soft skills' in a workplace while they work towards the opportunity to provide 'hard-skills' during work tenure. A receptionist can ask for work between phone calls – typing in data to spreadsheets or compiling printed workbooks into binders (and reading or glancing at the material while doing so – you never know what knowledge you can learn). While this may be low-level tasking, there may be opportunities to provide higher-level tasking to supervisors or management, or to learn more about the company and their work environment, as well as potentially be 'there' when a job opens.

7. Part-Time Job

Almost everyone starts off their work career in a part-time job after school. Whether you are a newbie out of school, or an older worker looking to change careers, part-time jobs may provide the opportunity to learn more about the company or a career field to absorb the knowledge and skills, as well as deciding whether or not the worker really wants to get into 'that' industry.

8. Ask to Help Out on a New Project at Work

While most full-time workers have approximately 40 hours to work and complete their tasks in that allotted time, there may be opportunities to learn another job or task by simply asking for a project that may not necessarily on a deadline to complete. Ask to be a member of a team working on specific programs or projects. For example: In the government contracting industry, the proposal to be submitted for consideration for a federal contract needs many hands-on team members to write up portions of the proposal, research details of the quote or bid parameters, and analyze what job descriptions currently in place will match the contract worker's parameters for tasking.

9.   Head to the Classroom to Earn Your Next Job

If all else fails to learn a (new) skill, then look for classes that provide the knowledge or skill sets. For example, to work at the local shipyard or auto manufacturing plant, look for cooperative programs where the services company will pay for a vocational school program in exchange for X years of working for the company. Newport News Shipyard coordinates with a local community college to assist future workers attain a combination Associate Degree and Welding Certification (ranging from MIG, TIG, Nuclear, and more). Once the worker completed the program, they are 'obligated' to work for the services company for a minimum number of years. The entry salary may be slightly lower than if the company hired a fully-qualified worker off the street for the length of service designated as the 'pay-back' period.

10. Network

Nothing beats a family member or friend that knows someone who knows someone looking for a hard-working, willing to learn, worker. Start asking family members who work for a large company who may be able to ask around for internship positions (or even a real work position). Network at church or your local YMCA or gym. Ask the person if they would be willing to provide a written reference. Locate the neighborhood gossip

– they may know some juicy details about available work.

Another way to get real experience (especially in labor and services industry) is to sign up as a provider for the online short-term job applications (e.g., Takl). You will have to answer questions, go through a short training instruction, agree to policies about high-level quality work, and then show up on schedule to ensure continued work. But, the income from these short-term tasks could add up significantly as well as provide some valued work experience on your resume.

(Resources on internship legalities)

Brockhausen, C. & Kalten, B. (2016, Sept.). *More California cities, Chicago, Minneapolis and St. Paul enact paid sick leave laws.* Retrieved from www.towerswatson.com/en-US/Insights/Newsletters/Americas/insider/2016/09/more-cities-enact-paid-sick-leave-laws

Gulati, A. (2015, Jun. 4). *Are Your Summer Interns ACA-Eligible?* Retrieved from www.shrm.org/resourcesandtools/hr-topics/talent-acquisition/pages/summer-interns-aca-eligible.aspx

Minton, Peter I. (2013, Apr. 19). *Six Legal Requirements For Unpaid Internship Programs.* Retrieved from www.forbes.com/sites/theyec/2013/04/19/6-legal-requirements-for-unpaid-internship-programs/#34ad93546bf1

EQUATING VOLUNTEERING TO WORK
EXPERIENCE ON YOUR RESUME

Youthful job seekers don't have much work experience per se, so don't know what to put on their first resume. They may have an asset they don't realize is just as experienced as 'real' or 'paid' work – their volunteer experience. More mature and experienced workers don't realize just how important volunteer work is on their resume and how their involvement can open employment doors. A few hours a month can add up over the years.

Whether you are a teenager with little work experience, but plenty of time to offer charity organizations or a local NPO, or a corporate executive that volunteers on a NPO Board of Directors, the participation and experience gained is a vital and valuable work experience. If you want to offer your time and skills, try the local newspaper or a quick Internet search to find a charity that needs your vital KSAs to get ahead in their goals and objectives. Then add it to your resume as another 'work experience' bullet. You will get far more out of the experience than you expect!

1.   Even the Boy Scout or Girl Scout troop or the little league baseball team can be a volunteer event that equates to 'work experience. It's a lot of hard work to corral a

bunch of hyper-active kids into a team of
willing learners or workers.

2.   Volunteer experience on one's resume
      indicates several things. The volunteer is
      involved in the community. The volunteer
      shares their skills or hands towards a
      unique cause. The volunteer is not scared
      of hard work – meaning they aren't couch
      potatoes with little-to-no ambition or life
      goals.

3.   Volunteer experience on one's resume
      indicates the job seeker has a larger group
      of social contacts. The larger the social
      group, the more the job seeker can reach
      out to others to inquire about 'real job'
      opportunities.

4.   Volunteers hone their knowledge, skills, and
      abilities (KSAs) in environments or
      industries that open their mind to different
      viewpoints and new ideas. Their volunteer
      work provides a positive impact on their
      community, or a geographic location or
      recipients of the volunteers' efforts.

5.   Many non-profit organizations (NPOs)
      'desperate' for volunteers, it's easy to pick
      up the phone and call to offer your services.
      Volunteer services can be simple as
      providing ideas in brainstorming sessions,
      picking up a hammer to assist in physical
      labor, or scouting for other volunteers with
      special skills to reach annual goals. Or, the
      need could be as complicated as providing

accounting certification audits for the NPO so they can move forward in applying for grants, or even state and federal funding.

6.	Volunteering has many benefits – to the volunteer or the job seeker. As a member of a Non-Profit Organization (NPO), doors are open to business or social circles that one would normally never cross paths (i.e., meeting big corporate executives at a donor appreciate event). Use these new connections to reach out to those corporations human resources departments via cover letters of introduction. For example, "I recently met with your CEO, Dr. Brown, and he indicated that the company could use a few more hard workers such as I when he noted my volunteer work for the XYZ Charity. I have enclosed my resume, as well as having loaded it onto the company's ATS and would be delighted if your office or recruiting representative can see my strengths and experience matching any of your open or future job opportunities."

7.	The volunteer can learn or develop new skills in parallel uses (i.e., an experienced for-profit accountant can learn about non-profit financials and taxes). The work may also open one's eyes to a social world one might never be exposed to otherwise (i.e., health and nutrition needs for at-risk, inner-city youth and the homeless).

8.   As a volunteer, it's also important to share
      experiences. Talk with others about what
      you have learned, what you achieved for the
      NPO. This opens up speaking
      engagements to expose yourself as a vital
      and experienced professional to a room of
      potential new employers. Your diversity of
      experiences will enable future employers to
      study your skill sets and your capabilities to
      work in a broad scope of environments –
      including budget restrictions (getting more
      done with less). Your value as a job
      candidate grows with your volunteer activity.

9.   A recent study of LinkedIn members asked
      whether a job candidate with volunteer
      experience would important and 41% noted
      the candidate would be looked at more
      carefully. The researchers indicated it was
      LinkedIn's "corporate mission to connect
      talent with opportunity," and further
      indicated "volunteer experience …
      showcases skills, initiative, and can …
      identify a shared point of passion with a
      potential employer or business partner."

10.   The same LinkedIn survey of nearly 2,000
      professionals in the United States indicated
      89% of these professionals had personal
      experience volunteering, but only 45%
      include volunteer experience on their
      resume, and "20% of the hiring managers
      surveyed agree they have made a hiring
      decision based on a candidate's volunteer
      work experience." The conclusion was …

volunteer experience is a key piece of one's professional identity.

JOB SEARCH

AVOIDING AGE BIAS IN THE JOB SEARCH

Age discrimination happens at both ends of the age spectrum. Once you turn 50, and you start to look 50, it gets harder to compete with younger job seekers. The younger competition may look a little sharper, have less wrinkles and more hair, and exude youth (seemingly more energetic and physically fit). Psychologists have also identified age bias for those 'too young' to have the minimum years of experience needed in a position.[3] Work up your enthusiasm – get the steam rolling!

Unfortunately, as age increases, so does the average duration of unemployment for working-age job seekers in the USA. An article in the American Psychological Association's Psychological Bulletin – Age and Reemployment Success After Job Loss: An Integrative Model and Meta-Analysis indicated the older one gets the odds of being re-employed decrease by 2.6% annually for each increase in age year.[4] The rate of unemployment among older workers was lower than younger counterparts, older unemployed

---

[3] Cavaiola, A. A. (2018, Jun. 11). Age Discrimination in the Workplace: Part 1. *Psychology Today. Retrieved from* https://www.psychologytoday.com/us/blog/beyond-bullying/201806/age-discrimination-in-the-workplace-part-i

[4] Wanberg, C.R., Kanfer, R., Hamann, D.J., & Zhang, Z. (2015, Apr.). *Psychology Bulletin, 142*(4), pp. 400-26. doi: 10.1037/bul0000019. Epub 2015 May 25. Abstract retrieved from https://www.ncbi.nlm.nih.gov/pubmed/26011790

persons spent more time searching for work. In
February 2010 (a year after the market crash and
at the beginning of the world-wide 2009 recession),
workers aged 55 years or older averaged
joblessness of ~35.5 weeks, compared with 23.3
weeks for those aged 16 to 24 years and 30.3
weeks for those aged 25 to 54 years.[5]

Following are some tips to avoid age bias
on your resume, as well as in your face-to-face
interview(s).

1.   Ensure your resume is 'modern' and up to
        date. A resume with an old-fashioned
        layout and format and using older style fonts
        is going to 'look' old. Use san-serif fonts
        (Arial) and fonts set at a 10.5 to 12 point
        size, so the resume is easy to read. Keep
        margins no less than .5 inches (.8 is best
        minimum width).

2.   Use cell phone numbers (not landlines).
        Landlines can be used to reverse look-up
        addresses. Use a g-mail e-mail address
        (not AOL or Yahoo). AOL has been around
        for decades, so an AOL e-mail may imply
        you, too, have been around for decades.
        It's best to establish a modern e-mail
        account *just* for your job search, which you
        can always set up to bounce to your

---

[5] Issues in Labor Statistics. Summary 10-14 / March 1010, *US
    Department of Labor, US Bureau of Labor Statistics.* Retrieved
    from https://www.bls.gov/opub/btn/archive/record-unemployment-
    among-older-workers-does-not-keep-them-out-of-the-job-
    market.pdf

previously established e-mail account on AOL or Yahoo. And – for gosh sakes – don't use any numbers in the new e-mail address that could be interpreted as a potential birth date (e.g., JohnBrown1955@). These incidences are common, and recruiters can usually figure out how old someone is by simply interpreting the email address.

3. Prove you haven't been sitting on the sidelines when technology is gaining in leaps and bounds, as a strong business and career skill. Research, identify, and complete adult-education classes to compete with 'younger' workers who may have learned already learned the technology in formal schooling.

   a) Work on your office suite software skills – word processing, spreadsheets, and presentation applications (a year's subscription to MS Office is ~$100 (USD); well worth the price to have access, and ability to use, for personal as well as business tasks)

   b) Learn how to use competitive business software packages – Microsoft Office, Open Office, and Google docs (MS Office is the business standard, so only use that package for resume writing and job applications).

   c) Learn basic accounting software packages – QuickBooks, Peachtree

– if you are in the bookkeeping or accounting field; brush up on the latest tax codes and laws via online classes or take a local tax class

d) If you can't afford to subscribe to Adobe Creative Cloud applications, then look for the free alternatives – e.g., Gimp for photo manipulation.

e) Ensure you have a LinkedIn account profile – fully loaded (showcases not only your expertise, but also your tech savvy in the profile).

4. Your resume should only date back 14-15 years (max), but you can discuss older work without the dates. The easiest way to do so is to list jobs to the 15 years ago date, then create a new section entitled "Other Professional Experience." Continue listing job titles, company names, and 1-2 bullets of career-relevant job accomplishments under each job title, even if they go back 20-30 years – but delete the dates. Leave dates off formal educational degrees – especially if over 15 years in the past. List dates of career related training going back 10 years, but no more. Training you received over 10 years ago may be no longer in use or it would be best to obtain refresher training on the topic for changes and updates.

5. In the interview, talk about how much longer you want to work. Do *not* say, "I am looking for a job to get me through the next few years to retirement." Explain that at this

'stage' in your career (*don't say* 'near retirement age') you are looking for stability in a company where you can stay around for a long time. You do not want out of the job market, because you 'want to be doing something productive.' What better than to be working in a focused, career position where you can bring your *wealth* of experience (*don't say* 'years') and your skill sets to benefit the company. During the interview, focus on what words and language you want to *avoid*. Do *not* remind or infer to the interviewer that you are old, nearing retirement, or finished working by using age-related words.

6.   In the interview, talk about legacy problems your *wealth* of experience has resolved. It's ok to discuss work further back than 15 years, just do not provide any dates as to when you conducted those solutions. Some things may be unavoidable to 'date' (e.g., the year 2000 date system in computers (millennium changeover, where COBOL programming was needed).

7.   Research the company and target outreach to 'older' employees. Networking is an awesome job search tool, especially to those in positions that know who is hiring. Mature workers may be more open to communicating with potential new employees (co-workers, peers) in their own age bracket. Use LinkedIn to search companies and identify current employees who may seem to be in the same age

group. Reach out and ask if the company has any employee referral policies (reward system). Would they be "open to reviewing your resume and pushing it to human resources or the hiring manager for consideration?" as well as earning an employee award for recommending you. If they aren't interested in pushing the resume, ask whom would be an ideal person in the company to push your skills sets to versus a direct human-resources contact. Ask permission to use their name as the source for the referral to the hiring manager.

8. Ensure any photos on social media accounts are 'youthful' looking (we are not talking 20-year-old, throw-back photos). Ensure the current photos have facial wrinkles smoothed out, the neck wattles hidden (scarves and neckties are 'our friends'), and sit up straight and smile. While you are reviewing your social media pages, look for compromising photos or posts that may 'turn folks off' for political, religious, or unpopular viewpoints. (Best case, privatize your social media profiles, altogether if you don't want to delete the profile.)

9. Change your look for the better.

    a) Get professional treatments to erase some of the pockmarks, spots, and roughness of your skin (light acid facials), use facial creams that smooth out the skin or erase age spots.

b)   Get a modern haircut. Men – if you are smoothing those last 20 hairs across your bald spot – just go ahead and shave it all off (get "the Rock" look – it's sexier and more professional, and less 'wimpy' looking). No hair actually makes you look younger versus the monk's tonsure).

c)   Get a modern haircut. Women – if you have long hair, either 'put it up' in a face-flattering style, get a wedge cut, cut it shoulder length, or straighten it. The long, straight bangs across the forehead with long hair and frizzies-on-the-end look will date you back to the hippy generation.

d)   If you are a long-term heavy smoker, coffee or tea drinker, or took prescriptions that resulted in yellowed teeth – use teeth whiteners to brighten your smile. The whiter your teeth, the more youthful you come across. (Dentists sell professional kits for about $250.)

10.   If you can't afford new clothes, look for a local non-profit that helps those in lower-economic situations prepare for job interviews by providing free professional suits and dresses (search on the Internet for the group: "Dress for Success" in your city. Dress for the position one-step above for

which you are interviewing, e.g., if you are applying for a receptionist position, dress for management; if a welder's position, dress for the supervisor's level.)

CREATING JOB ALERTS

One of the best tricks is to let technology work for you in finding great jobs in the creation of a 'job alert' in whatever system, platform, social media, or online resume database in which you are uploading your resume. The job alert is a filtered trigger that lets the resume owner know that keywords are within the job posting that a company's recruiter or human resources representative has just publicized on a recruiting platform.

Keep track of user-names and passwords used to sign up for these job alerts. There may also be a one-click option to opt out of email alerts from specific systems. Otherwise, job seekers may have to sign in and untoggled the 'on' button for alerts or send an email directly to the issuer to cease future notifications.

There are several options and type of job alerts one can sign up for or filter for delivery.

1.	Email news feeds. Some non-profit and for-profit organizations will provide job seekers the opportunity to sign up for email notification of newly opened positions for either (a) direct hire or (b) as a third-party notification for one or more organizations. For example, there are a few veteran-based entities that collect resumes from job seekers and send out those resumes to a collection of recipients (recruiters and headhunters). The emails will also be targeted towards job seekers by companies targeting applicants for newly published job requisitions as part of their Equal Employment Opportunity (EEO) and/or Affirmative Action Plan (AAP) policies.

2.   Private company job alerts may be delivered to those job seekers who place their email on a specific business' mailing list when new jobs are posted in the company's help wanted website or Automatic Tracking System (ATS). When job seekers post a resume directly in the ATS for most companies, they may see an option to toggle 'on' for 'keep me notified of any future positions that may open up.' This enables the job seeker to be notified of any specific type or all publicly posted jobs in the future.

3.   Social media job alerts – LinkedIn. This business networking social media site has really ramped up their job and recruiting functionality in the last 3-4 years (as of 2019). Recruiters love searching for job candidates on LinkedIn and your goal is to ensure your profile is fully loaded (and managed weekly), as well as the 'open for career' discussions button clicked on. Look for the 'Jobs' tab in the string of tabs at the top of your LinkedIn profile. Click to go to the Jobs page. Your first screen will enable

you to toggle 'on' the "Let recruiters know you're open" button. This provides an option to recruiters to send you In-mails to ask if you have an interest in their open positions.

(See sample screen shot below.)

You will additionally see the tab for Track my jobs and Career Interests. You can plug in some keywords directly relevant to your skill sets and experience to create the job alert.   Initially you can 'search' for jobs with those skill sets, then you can filter the search by geographic location or more specific job titles.

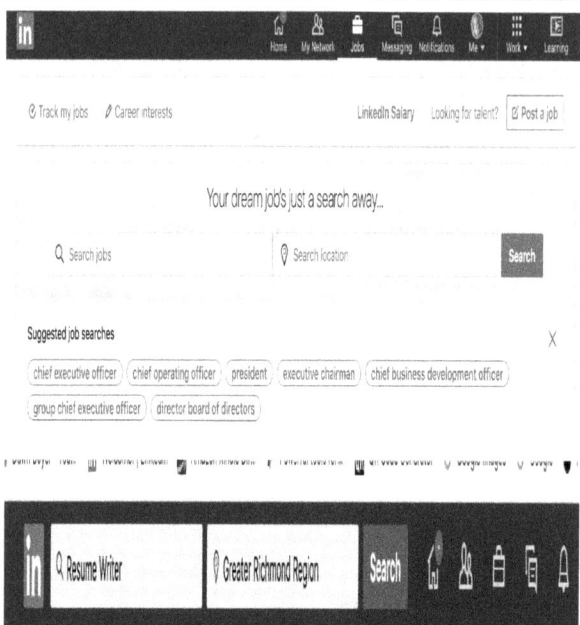

Once you have specific job search criteria
identified, you can then create the 'job alert.'

Using the keywords you used in your initial
job search, click on the "Job Alert On"
button, then indicate how often and how you
want the alerts directed, then save your
choices.

Create search alert   ✕

government contracting proposal manager in Washington, District of Columbia, United States
25 miles (40 km)

Receive alert

Daily   ▼

Get notified via

Email & notifications   ▼

[Cancel] [Save]

---

4.   Follow Companies on LinkedIn: Plugging in
       a specific company on LinkedIn will also
       create another form of alert. Search for the
       company name, then click on the Follow
       button, and then watch for "Job Results"
       and click on "See All" to review the most
       recently posted positions. This Company
       Follow also shows who you may be
       connected to ("1st") that you can contact to
       inquire more about positions in that person's
       department or business unit, or to ask if the
       company has a 'employee referral' program
       in which they can forward your resume to an
       appropriate hiring manager and human
       resources (if hired, they are qualified to
       receive 'hiring bonus' awards for the new
       hire referral).

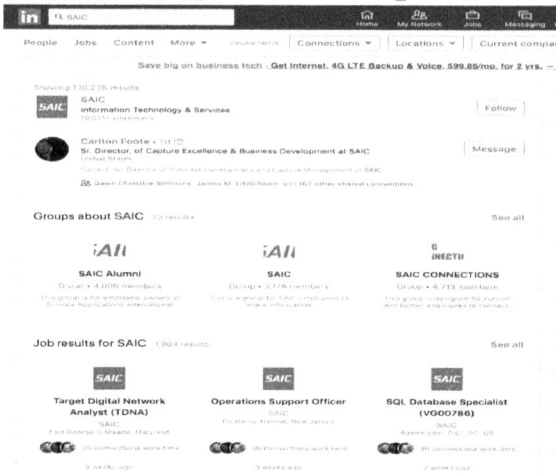

5. Social media job alerts – Twitter. The notifications method on this social media platform is more identifying companies or recruiters who are using Twitter to automatically notify followers of job openings and following them.

   In the Twitter "Settings" page – ensure the box is toggled on for Tweet notifications for 'people you follow' (recruiters, headhunters, placement specialists).

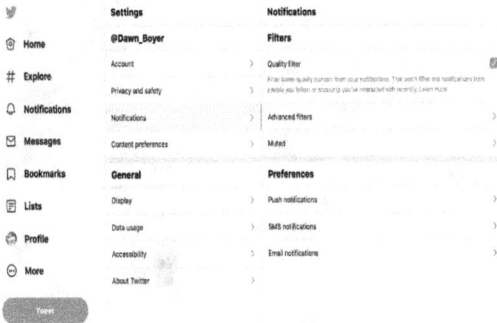

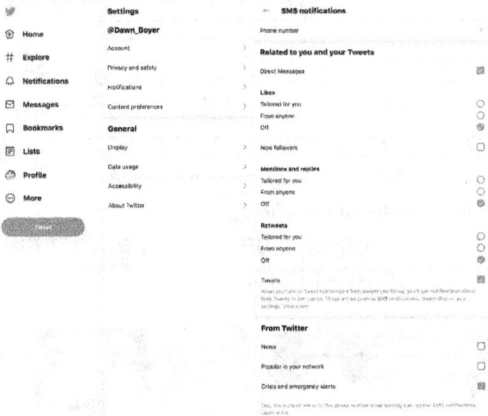

6. Social media job alerts – Twitter. Ensure you are *following* companies or recruiters that regularly post job notices on Twitter. You will have to check your Twitter feed regularly, and/or use the hashtag and keywords to search for jobs posted on Twitter. Plugging in a hashtag for Job Search (#jobsearch) will result in a list of recruiters, companies, or placement specialists you can follow for the fastest updates.

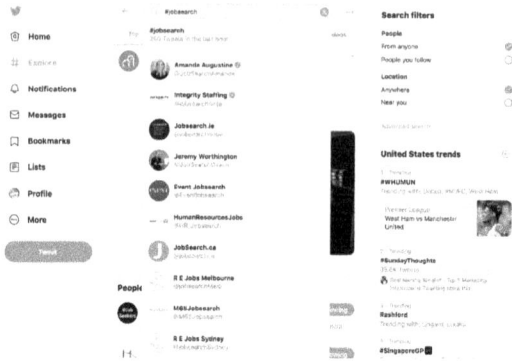

7.   Follow Companies on Facebook: Some
      companies have specific business-branded
      pages on this social media platform (some
      companies you would thing wouldn't bother
      have full-blown developed pages!). Search
      for the company name to see what they
      have on this platform.

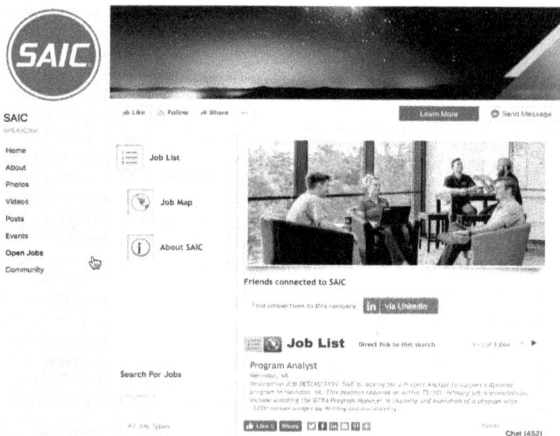

8.   Follow Business Pages on Facebook:

Other companies or entities may have job-assistance-related pages to help job seekers.

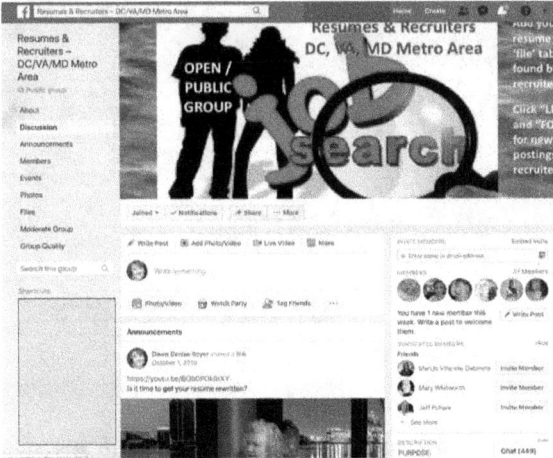

9. Some entities offer job alerts – huge Internet browser's themselves – e.g., Google has the power of their own search engine to post open positions where you can create job alerts.

10. Additionally you can have Google do all the hard work for you even in non-Google jobs – for setting up alerts with keywords. You do need a Google email address. This may be the perfect time to see up a specific email address ONLY used for your job search and placed on your resume.

    How to set up the Google Alert:

    a) Go to Google Alerts.
    b) In the box at the top, enter a topic you want to follow. IF you want to have exact matches, place the keywords inside quotes … e.g., "Database Analyst" or "Human Resources Manager" – otherwise any alerts will pick up just one of the words for each 'find' and not necessarily the

combination.

c) To change your settings, click Show options. You can change:

    I.   How often you get notifications

    II.   The types of sites you'll see

    III.   Your language

    IV.   The part of the world you want info from

    V.   How many results you want to see?

    VI.   What accounts get the alert?

d) Click Create Alert. You'll get emails whenever we (Google) finds any matching search results.

Example following:

FIRST STEPS AFTER LOSING A JOB

If you rely on work income to support yourself or your family, losing a job via layoff, termination, or you suddenly quit unexpectantly can be emotionally, as well as financially, devastating. One can go through the same emotions and stages after losing a job as one does when losing a family member through death. These emotions are not always in a specific order, but seem to be common to those who suffering a loss.

Initially the shock or disbelief kicks in, sometimes accompanied by denial ("Did I really just get fired?" or "This has to be a mistake, maybe they got the wrong name on the layoff list? I am one of their most valuable employees!" Then anger and/or bargaining sets in. ("How dare they fire me! I wasn't the one who stole all the money out of the petty cash drawer!" or "Maybe if I go back and beg or grovel they will hire me back?") Guilt may be part of the emotional upheaval ("What am I going to do now? My family depends on my paycheck and now my kids can't get the dance lessons I promised them!"). Depression is one of the steps in the progression. This emotion severely affects attitudes when looking for a few job. If a job applicant shows up with a defeatist attitude to an interview, the hiring manager will move on to a candidate with a chirpier disposition. And then acceptance will finally sink in.

It's important to get through all the negative, emotional steps as fast as possible and move on to acceptance and work towards getting that next career position. It may be that after being hired into a new company, one may look back and realize that getting fired or laid off was the best thing that could have happened.

Regardless of layoff, termination, or quitting a job because you just couldn't stand it there any longer, you need to get a new career position as fast as possible, so take these steps to enhance the speed, as well as the number of times recruiters and hiring managers can see your resume and reach out to you for your job skills.

The following are tips that will assist job seekers in getting over the initial shock and work towards practical actions to getting back on their feet in their career.

1.   If you were fired for something other than a serious offense (murder, embezzlement, grand theft, violence in the workplace), most states will give the benefit of the doubt to the worker who was let go, and issue a decision to allow unemployment benefits. Depending upon the state, benefit payments could start immediately or up to 15-30 days after the last date of employment with the former employer. The first thing to do, on the date of termination, is to file for unemployment benefits. Once the waiting period is completed, one can qualify for up to a set maximum weekly unemployment

benefit as long as the unemployed worker can document their attempts to find work (e.g., the Commonwealth of Virginia pays up to $378 weekly for up to 26 weeks, while the state of California pays up to $1,252 weekly for between five to 18 months).

Another method of being 'fired, but not being fired' is via 'constructive discharge.' This means the employer makes it so difficult to perform or do one's job tasks, that the employee will quit in frustration or under physical or emotional duress. Piling on impossible to complete by a deadline tasks (e.g., you need to fold, stuff envelopes, and mail 2,000 mailers between Friday at 4:00 p.m. and Monday at 9:00 a.m., forcing the employee to take work home for the weekend and asking for help from family and friends to complete the impossible task). Or, indicating if the employee took any more personal leave to assist a family member or take a child to daycare, they would be terminated for excessive work absences.

Some states will allow an unemployed worker the choice of having state and federal taxes pulled from unemployment benefits before distribution (earned income) or wait until after when the employee files annual taxes. Any taxes are deducted from the current year's refund (or added to IRS debt if one owes).

2.   Ensure you are set for all the exit paperwork

from your previous employer. If you had health insurance, you are eligible to continue your health insurance coverage under COBRA, but will have to pay the entire monthly premium out-of-pocket, in addition an (up to) 1% processing fee.

3.   You should have been updating your resume on a quarterly, if not monthly, basis. Ensure your resume is professionally written (not slapped together from a template from the Internet). Spending $200-$300 on a new resume means one less week without a paycheck coming in if recruiters and headhunters find the highly qualified candidate with the professionally written faster on their job boards or resume databases to call you in for an interview. (In essence, don't try to save a nickel to earn a dollar!).

4.   Ensure your professionally rewritten resume is posted on as many major job boards as possible. Recruiters and headhunters 'FARM' resumes – the more they have in their database or have access to in subscription databases (Monster, Indeed, CareerBuilder) the faster they can fill job openings.

5.   Update your LinkedIn profile. If you have never created a LinkedIn profile, it may not be a major return on investment (ROI) at the point you have lost your job. But, create it or update it anyway. Complete all the job descriptions from your freshly rewritten

resume. Ensure that all 50 of the allowable skill sets are added to your profile (LinkedIn's search engine uses this section primarily for key word searches by recruiters.) Upload your resume into your profile. Ensure a direct sub-header is written in the limited characters available under your name – e.g., use keywords that indicate your professional specialty in that text box.

6. Dig out your rolodex (or contact list). Start looking through the list of professional business contacts for anyone who may know someone who is hiring. Start making calls. "Hey Harry, how are ya? Great job on that production meeting and the project last month. I have a question. Do you know anyone who may be looking to hire a '(general job title)? I know someone who is in the market and has some incredible credentials … I don't want to share their name for privacy … but who can I call to make introductions? Great! Can I tell them you referred their name?"

7. Look at your last employer's competitors in the market. Those are potential employers who may be very interested in your experience and skills sets learned at the last employer.

Companies often require employees to sign non-compete agreements (usually with two-year limits). Those NCA's may not be valid (or legal) if there are only two entities in a general geographic area where the worker is able to be employed. For instance, if there are two hospitals in one remote county, one hospital cannot force a medical doctor to sign a non-compete against working in another hospital within a 50-mile area, especially if that other hospital is the only other workplace option for that doctor – and – it would cause an undue hardship for the doctor to move to obtain work outside the 50-mile radius. A company cannot legally enforce an NCA – if it causes unfair economic restrictions on an employee (the ability to work for any company of their choice). On the other hand, the company can enforce the employee from sharing proprietary information (e.g., research and development, proprietary secrets such as recipes or processes) from the last employer with their new employer.

8.   Look at your budget. A media story in 2019 about an economic research study, concluded that if faced with a financial emergency, a typical family in the United States would not have the ability to access or come up with $1,000 in credit or from savings. If one is living paycheck-to-paycheck, this may be a bona fide reality. Another story the author read indicated for every $10,000 in salary, over $40,000 annually, a job seeker should expect a month of searching for that next job. If one is earning $80,000 annually, one should expect to be looking for work for at least four months. This makes it critical to have at

least four to five months of savings in an 'untouchable' account for this type of emergency.

One can also cut back on luxury items – get rid of the subscription music apps, cable television, and memberships at the local gym. Don't hesitate to take a 'interim' position for much lower than expectations salary just to get food on the table and gas in the car.

If one has a 401(k) retirement account, one can borrow against the funds. The option is to borrow the money, and start repaying those borrowed funds immediately upon getting the new job, or pay taxes on those borrowed distributions in the current tax year's filings as 'income.'

9. Go back to school. In some cases, when an employee loses career job, it may be the perfect opportunity to switch careers by going back to school to learn a new trade, skill, update knowledge, or pursue higher degrees for their current career. Whether the school is in academia or a vocational trade school, most accredited schools will work with students to obtain Pell Grants or Student Loans to finance their schooling for tuition, books, and other fees, as well as potentially enough funds to live on (basic living expenses) during their full-time schooling.

10. Go on a well-deserved vacation! If you are

not constrained by finances, now may be a perfect time to get away and relax without work-related responsibilities to worry about. Seldom do adults in today's 24-hour work availability have the opportunity to truly be free without constraints or deadlines. If you can't go on vacation, take the time to work on hobbies you have missed or didn't have time for while you were working full-time. Take some time to spend with your kids, your better half, or relatives you haven't seen in a while. Enjoy the time, recharge your battery, and relax.

HOW TO DETERMINE THE BEST
ASKING SALARY FOR THE JOB

The (literally) $60,000 question is what salary should a job seeker ask for when they are discussing employment and compensation once they reach the interview stage.

Companies – even small businesses - normally perform an analysis on jobs they are posting to fill with the most qualified candidate. This analysis compares (required) job skills, background, education, abilities, and years of experience to ensure that salary and compensation matches a general market-level compensation level for the employee. Some companies will hire compensation analysis companies who are privy to multiple industry salary data (public and private) to provide researched, up-to-date, market ranges of salaries for specific types of jobs. These salary ranges are based on other factors such as geographic locations (Cost of Living Adjustments; COLA), years of experience, number of formal degrees, training and skill levels, as well as, in the government contracting or federal government, any security clearance (and levels).

Overall, if current job holder has a Master's degree and has 20 years of experience, but the targeted job candidate has only a Bachelor's degree and five years of experience, regardless of gender of either employee. Compensation should match the 'open market' competitive salary level and compensation for the employee at that level of experience and skill sets. Companies may look at some positions (human resources reps) as 'overhead' expense and will strive to pay as little as possible in salary and compensation to non-revenue generating staff costs down. You may not be paid your market value in the beginning, but think of it as obtaining valuable experience in the trenches. This is potentially true for those 'older' workers who are striving to move into a new career field, also.

1.   Job seekers need information to target the best range of compensation without accepting too little or accidently asking for too much during a job interview. Just because a job seeker has a degree in any particular field that normally pays very well, does not mean they will be able to walk into a position immediately after college graduation and get paid that average industry salary. New graduates may have to accept a position as an associate or assistant before working their way up in the ranks amongst the competition – even from those without career degrees – especially if the field is flooded (e.g., customer service and sales representatives, realtors, and human resources practitioners are common, with or without college degrees).

2.   When the recruiter calls to inquire (or emails), the job seeker should ask – diplomatically and tactfully – "What the

"*minimum* salary range?" is for the position.
You don't want to waste your time or the
recruiter's time, if the salary minimum is
more than 10% below what you would
accept for any position (e.g., you want a job
that pays $70K (USD), and the recruiter
quoted the salary minimum is $55K. There
is a good chance they would not be able to
stretch the salary range for this position to
the $70K plus benefits and other related
compensation.

3. Imagine receiving two or more job offers at
the same time. It's a good problem to have.
But how to decide which offer is best? What
other factors, besides salary, should they be
sure to consider?   If a job seeker receives
multiple job offers, they are doing something
'right' and now they need to make a vital
decision to see which 'sand-box' they want
to play in - and make a wise decision based
on their own career goals. Salary may be
secondary to the importance of the answers
to the above questions, because there may
be more intrinsic value over the long-term
employment with one company versus a
higher-salary at the second company. The
applicant should ask these plus other
questions of the interviewing manager or
recruiter in the first interview and write down
the answers for comparison if there are
multiple offers (although, yes, this is rare for
an AP to happen). When the job seeker is
in the first interview, they need to get the
answers to the following questions:

a) Is there full- or shared-costs for health and welfare benefits to the employee and/or the employee's full family? If the health and welfare benefits pay the entire monthly premium for the family, but the hourly wages are $2-4 an hour less, the employee may be 'ahead' because paying for part or all of the benefits at the higher-paying (per hour) company may end up with less in the employee's pocket.

b) Is there a Paid Time Off (PTO) leave policy and/or flex-time if the employee has a personal doc appointment or family emergency; in other words, is there another employee on staff that can fill-in for emergencies (lessons the guilt for an employee if they are absent).

c) Does the company have tuition reimbursement for increasing the worker's skills sets - computer classes (Excel, Project, Word), community college classes (towards degree programs), or other learning opportunities? The cost of tuition reimbursement to increase job skills and enhance the skill sets and knowledge to open the job seeker up for broader career possibilities in the future is also a huge bonus point.

d) How many weeks of paid vacation is offered annually, and how does the employee obtain more or becomes eligible for more (years of service)?

4.   Non-salary compensation is another factor
        that job seekers need to ask about or
        consider. Does the company have a cross-
        training programs to learn new skills and
        take on projects that others don't want or
        have no time to complete as learning or
        promotional opportunities for employees?

5.   What should job seekers be leery of and
        what are the potential pitfalls of applying to
        a job postings that seem too good to be true
        for salary and compensation?   Huge
        salaries or compensation packages that are
        offered sight unseen, even before an
        interview. While it sounds wonderful, rarely
        is anyone going to graduate from college
        with a general degree and walk into the job
        market demanding a six figure salary -
        seriously, this doesn't happen unless the
        graduate has a rare and unique job skill no
        one else has or you are the son or daughter
        of a politician and the parents have already
        networked the position for their offspring
        (think Chelsea Clinton or Hunter Biden).
        Scammers will offer to pay the job seekers
        up front - they will send a check for a large
        amount of money via US Mail or sometimes
        UPS or FedEx (to avoid the mail fraud
        charges if caught), then contact the job
        seeker telling the job seeker they
        accidentally sent too much money, could
        the job seeker send half back to help pay for
        food for the folks they are supposed to be
        working with - before the job starts.

6.   A job candidate always negotiates salary
        when interviewing for a job. Salary
        negotiations should start before the
        interview - yes, recruiters are reluctant to
        provide salary levels the company is 'willing'
        to pay, because the recruiter's job is to
        obtain the least expensive candidate for the
        position they must fill, regardless of any
        current salaries of any employees already
        working within the company with the same
        job title, while simultaneously being
        cognizant of EEOC equitable pay for both
        genders.   It would be best for an applicant
        to ask the recruiter - before or during formal
        interviews – either: what is the company
        salary range for this position, or what is the
        minimum salary that will be offered for this
        position? The job seeker should
        acknowledge to the recruiter they
        understand the salary will be contingent
        upon experience, skills, education, and
        other factors. If the recruiters are willing to
        provide salary range information, the job
        applicant can make a quick decision upon
        whether to provide any indicators' of further
        interest. Job seekers can start the
        conversation thus …

        e)   "My last position baseline salary was
                within this range, but with my XX
                years of experience, I would need to
                be considered for the high range of
                your salary considerations for a
                qualified candidate." This confirms
                you are willing to continue the

interview and salary would be within a reasonable negotiation range.

f) "My current salary is approximately 20% above the minimum salary range you considered, and my assumption is that the high-end of the salary is approximately 15-20% above the stated minimum salary. It may be tight for a compensation fit. What other compensation does the company provide and what are the normal annual salary increases based upon above standard performances? (If the additional perks are valued at between 2-6% of the salary, those added perks could be more valuable than the payroll cash – especially if 401(k) matches, tuition reimbursements, add up to more than that percentage.)

Once you know the salary ranges before you interview, you can more comfortably enjoy the telephonic or face-to-face interview without stressing over wasting time without being disappointed at the end of the hour or more with a low-ball salary discussion.

7. Does a job candidate have to submit salary history details? Ask the recruiter for the relevance. You could even note past salary concerns would be the future employer may not think your current worth matches the increased and more competitive salary at this point in your career. Ask the recruiter if

they can supply the job's salary range and you can assure them you are doing so to avoid wasting their valuable time in recruiting you if the range is not within your expectations. If they can only offer the baseline (minimum) range, then you can quickly perform a calculation as to whether a 10-20% range would reasonably be their top offer for baseline salary and decide to continue the conversation – or not.

Asking the recruiter about the relevance of your salary information may produce a reaction of them backpedaling from the question. If they persist, you can next ask them if you would be taken out of consideration if you declined to provide that information. Depending upon how 'desperately' you want to work for that company or just to get a job will provide your impetus to provide that data. or a 'range' for which you would be comfortable in providing (e.g., I will share the dollar-based value of my current total compensation package, including gross wages, value of benefits, and matching 401(k) pension to indicate my minimum salary consideration with your company if offered a position).

There is a new trend in employment law that is trending that makes it illegal to ask for salary history in many states (does not include federal job applications via USAJobs.gov), including: Alabama, California, Colorado, Connecticut,

Delaware, Georgia, Hawaii, Illinois, Kentucky, Louisiana, Maine, Maryland, Massachusetts, Mississippi, Missouri, New Jersey, New York, North Carolina, Ohio, Oregon, Pennsylvania, Puerto Rico, South Carolina, Utah, Vermont, and Washington (state).

8. Don't put 'absolutes' in front of the recruiters (I can't work for less than $XXX) before a full-blown conversation about the job itself, and a full explanation of the salary and compensation (perks) are discussed. The company may be hunting for a candidate willing to take a lower salary in exchange for a huge potential in the long-run such as on-the-job training for a position without candidate experience (based on the resume showcasing 'capabilities'); or the compensation perks outweighs the paycheck take-home amount (company pays 100% for all health insurance benefits for candidate plus all the family).

9. When the offer letter comes, call the interviewing manager and ask for a slightly higher offer to accommodate specific concerns. For example: "My commute is far longer than current position, so I need to negotiate associated additional fuel or commute costs" or "This position requires a more professional wardrobe than my last position – is there any accommodation for the higher costs of my business wardrobe and/or dry cleaning costs?" Make the additional salary request a directly relevant

'job-related' concern. Sometimes just asking for $1-3K more annually than the initial offer is an acceptable price-point for the offeror and hiring managers expect a counter-offer.

10. Advice for job seekers who need or want to change careers. Determine what type of work you are so passionate about that you would be willing to drop your salary in drastic measures just to get into the industry or you actually want to reduce your overall responsibilities. In many cases, if you do not have the experience under your belt, you *will* be starting from scratch and on par with new workers straight out of high school or college. You may need the re-training and/or re-education and companies are reluctant to train a new worker in skills sets at a reasonable salary when they can hire much younger folks (I know, age discrimination).

While the author strongly recommends the Objective line in a resume *only* include the job title sought, underneath there could be a second, *short* line indicating – "Looking for new entry-level, career field with associated job-level compensation to learn new skills and capabilities in lifelong field of interest." A short line on the cover letter relating the same information may help, also.

BONUS TIP!

11. Any resources recommended for research
on salary negotiations? To find 'ranges' of
salaries for general types of job titles and
then chopping off the 'outliers' (extremely
low and high salary metrics), you can obtain
a reasonable range of baseline salaries to
start negotiations.   There are several USA-
based sources you can explore to find
salary ranges for general types of jobs.
Glass Door requires a sign-up, profile, and
for you to add your own salary information
(anonymously) to help them build up their
database. The Bureau of Labor Statistics
works to provide the most recent job salary
ranges (usually within 6 months to a year
and a half after reporting by USA-based
companies), and Salary (dot) com is a site
that charges HR and Companies for
information, but individuals can request
broad salary range information based on
input to the database from company
subscribers. (Note: take Salary's data with a
grain of salt because they average the
entire country, including the higher salary
geographic areas of DC, New York, and
San Francisco in the output – which are
normally between a 20-25% higher
geographically-associated cost-of-living
[COLA].)

- Bureau of Labor Statistics
  (https://www.bls.gov/data/#wages)
- Glass Door
  (https://www.glassdoor.com/index.htm)
- Salary (https://www.salary.com/)

HOW TO LOOK FOR A JOB
ON THE 'DOWN LOW'

Some job seekers are worried that their current employer or boss will find out they are seeking a new career position – whether inside the same company or for a new employer. This fear sometimes prevents them from searching for a new job, including avoiding posting their resume on the major resume job boards. There are several options that job seekers can use in their new job search, as well as some realities about what can be seen in those large resume platforms. This keeps the job search as secret as possible.

1.   If you network and reach out to potential companies for consideration for a position for a new employer, you can ask what the company policy is for background checks and ensuring that the interviewing process is held in the highest confidence. Company representatives can't *legally* reach out to current or past employers for references or job information confirmations without a signature from the job seeker authorizing the referrals' contact. Any reach-back contacts to past or current employers should be *after* the future employer has provided the job seeker an offer letter of employment, which will include contingencies noting if the background

check does not meet minimum
expectations, the offer may be revoked.

2.   Build your LinkedIn profile; increase the
      number of connections to people with whom
      you have worked with, done business with,
      or interacted with in business events or
      organizations. Most folks won't hesitate to
      accept an invite to connect on LinkedIn if
      they know you. Make sure the profile is
      built up to a strong presence and you
      actively go into the account on a weekly
      basis to see who has been glancing at your
      profile. If recruiters or company
      representatives peek at your profile, then
      visit the company's websites to view their
      publicly posted open positions. They may
      not have time to reach out to all the profiles
      they review, and if your profile doesn't
      showcase your capabilities enough,
      perhaps you need to apply for a position
      with your refreshed and more-robust
      resume.

3.   Another benefit of LinkedIn is you can
      toggle on the 'recruiters may contact me for
      potential job interest' button. This opens up
      the possibilities for recruiters using LinkedIn
      to search for job candidates to reach out to
      'touch base' with you via their 'in-mail'
      subscriptions. This is another reason why
      you should accept invites to connect from
      folks you may not know. Connecting allows
      'free' unlimited in-mails between connected
      (linked) profiles. Otherwise, free or first
      level subscriptions are limited to about 10

'in-mails' monthly. Recruiters take advantage of this often. When you get an invite – check out the person's profile – and if they seem like a legitimate profile, then accept the connection.

4. Another LinkedIn benefit – especially for the paid business account level (circa $100 annually?) – is the ability to sign up for job alerts. This is a private service between LinkedIn and you. No one else knows or can see you are receiving these emailed job alerts posted by companies using LinkedIn as their recruiting, marketing funnel.

5. What if my boss sees all my activity on LinkedIn; won't they get suspicious and think I am looking for a new job? The boss will not be able to view your profile's 'activity' from others viewing your profile. They can see if you are building up your profile to a more robust page. If the boss gets suspicious you are building up your LinkedIn profile for a job search, then the boss is already suspicious you are searching for a new job. If asked, note you are working on keeping up the list of your achievements for the current job and posting them on LinkedIn provides a great way to keep up with the list for your annual performance evaluation.

6. Ask human resources what major job boards or website the company is using to resource candidates. ("Hey, I have a friend who is interested in working for the

company – which resume platform does the company use – Monster, CareerBuilder, or Indeed or something else? Or, do you only use the company website to solicit resumes from candidates?") Once you know what platforms the company uses, then you can either (a) avoid that resume database platform (e.g., if your company uses Monster.com, then post your resume on CareerBuilder or Indeed) or (b) you can anonymize your resume when you post it on job boards (see next bullet). Some resume platforms will allow this with a toggle button, while others do not have that option.

7. If you can't find an anonymity button or option on the major job boards to which you want to post your resume, then anonymize your resume using these tricks.

   a. Save your current resume, e.g., "Anonymous Resume Sept 2019" as the file name. Open and review the 'file properties' to ensure you do not have your name or any point of contact information in the file information text boxes.

   b. On the resume – type over your name with the words "Anonymous Job Seeker" (or any form of acceptable and alternative text).

   c. Delete any street address and only leave "City, ST" identifiers. This allows recruiters to pinpoint your geographic location in case they need you to start work immediately without waiting for relocation delays.

d. Create an email address you will check for messages related to jobs – or – create a new email to bounce directly to your regular email; then post the new 'anonymous' email (created without any unique identifying data such as name, birthdate, etc.) on the resume before you post it to the boards.

e. Anonymize the company for which you work currently with the words replacing content, e.g., "Company name privatized to avoid ethics issues; will share with serious employment inquiries."

f. While a good detective could always go back to your personnel file in the company HR offices to compare the anonymous resume online with your older resume in the file, it's a long shot that could even occur.

8. Find niche resume database platforms and online job boards to post your resume. If you are still worried about your current company finding you are searching for a new job on Monster, CareerBuilder, and Indeed, and you think your recruiting department has subscriptions for them all, look for smaller resume services that target specific industries. For instance placement

agencies, e.g., Robert Half and Associates. Sometimes the temporary staffing companies deliver more personal and 'quiet' services in finding candidates for companies to hire and these recruiting companies always anonymize the resumes before sending them over to companies for consideration of the skills and experience. This enables you, the job seeker, to review the company's credentials before you give the go-ahead to the temporary agency for setting up an interview as well as tell the placement agency to not forward your resume to your current employer.

9.   Apply directly to companies for jobs posted on their company website employment page. Companies usually have jobs posted on multiple advertised entities on the public market. Recruiters guard these resumes closely – because of the private and identifying information. Some applications have text boxes for adding notes from the job seeker to the potential future employer. The job seeker can emphasize keeping the job search confidential during the process in that private note space.

10.   Sometimes telling the boss or the company you are beginning to look for new career opportunities is better than hiding your efforts. If your company is looking to scale back the workforce, you are in a good position to ask for help from your peers and management staff to identify positions in other companies for which you are a good

fit. If a reduction in force or merging of
business units is in the near future, then
letting your manager know you are open to
promotional opportunities within other
business units (parallel move or move up),
they may have a positive mindset and help
you in those efforts.

JOB FAIR ADVANTAGES

There are mixed feelings about whether job fairs are a 'waste of time' for employers or the job seekers nowadays. Job fairs can be expensive for companies to attend, set up a booth, and send employees (overhead labor hours) to stand at the booth. Companies are *still* attending job fairs, or conducting in-house job fairs, to look for qualified job candidates for current and future positions. Job seekers are *still* getting the impression there isn't a payoff. There are still advantages for both parties for why job seeker's still need to attend job fairs and the advantages.

1. Companies now have online resume automated tracking systems (ATS) to handle recruiting efforts and the deluge of job applicants for advertised jobs. These electronic databases assist recruiters in finding the best applicant for a position based on key skill words and queries they perform on those words. But company's still attend job fairs for several reasons:

    a) The employer is desperate to fill a position 'yesterday' and has loaded its guns with several managers to find a candidate and interview them immediately (some employers might not be on an attending list, but attend at the last minute).

b) Employers wish to get their job openings virally marketed. Hard-copy lists do get circulated by job fair attendees to friends, family, peers, and co-workers.

c) Branding the company to get their name 'out there,' and to become recognizable to future job applicants when the time comes to solicit for resumes and recruit for positions.

d) Give attendees an idea of the type of people who work for the companies; provide warm fuzzies to job seekers visiting the company booth.

e) Recruiting for affirmative action to balance out gaps in AAP staffing and to documents the company has made efforts in recruiting those candidates

f) To 'resume farm' for job openings in the future, even if not open or posted now, to encourage today's job seekers to load resumes into the system for future consideration.

g) To 'peek' at other companies in the same business arena (industrial spying 'lite') to see what jobs are open or for which they are 'resume farming.'

h) HR departments schedule a minimum number of recruiting activities annually, and job fairs may be on the list for

currently funded events. Employers
may have paid for the job fair booth
months ago, and they can't get refunded
(sometimes employers don't bother
showing up if it costs more to fly in a
recruiter with no jobs to fill), so just
leave the booth unmanned with a
banner or flyers the organizer can put
on the table for the company.

2. Job seekers are puzzled employers no
longer accept hard-copy resumes –
especially in the defense industry. There is
a law enforced by the OFCCP, EEOC, and
DOL agencies driving this business
decision. Any hard copy resume accepted
(in a job fair) is a 'considered for hire'
candidate, whether qualified for the job or
not, and thus EEO information must be
recorded and documented for AAP reporting
(annually).

What does this mean to the process?
Companies circumvent a time-consuming,
manual recording of candidate data by
forcing job seekers to apply online where
the information is automated, self-reported,
provide easier to compile reports, and
unqualified candidates can easily be
disqualified in the system through filtered
questions and answers.

3. Job fairs are common recruiting tools. Some
job seekers travel from other cities to
attend, or they drive to Washington, DC or
the 'technology triangles' in some states for

what they believe may be a 'good venue' or 'cadre of hiring companies.' Job seekers often complain a job fair wasn't up to snuff, they wasted their money, employers didn't have any jobs, no one accepted resumes, or wanted to interview them. Walking in, job seekers should have "0" expectations. Prepare for positive actions to make it worth your while, regardless of the number or type of employers, interest, or number of job openings.

4.   Take hard copy resumes to the job fair for those few companies decide to accept resumes for a 'quick review.' Make sure cell numbers and an email address are at the top. If you can obtain some business cards (with a concise list of capabilities on the back of the card and your website URL for your resume), provide those at each booth. Dress for success at these events – do not walk in the door in sloppy clothes, leisurewear, or beach get-up.

5.   Actions to take during the job fair to get that return on investment and make yourself memorable:

      a)   Soak up the knowledge for those golden nuggets of information from speakers and special presentations offered for free to attendees. Ask representatives to glance over your resume for any advice they can offer if they won't take the physical hard copy at the job fair event.

b)	Visit every booth – regardless of whether you have an interest in or haven't heard of a company – and pick up company information to review later. Talk to each employer representative; ask if the company has subsidiaries not represented at the job fair, but that may have job openings; don't expect any quality interviews at job fairs – usually there are too few reps manning the booth to afford quiet, to-the-side, mini-interviews.

c)	Practice your elevator speech – you have 60 seconds to make yourself memorable; do *not* read your resume to the reps – most won't have time for interviews.

d)	Recognize that employer representatives at job fairs may be non-HR or non-recruiters sent to watch the booth and may know little about any job openings; often companies send the lowest-paid company rep to save overhead costs – ask for information about the company and business units instead of specific jobs in this case.

e)	Ask for names in the company; if you know anyone in the company – ask about them directly and how you can get in touch with them.

f) Research every company by picking up company brochures; get a business card from everyone in the room; you'll need those after you leave to reach out and email resumes direct. Find out if the company is looking for candidates for now or further down the road; are contracts ending or beginning; are the company ranks expanding or shrinking?

g) Soak up the give-away goodies offered at the job fair – if for nothing else, to walk away with something useful (flashlights, yellow highlighters, refrigerator magnet clips, thumb drives, etc.) – but don't grab and run –spend time with rep, ask politely for a give-away, and thank them.

6. Several actions should be performed at a job fair; here's advice for after the job fair. These follow-up actions provide tools and advantages other job seekers won't know to use. These tips are valuable whether you attend a job fair locally or drive to another state to attend a huge or broadly advertised event.

Search the Internet and social network sites (LinkedIn) before the job fair to see if you can find a name of a person working in the company and their department – use that name at the job fair to ask if 'John Doe' has any jobs requiring your capabilities in their department, but not yet posted; use that name after the job fair to refer to the event, and your interest in a position, via in 'in-mail' on LinkedIn.

At the job fair, get business cards from everyone for point of contact (POC) information by picking up a card at each table; connect with them on LinkedIn (write a personal note as to why you are asking to connect); and they may be able to later connect you with a hiring manager. If you get a name from the job fair rep, perform a Boolean search on the Internet (and LinkedIn) for that contact in HR, recruiting, or other departments to contact directly to forward your resume.

7.   If the POC other than HR gets a resume, there is a likelihood the person will forward it to HR, possibly perceived as a (employee) referral. Mail your resume and a cover letter to each employer rep for whom you grabbed a business card via snail mail, thanking them for the opportunity to discuss their company and potential job openings.

They may not remember you, but that's okay – now they have your hard copy resume and cover letter and may look at it for further consideration. Once they have a printed copy, and know it's posted to the company's online resume database, they may be inclined to forward the package via inter-office mail to a hiring manager who may have an interest in your capabilities.

8. Research every company by picking up company data you may need later. Job fairs are one of the richest sources of finding POC information within a company – there may be a name for a CEO, VP, or program manager in the handouts, company Internet website, or addresses for work sites, where you can send notes and resumes directly.

9. Send polite thank you notes to company executives on the professionalism of the job fair rep. The executives may show or route the note to the job fair rep. Of course the rep will want to review your profile in the recruiting system to see who said that nice thing about them – boom – you and your credentials are now under their noses and they are reading your resume.

10. Some job seekers are looking to move up to higher career levels. If you are waiting in a job fair line, start up a friendly conversation with the next person – Are they leaving a company? Is their contract ending? Where did they work before? Who did they work for ("…I think I remember someone who used to work for XYZ – what is your bosses' name…")? You might hit a gold-mine – if a program assistant is now looking for a program manager job because they need to move on and make more money – and now you know the name of the company and

what supervisor to send your resume. That employer will need to fill a job quickly.

JOB OVERQUALIFICATION, AGE DISCRIMINATION, AND THE LAW

Overqualified (adjective): overqualified; adjective: over-qualified; having qualifications that exceed the requirements of a particular job. "an overqualified person will quickly become dissatisfied." (dictionary.com)

Applicants see a job they're interested in, but based on their education and experience they are what they consider to be slightly over-qualified. How can they sell themselves if the job is one they really want because it offers them an opportunity to expand their knowledge and experience in an area they want to learn more about? Being told you're overqualified for a job can be akin to someone saying you are too awesome to date. Hiring managers may believe job seekers are using this job opportunity as a temporary gig until a more senior position opens up elsewhere, or that you expect to earn a salary that's commensurate with your experience.

Age Discrimination. Age discrimination involves treating an applicant or employee less favorably because of his or her age. The Age Discrimination in Employment Act (ADEA) forbids age discrimination against people who are age 40 or older (by employers with 20 or more employees in their labor pool).

It is illegal (in United States federal and state employment law) to imply a candidate is 'overqualified' as it 'stinks' of age discrimination. A company indicating this to disqualify an applicant could potentially set the company up for an age discrimination lawsuit (especially if the applicant is 40 years of age or older). To circumvent the illegality and age bias, most ATS systems usually allow the recruiters to ask job applicants what salary they are seeking (within a range). The company may believe the job applicant may be 'over-qualified' if they want a salary commensurate with their years of experience (considered over-qualification in comparison to others seeking the same salary range with lesser experience).

The Age Discrimination Act of 1975 prohibits discrimination on the basis of age in programs and activities receiving federal financial assistance. The Act, which applies to all ages, permits the use of certain age distinctions and factors other than age that meet the Act's requirements. The Age Discrimination Act is enforced by the Civil Rights Center.

The Age Discrimination in Employment Act of 1967 (ADEA) protects certain applicants and employees 40 years of age and older from discrimination on the basis of age in hiring, promotion, discharge, compensation, or terms, conditions or privileges of employment. The ADEA is enforced by the Equal Employment Opportunity Commission (EEOC).
https://www.dol.gov/general/topic/discrimination/ag edisc

Age Discrimination. Age discrimination involves treating an applicant or employee less favorably because of his or her age. The Age Discrimination in Employment Act (ADEA) forbids age discrimination against people who are age 40 or older. It does not protect workers under the age of 40, although some states have laws that protect younger workers from age discrimination. It is not illegal for an employer or other covered entity to favor an older worker over a younger one, even if both workers are age 40 or older. Discrimination can occur when the victim and the person who inflicted the discrimination are both over 40.

Age Discrimination & Work Situations. The law prohibits discrimination in any aspect of employment, including hiring, firing, pay, job assignments, promotions, layoff, training, benefits, and any other term or condition of employment.

Age Discrimination & Harassment. It is unlawful to harass a person because of his or her age. Harassment can include, for example, offensive or derogatory remarks about a person's age. Although the law doesn't prohibit simple teasing, offhand comments, or isolated incidents that aren't very serious, harassment is illegal when it is so frequent or severe that it creates a hostile or offensive work environment or when it results in an adverse employment decision (such as the victim being fired or demoted). The harasser can be the victim's supervisor, a supervisor in another area, a co-worker, or someone who is not an employee of the employer, such as a client or customer. An employment policy or practice that applies to

everyone, regardless of age, can be illegal if it has a negative impact on applicants or employees age 40 or older and is not based on a reasonable factor other than age (RFOA).
www.eeoc.gov/laws/types/age.cfm

1.   There are ways to avoid potential age bias in job shopping. Ensure your resume is worded properly to avoid the indications of your age.   Never note more than 25 years of 'anything' on your resume; if you take a college degree date and the 30 years of employment, a recruiter can add up and figure out you are over 50 years of age. Instead, if you have been in the military for 35 years, then note a 'ceiling #' of years then add a plus sign: "20**+** years in the US Navy"

2.   Education can be listed, but not 'dated.' If your college degree is not within the last 10-15 years, then don't add a graduation date, but if it is within the last 10 years, DO note the date. Recruiters may assume the job seekers is younger because of 'more recent' college degree.

3.   If you have only had one job in the last 15 years use volunteer experience to round out your diversity and versatility. Provide as much leadership- and management-related task descriptions as possible, but if you are trying to de-emphasize leadership level tasking to move into a lower-level position in a future job, then discuss the mid- to lower-level types of tasks you completed or

accomplished.

4. The older job seeker should absolutely have computer skills - too many older workers nowadays can hardly use the basic office software packages. It is imperative the basic office software be at least an intermediate skill, but the older worker may want to pursue other computer software learning programs (local adult education centers and community colleges) to at least open their skill sets (and minds) to learning new things. The minute an older worker opens their mouth and admits to not having used the computer much or not knowing many software programs, they have immediately 'dated' themselves.

5. Another plus - list all the types of training you have offered to others in the job - including mentoring as an 'added value.' So many companies want to perform internal training for their staff, but can't afford outside education costs; having an internal staff member who is skilled at training and mentoring is an added benefit. If someone is older and considered 'over-qualified', the perhaps their ability to teach others their skills would be an enhanced non-age-related skills.

6. In filling out applications - for those entries that require dates that will 'tell someone's age' – the author suggests trying to leave them blank (if possible in online applications), or adding in fake dates

01/01/2000. In the description line, note "Real Dates not provided due to potential 'age-bias'; will be happy to provide the true dates to HR once offer letter in hand."

7. If a job seeker knows what position applicants are indicating willingness to accept as salaries, the (older) applicants can indicate acceptance of the salary range, and have a higher chance of being reviewed. Some companies may see a very qualified applicant, but cannot pay what they believe the applicant may be seeking, so to circumvent the legal issue, the recruiters can reveal to the 'over-qualified' applicant, "the salary range is between $XX and $XX; we are unable to pay any more than that - are you still interested in being considered for this position?" If the applicant has the chose to withdraw from consideration for salary reasons, then the company avoids age discrimination issues. If the applicant decides to accept whatever the salary range is, including the maximum, then the company should continue to review the application and move the job seeker to qualified candidate status.

8. This may sound cheesy, but for gosh sakes – look at yourself in the mirror. Do you 'look old'? Do you have graying hair, slumping shoulders, are you bent over, walk slowly, talk slowly, and/or are overweight? You may be your own worst enemy when it comes to the job search.

9. Some job candidates insist on putting the Jr. or Sr. behind their names. This could potentially indicate age. These initials are not vital on a resume – unless your son or dad is also searching for a job at the same companies or in the same industry / field. Leave that information off the resume – it's not important.

10. Don't go back more than 10-15 years in your job history. Most recruiters or headhunters are only interested in applicants most recent and relevant employment. Any experience or skills older than 15 years may no longer have any relevance in current business practices (especially in the 'tech' or 'IT' world). Instead of listing an objective statement, simply list the number of years in 'general' types of jobs (e.g., 10+ years supervisory management vs. Manager at XYZ company), regardless of the number of years of experience.

JOB SEARCH STEPS
AND RESOURCES

Twenty years ago, the choices for searching for a job were somewhat limited: (a) look for open positions in the newspaper, then mail in one's resume to P.O. Box provided, (b) print dozens of paper resumes and mail them to potential employers, (c) calling businesses to ask if hiring and could 'one come fill out an application?', (d) visit the local state-run employment commission, or (e) network with friends, family, and strangers to ask who was hiring.

Fast-forward to the digital age. Most of the 20th Century job-search methods are obsolete as we move past the second decade of the 21st Century. Companies no longer accept paper resumes. The government instigated legal employment-practice mandates forcing businesses to keep records on every resume and job posting. To keep up with the tsunami of documents and data, companies moved recruiting processes to Automatic Tracking Systems (ATS) to document the paperwork. The ATS platform also enabled recruiters to increase productivity via Boolean searches on keywords, and send out mass communications to system-registered job seekers when a position opens.

Massive (and smaller competitors) online

resume collection websites entice job seekers to post their resumes so employers who are subscription holders can search for candidates within those thousands, if not millions, of job seeker resumes. Other companies cater to job seekers and hiring companies by selling RSS feeds of resumes to recruiters directly to their e-mail box. Social media has opened up new sources for job seekers to search for open positions, while employers have taken advantage of newly created funnels of qualified candidates, also.

Job seekers can use steps to prepare and work towards their next job or career promotion. The following tips will provide some guidance for where to start and how to look. Knowing, via a checklist, what actions to take provides the best return on the job search time and efforts.

1. Collect referrals and recommendations. The best place to collect and store referrals are on LinkedIn. You can also obtain company letterhead referrals to keep copies on hand. Keep a list of co-workers or peers willing to provide referrals for your work standards and professionalism. Keep that list updated annually for cell numbers, emails, and current employer(s) and job title(s).

2. Compile certifications or records for skill sets. Track down school transcripts for education or training. You will want to list these on your resume, as well as on any employment performance reviews, to keep track of these for showcasing your increased capabilities based on the

education, training, and/or job skills.

3. Ensure your resume is professionally written (don't be stingy – hire a good resume rewriter!). Ensure clean formatting, spell-proofed, and grammar-checked for clean language and writing style. Ensure the resume is between 1-4 pages for a private sector resume that showcases 10-15 years of experience. Update the resume every time an important work goal is achieved. Add the special achievements to your resume when you meet important work-related goals such as increased revenues, reduction of manpower, or added productivity.

4. If the job seeker has social media profiles, ensure those are scrubbed or privatized so future employers can't find any compromising or unprofessional posts. If one is unsure about what may be on social media profiles historically, the best option is to simply delete all the accounts. If a job seeker decides social media is vital in their life, let connections know about the profile(s) deletions and the new accounts for professional and private profiles. Some people can live without them, while others need the accounts to keep up with family and social circles.

5. Ensure resume-connected resources are updated regularly – especially LinkedIn. The job seeker's LinkedIn platform should be loaded with as much information from

the resume as possible. The LinkedIn
profile should have all 50-allowable skill sets
populated in the Skills section. The updated
resume should be attached to the social
media profile. Whenever a resume is
updated, update the most current version
posted on social media and/or in resume
databases.

6.   Identify which online resume databases to
       job seeker wishes to post their updated
       resume. Don't settle for just one … hedge
       your bets by researching as many as
       possible, and not just general platforms, but
       niche markets. Load the resume into all of
       them. If a job seeker's skill set is unique
       and in a niche market, the job seeker may
       be inundated with messages from
       desperate recruiters or listening to crickets if
       the skill set is too general or not enough in
       demand.

7.   Network! Research your phone list or inside
       connections on social media. If one has
       been active and providing some amazing
       posts on social media, the reach out for a
       new position may be rich in responses.
       Make phone calls – ask where can you look
       for potential jobs, not-yet-advertised
       positions, or if contacts' know anyone who
       knows somebody.

8.   One hidden gem and mostly undiscovered
       resource for job listings is the state
       employment agencies located in most major
       cities in each state across the country.

These offices have online and in-person locations, with computers, to search for jobs, register for classes on how to perform job searches, and more important – they have a database of open jobs advertised by companies across the state. Some companies use the state-based employment agencies to post public jobs as part of their Equal Employment Opportunity (EEO) and Affirmative Action Plans (AAP) for diversity recruiting. Smaller companies can't afford expensive ATS platforms or subscriptions to the larger resume databases, so may use the state-based (free) sources to post their open positions.

9. Visit websites of companies located near the job seeker's desired work location. If you don't have computer to use at home, visit the local library to study local business listings to identify companies with potential interest in your skills. Make a list. Visit each company's website and search for the 'recruiting page' to study open positions and to upload the resume into the company's proprietary database for current or future job opening considerations. Don't discount companies that are located in far-away cities. Sometimes large Fortune-500 or Fortune-1000 companies may have local offices in unexpected locations.

10. Be aware of job sites that attract scam and con artists (including Craig's list, which is usually a ripe arena for these scams). Job seekers may apply and immediately get a

message identifying the job seeker as a 'perfect candidate' for a job and when can they start work? Be wary of ANY entity offering to hire before meeting in person or interviewing. These situations are ripe for desperate job seekers who believe the contactor is a legitimate employer. Be wary of those who offering to send a first paycheck in advance ... especially if they haven't collected the first piece of employment information about you – including social security, legal application information, or conducted any valid interview questions. In this case, scammers send 'fake' checks, hoping the victims will deposit the check at an ATM after hours, then contact the victim stating they overpaid and need the difference back immediately via money transfers, Western Union, gift cards, or other 'cash-equivalent' methods of monetary exchange.

PASSIVE JOB SEARCH
ACTIVITIES AND PREPARATION

Are you going to become an active job seeker or a passive job seeker? Both have their resume either professionally written or updated regularly throughout the year with new accomplishments or achievements from their current employer or new career milestones or training/education achieved. The differences:

Active job seekers will post their updated resume in major resume databases (public, Monster.com, CareerBuilder.com, Indeed.com, Corporate Gray, etc.). Additionally, they will actively (similar to a part-time job or full-time if they are unemployed at the moment) look for job requisitions that have been publicly posted by companies in the career industry in which they are seeking a new position. Active job seekers will actively watch their own company for promotional opportunities. Active job seekers will actively network with their friends, family, tactfully and under the radar with their co-workers or peers in the industry, and/or with potential new employers via their clients. The active job seeker will ensure they have available paid or unpaid time off to use for those last minute interview appointments. Active job seekers will be available before work, during lunch, and after work, and weekends for communicating with hiring managers or headhunters.

Passive Job seekers will post their
resumes to resume databases, but will not actively
spend time on applying to open / publicized jobs.
Passive job seekers are somewhat content with
current situation, but will have an open mind if a
'too good not to follow-up inquiry' comes along.

1.   Never say no to an opportunity. Regardless
        of how long you have been in your current
        job, if something comes along that is your
        passion, at the right salary level, regardless
        of whether you have been with the current
        company six weeks or six years, you want
        to be ready to hand over an updated
        resume on the spot. Even though the
        author has been in consulting for 10 years,
        her C.V. is updated for every new
        publication, article, book, and cited work.
        You never know when a job offer comes
        along from someone you just met at a
        conference, a chance encounter at a client's
        office, or at a party.

2.   Create and maintain a LinkedIn profile. It's
        an amazing tool once you understand the
        power of this business professional
        platform. Folks think it is a: (a) sales
        platform, (b) recruiting site, (c) a dating site,
        or (d) a recruiters resume database. It is
        definitely not a dating site, and many
        professional women shied away from it
        because of inappropriate messages, but the
        'reporting' function for these ''nonconformist'
        stalkers works well. The platform primarily

focuses on Business-to-Business (B2B) connections between working professionals as its premise. Recruiters have found this to be a gold-mine for qualified candidates because the profile owners not only load resumes (which the recruiters can download), but also expand into groups (with participation and discussion recruiters can review). Salespersons can research point of contacts within a company to explore business opportunities (although naive sales-persons barrage you with pitches – which is *not* proper networking etiquette). And, LinkedIn offers a 'jobs' tab that helps with researching posted positions as well as researching businesses with company profiles.

3. Keep your rolodex, your LinkedIn connections, and/or your phone contacts up-to-date. While you expand your role in your current job, ensure that any peers, coworkers, and business clients are added to your (a) LinkedIn connections (if they are willing) and (b) added to your personal phone or address book. If you ever separate from your current employer, you can start down the list and start making calls to past clients and connections to start an active job search. Keeping these connections updates helps you passively keep connected.

4. Create and maintain job alerts. Regardless of whether you are deliriously happy in your current job, or just want to see what is out

there, create job alerts in the major resume databases as well as in LinkedIn. These job alerts can often be set for instant, daily, or weekly emails. You can review them as they come in to see what company is hiring, what types of jobs are being posted and whether you find something that will trigger an "OMG – I always wanted a job doing that!"

Sometimes recruiters catch up to job seekers just a 'little too late' in some cases. The author once accepted a job as a high-level manager, and four weeks later was sought out by a recruiter for a very lucrative career position, but had already 'settled' in and decided to stay. WHY is this good (to have kept the job alerts)? You can conversationally chat with the recruiter to find out inside information about the company, the salary range you might have qualified for, what type of perks the company offers employees in those positions, and other information you may not have been able to ask in actual job negotiations. This information provides great data for competition research, also.

5.   Update your resume with each new added skill. You should treat your resume as if it were a performance evaluation you have to present to your boss every month to be judged on what you did right in the job to keep the job. Every month, you should add major accomplishments and achievements, and what those meant in results to your employer - increased revenue, decreased

overhead costs, increased productivity, new clients, training of peers and/or coworkers so they can do their job better. What have you done that is not in your *job description* that was a positive thing for your company / employer. How did your employer gain by your industriousness? If you do this monthly, then annually, you have an updated resume for your current job, and you won't have to struggle to remember everything you did at the end of the year.

6.   Every month, after you have updated your resume – reload that resume into the major job boards. The trick to getting seen more often by recruiters who use the major job boards for finding qualified candidates is to update the resume at least every 30 days. If you have a resume in Monster.com, then take the current resume, add a blank line or an update to a new project completed or even additional training. This tricks the website search engine into thinking it is a 'fresh' resume versus an older one which gets pushed down due to age in the database. This keeps your resume in front of more eyeballs.

7.   Every month, after you have updated your resume – reload that resume into your LinkedIn profile. Delete the old and update the new resume in LinkedIn. LinkedIn will return results of searches by recruiters more often to profiles that have been refreshed, new content added, and to a profile owner who signs in and browses around in the

LinkedIn profile more often. A peek a week is the goal, and updates monthly or at least quarterly.

8. Write white papers or advice articles and post them on LinkedIn to get notice for your skill sets. LinkedIn profile owners get a huge amount of notice when they post often. One connection to the author posts a photo – no writing or content – just the photo, and they are probably from a stock photo site … but the photos grab your eye, and then you look at who is posting it. The author posts weekly slides about job hunting, resume writing, and other job search tips. Active LinkedIn profiles can get as many as 100-600 views weekly!

9. What else should you do to perform passive job searching? The author can NOT stress enough education, training, and certifications on anything and everything you can find to increase your skills sets, education, and capabilities. Use YouTube free tutorial videos to learn how to increase your ability to use MS Office or other software. Google for free software training on anything the company uses so you can find and develop new skills. If you are government contractor or government employee, search out the DAU (Defense Acquisition University) for free classes. There are MOOC (Massive Open Online Courses) provided by some universities to 'audit' a course for free. Subscribe to on online training site (e.g., Lynda.com) and go

through the learning modules for any
specific type of software you think could be
useful in a future position or a totally new
career path. (LinkedIn owns Lynda.com now
and a paid LinkedIn subscription gets you
free access). Check the local city adult
education offerings for computer classes,
accounting packages (e.g., QuickBooks),
see if local businesses offer free training
(Jackson Hewett and Liberty Tax offers free
tax classes). *Do not stop learning* or you
lose your ability to learn job skills. Don't be
scared of computers to learn, self-teach,
and educate yourself on software,
hardware, and soft knowledge.

10. Keep a folder of all of your best work so you
can add it to your portfolio. A portfolio is
mandatory if you are an artist, but a portfolio
is not something a recruiter will ask for if
shopping for candidates in a non-artistic
field. What recruiters want to see are
examples of projects and programs one has
managed. Sometimes the information is
proprietary to the company (current
employer), so it would not be ethical to
show to recruiters in a 'current work'
portfolio. Recruiters are looking for how you
saved a project, how you increased profits,
how you decreased overhead or man-hours,
and technology used to increase
productivity.

READING AND INTERPRETING
JOB DESCRIPTIONS

"I was told to copy the job description to ensure keywords were in my resume …" is something the author often hears from resume clients. Job seekers copy and paste the content directly from the online announcement, but can't understand why they are ignored when they send in their 'plagiarized' resume. Copying and pasting a job description won't help. When recruiters see 'copy and paste' resumes, they recognize their job descriptions, and reject the resume. Recruiters want to read applicant job accomplishments, task capabilities, and achievements … written uniquely to a job seeker's specific background, skills, and experience.

Job seekers can analyze the important words from an open position announcement by scrutinizing the job requisition for general and specific requirements sections. Ignore the benefits and company description. Target the 'must have' qualifications for clues to keywords recruiters are seeking.

For example, the job requisition "Budget Analyst" (posted on usajobs.gov) notes:

- Assist in work to be accomplished; communicate assignments, problems to be solved, issues, and deadlines.
- Coach team in selection and application of appropriate problem-solving methods and techniques; resolve employees complaints.
- Maintain program and administrative reference materials, project files / relevant documents; prepare reports; maintain records of accomplishments / administrative information.
- Represent the team for the purpose of obtaining resources; securing needed information or decisions from the supervisor on major work problems / issues.
- Represent team findings and recommendations in meetings; deal with issues that have an impact on the team's objectives, work products and/or tasks.

This description is in the generalized job section. It is heavily advised to NOT copy general job descriptions into any resume.

- "Assisted in work" could equate to a team member assigned specific workload assignments to research, analyze, identify, and implement solutions to problems, methods, and technical issues.
- "Represent the team" can be interpreted as presenting reports on specific topics to a group.
- "Maintain program and administrative reference materials" could equate to a document-database librarian or database maintenance tech with software skills, and alphabetical- and

numeric-filing capabilities, and ability to recognize documents 'classes.'"

- "Prepare reports and maintain records" of work accomplishments equates to filing documents in a manual or in digital format (e.g., create electronic files on a server or SharePoint website in a logical, organized manner."
- "Research qualitative and quantitative" equates to an ability to ask questions, perform statistical analysis, and possibly conduct Lean Six Sigma studies or process improvements to work tasking, production (lowered man-hours), recommending automation processes for work-task processing, and improving customer service timing and services."
- "Resolve simple complaints" could subjectively equate to 'being a people person' (please don't use that cliché' term!).

The remainder of the job description is more 'generic' capabilities. The ability to "communicate orally and in writing; make presentations clearly; manage time, balance priorities, and work under tight timeframes and conditions; use of computer for word processing, spreadsheets, graphics, and communications programs; use of analytical and problem-solving techniques; use of automated financial systems" can easily be interpreted as strong work capabilities that are discussed in the same bullets explaining specific skill requirements.

Copying and pasting the original job description won't help job seekers. Describe 'how' a specific task or responsibility matches the job description's mandatory experience requirements to showcase an ability to interpret, analyze, and write to satisfy the recruiter's need for documented *capabilities*. Recruiters can read between the lines for skills, experience, and education via those keywords describing the experience.

What is missing in this 'general' job description? Anything related to financials, accounts receivables or accounts payables, budget oversight, monetary or financial analysis. Now review the '*must-have*' job description details. Target the mandated job skill requirements and write about tasks accomplished related directly to that experience using the keywords. And use objective terms in describing accomplishments, not subjective descriptors that can't be proven as fact./

- "Knowledge of budget concepts, process, financial coding structure, and interrelationships among appropriations" means describe the accounting system (name brand software) and the line item coding, accounts receivables / accounts payable, budget appropriations (funding) and funding designations (to / from business units) and obtaining approvals for expenditures.
- "Interpret budgetary aspects of laws, regulations, policies, procedures, and provide guidance" means detailing knowledge of Generally Accepted Accounting Practices (GAAP), and experience as a Subject Matter Expert (SME) on Internal Revenue Service (IRS) law, regulatory compliance (including Sarbanes-Oxley; SOX), and internal company policies and procedures related to taxes, budgeting, finances, and accounting to advise peers and management.

- "Analyze and relate financial data to work plans, business plans, Strategic Plans …" means data research, analysis, auditing, and compiling reports to share in group presentations.

Read those job descriptions and rewrite your resume to the job postings minimum standards to showcase 'matching' capabilities.

1. Read the job description carefully – and if needed – copy and paste the full job description onto a blank document (on computer) and then highlight keywords that are job related – Accounts Receivables, GAAP, Accounts Payable, budget, compliance, SOX, compliance, taxes – to make a list. Then open your resume and search for each of these key terms in your own resume. If you know you have the skills or knowledge, but you can't find those keywords in your resume – you have just failed the recruiters' qualifications test for that job!

2. Once those keywords are identified in the job description, and you have the list of keywords, write descriptive bullets of what you achieved or accomplished, and how often, directly related to those keywords.

    a. Performed accounts receivables postings and balances daily for up to $5,000 of incoming payments from as many as 200 clients
    b. Created reports for company accounting book balances weekly, presented to

   Chief Financial Officer, resulting in
   historic comparisons for forecasting
   sales and revenue for upcoming fiscal
   year

 c. Used Generally Accepted Accounting
   Practices (GAAP) for performing
   bookkeeping tasks for company general
   ledgers, passing external auditor's
   review annually

3. It's important to add metrics into the
   resume. Metrics come in many forms –
   actual numbers associated with each task
   (compiled four reports weekly), numbers
   associated with what you do for others
   (assisted ~80 dinner guests at 10 tables per
   shift, four days week, during 4-hour shifts),
   or production numbers (achieved an
   increase in sales by 25% or $200K in three
   months from start date), or a list (worked on
   sales, revenue, income, and employee
   schedules).   Metrics not only tell what you
   did, but how well or at what level you did
   those tasks. You want to 'show, not tell'
   how well you performed at a task, and
   metrics are documentable records that can
   be substantiated to a degree to prove you
   did something well or at which you excelled.

   Once you have added keywords, and
addressed the minimum job description
requirements in your resume, it's time to describe
potential experience that may be directly related to
your past performance. Anything extra, above the
minimum job-related skills or capabilities
demonstrates an 'added value' asset to compete

with those other applicants.   Ensure you add these elements to your resume if you have answers to the questions below that describe related experience.

4.   Do / Did you manage or supervise others – if yes, how many and what are/were their functional job titles or responsibilities under your supervision?

5.   Do / did you train or mentor (formally or informally) subordinates or peers? Did you develop the training curriculum? How often do you train per topic, to XX of learners per class, for a total of about ## classes over XX years, and circa XX total learners trained?

6.   What was the value of the equipment, contracts, or projects over which you participated in, supervised, or managed? What was the value of the company assets to which you had oversight?

7.   What budget did you oversee, if any, annually ($XXXXK or $XXM)? Even if you didn't create the budget, what oversight or control over it do/did you perform?

8.   Where/how did you save money for your employer or the employer's client? How much money (USD value) total or in accomplishing unique jobs/tasks did you save for your employer or client(s) during tenure? Provide a quantitative estimate, e.g., saved $XXXK in office supply requisitions or reduced manpower by XX %

over (XX months or years?) and provide documentable data. Saying you saved thousands of dollars or hundreds of hours is stating a guess; make sure you indicate real numbers – not guestimates..

9.   What estimated amount of project work (with metrics) did you accomplish daily, weekly, monthly, quarterly, annually?

10.   What new processes did you personally instill and what were results? What was saved (man-hours, budget money), or what did the processes increase (productivity)?

RESEARCHING YOUR FUTURE
EMPLOYER AND THE JOB POSTING

Research the company you are applying for a position with thoroughly before going in for an interview. Be prepared with lots of questions – you are allowed to ask as many as the hiring managers are asking you. Don't let time constraints for either party pressure you. If you do not get all the answers, then ask for a second interview to pursue more information.

1) There are horror stories about jobs that seemed too good to be true. Be careful with where you search for jobs. (Craig's list is a scary place where creepers and stalkers post fake ads then ask job seekers to show up in remote locations to be robbed or worse.) Focus on applying for jobs directly via company websites and their employment pages online or the larger public job boards (Monster, Indeed, CareerBuilder). Ask logical and reasonable questions. Is the job 'promising' a minimum salary that seems higher than your experience would practically earn? Is the job promising hard-to-believe benefits? It could be a hustle. Con artists post a job that seems promising and with reasonable expectations (busy son needs part-time assistance with parents with Alzheimer's).

They may note little-to-no experience is required, and hire you sight unseen (without an interview) based on a few questions. Their communications may present an 'urgency' to get you hired. They may also offer to pay in advance – to automatically deposit the check to your account, even. (Yup – it's a con job to either get your bank account information). Or, they may send what looks like a legitimate back check (if there is no routing numbers or bank account number or bank name on the check – it's fake). The con artists are hoping you will deposit the fake check, then they will request a portion of that money via a cashier's check or wired to them.

2) Prepare a set of questions for the hiring managers or human resource interviewers. Although they are interviewing you for an open position, YOU are interviewing them for a long-term career position. You want to ensure you are comfortable with the people and the work environment. Ask the interviewers what 'pain' that you, as the new employee, can resolve for them (they need an empty chair filled or they have serious issues in the department they need someone with skills to fix or make go away).

3) Research the heck out of the company and if you can suggest a 'correction' in a typo on their website or marketing materials, then you can showcase your eye for details. If you can bring into the discussion points you found out about the company during your

research, they will know you - as the job candidate - are serious about the position.

4) The majority of job descriptions are written from heavily analyzed and researched compensation plans within the corporate structure and provide a 20,000 feet viewpoint of the position. The position may be somewhat vague in actual description, with some nuggets of more specific wording for tasking. Research the general job description that matches what the company job title is posted for a vacant job. If the job title is software engineer, don't focus so much on the company posting versus what you can find as a general job description doing an Internet search. The Bureau of Labor Statistics has outstanding job descriptions, with listings of salaries, typical job responsibilities, and baseline requirements for education and training. Use the general job descriptions you find on multiple job boards to write up your own job description and describe specifically what you accomplished related to those general industry positions.

5) Be wary of all job contacts, and do your research before you leave the house for any interviews. Look for the company website, perform your due diligence for how long the company has been in business. Look the company up in the state Securities Exchange system. Check with the Better Business Bureau to see if there have been any complaints. Check online with Glass

Door to see if any current or past
employees of the company have issues or
complaints about the company and work
environment. If you cannot find anything
about the company, you may wish to work
with the recruiting representative to conduct
a telephonic interview first, so you are in a
safe place while you learn more about the
company.

6) Research company employees. LinkedIn
can assist in this research. On LinkedIn you
can find employees of the company by a
direct search in the search inquiry box.
Typing in the company name will result in
lists of employees who work for the
company (currently or in the past). You can
read about the employees or potentially
reach out to them for two purposes: (a) to
find out more about what working for the
company is like from the inside, or (b)
asking if the company has an employee
referral plan for employees to refer potential
candidate for award bonuses. If the
employee reviews your resume and likes
what they see, they may forward the
resume directly to HR for consideration for
more than one open position and that email
will link them to any potential hiring action
for a bonus.

7) When you write a cover letter, there are
three vital sets of information recruiters and
hiring managers may want to see, other
than the grammar, punctuation, and spelling
within the letter itself. (a) where did you find

the information about the job (so HR can continue to market that successful market or demographic); (b) why do you want to come to work for the company (mention something the company logo, motto, website simple summary, etc.; and (c) mention whether you actually know anyone who works in the company who may have referred you (and may earn a referral fee). If you have done your research, these three pieces of information can help you help the recruiters pay more attention to you and your resume.

8) Research *yourself* – what would the company find out about YOU if they performed a Google search? When companies have access to third-party background checking vendors and social media is so rampant out on the Internet, just a few minutes of research will result in all types of information about a person. Online companies charge $19.99 to come up with as much information as possible in public records for a target. It may be worth it to pay for a search for yourself. If there is negative information online, now is the time to catch it, report it, request it be removed, or to hire an online reputation defender to work at removing all the negative information.

9) If a company is interested in your background and skill sets, and asks you as the job seeker to perform 'spec' (speculative; sample) work, ask dozens of questions about the spec work required.

Ask for references from current employees who performed spec work to gain employment with the company and ask those employees what their experiences were (positive/negative?). Research via GlassDoor for any negative reviews posted for pre-employment spec work. Was the company consistent in *hiring or not hiring* after they get the ideas and work completed. If the spec work seems like it would entail hours or weeks of work to complete, then the job seeker has two options: (a) tell the hiring company you will expect payment, as a 1099 contractor, for any work performed on their behalf, regardless of whether they are satisfied with the end product or not, or (b) tell them you would prefer not to work for a company who uses job seekers to perform work for the company without payment, because that demonstrates unethical business practices.

10) If a company is hiring for an overseas position, you must do your research for the living conditions, housing availability, and comparative salary ranges on your own to compare with the answers provided by the interviewers (e.g., if Britain is 30% higher cost of living average [COLA], then the USA-based salary should be bumped up while working in the UK). Do you fluently speak the language of the country in which the job is located? Do you have a valid passport? Will you need a work-Visa or green card for that host country? When interviewing for a position in another

country, you also need to ask about medical benefits, emergency health care, international banking, and access to company provided transportation or vehicles.

RESEARCHING YOUR NEXT
'EMPLOYER OF CHOICE'

Recruiter's jobs are to find a perfect candidate for a company or client needing a job filled. Recruiters must be respectful, courteous, accommodating, and pleasant to deal with as the face of the corporate entity. Their goal is to demonstrate and convince the candidate their company is an 'Employer of Choice' to applicants seeking positions.

What happens when the company has a 'bad reputation?' The best they can do is hope the job candidates don't know about the 'negatives' related to the business. Job seekers need to dig deep into the weeds to research everything they can find out about a company – not just what the company says about themselves, but what third-parties say about the company. This company – and its reputation – will follow you around on your resume for years, so be careful about who you go to work for in your career.

1.   Applicants hope for a phone call for an interview, but don't think to investigate the company. There are many venues to do the research. One of the best ways to learn more about the company environment is via social media. Job seekers can also perform

Internet research and review industrial guides. It's easy to log into websites focusing on providing data about the company, as well as checking social media pages such as Facebook and LinkedIn for employee (or ex-employee) commentaries.

2.   An Internet search for 'Rate My Employer' turns up GlassDoor.com and RateMyEmployer.com. You can also find company data at Business Wire, Hoover's Online, WetFeet.com, EarningsWhispers.com, Annual Reports Library, Forbes Lists of Best Companies, Thomas Register, and Wright Research Center for salary ranges and employee feedback. Use key search terms of the company name inside quotes and a plus sign combined with keywords (+Watch) to see if organizations have the company on a watch list for unethical business practices. Check with customer feedback sites, also, for what the business customers are saying (see list below).

3.   What are job seekers looking for? Is the company potentially on a government regulatory list of organizations that need to report regularly to the oversight agency such as the Securities and Exchange Commission (SEC)? What news stories have been published within the last year about the company – were they PR stories (positive) or investigative (negative) stories? Are there 'alternative' media covering stories for conspiracy theories or are they

'kooks' throwing out theories. Take what is read on the Internet with a grain of salt, read the reports, and write solid questions to ask the hiring manager during the interview.

4.   Job seekers should investigate the company's use on social media platforms – including all the top 5-10 major venues: LinkedIn, Facebook, YouTube, Pinterest, and Twitter. Are they open to direct messaging? Are there loads of positive or negative posts from social media users? Is the commentary theme attacks of the company based on reasonable business decisions or political activists or honest and sincere content based on the company's daily business and organizational goals?

5.   Job seekers should investigate the company's customer feedback sites such as Yelp, Angie's List, Merchant's Circle, Better Business Bureau, and Yahoo Local. A company's publicity team or social media manager should have RSS feeds set up on all the major search engines to notify the PR team immediately of company mentions. There should be a company course of action 'Investigate & Mitigate' plan for negative commentary. And, the company should publicly respond with a positive action and whether the action resulted in resolution of consumer issues.

6.   Do you remember the unhappy flyer, Dave Carroll, trying to get a response from United Airlines about a damaged $3,500 guitar? He

recorded a YouTube video – with 12 million views by the fall of 2012. United Airlines lost millions – and many customers – when all they had to do was respond to Carroll, apologize, and ask him what they could do to make him happy. Ken and Meredith Williams had a similar problem with a bank for a mortgage and posted a YouTube video. Within 48 hours it got the attention of a TV station, and immediately after, the bank stopped giving them the run-around.

7.   Who wants to work for a company that is heartless and unresponsive to their customers? How does that speak to managing their employees? Social CRM conducted a study finding that 70% of companies ignore customer complaints on Twitter. A *RightNow Customer Experience Impact Report* noted 89% of consumers went to a competitor after a poor customer experience; 50% of consumers gave the business only one week to respond. This emphasizes a need for a speedy response by the company. A job seeker can strive to showcase how they can reverse this type of public attitude or improve customer service when hired as a solution to the company's 'problem' if the job seeker sincerely wants to target this company as a future employer.

8.   If a job seeker was considering working for a company with negative reviews – how would the job seeker feel knowing the company had a severe lack of customer care? How does this translate over into

caring for their own employees? Are they training the employees to perform better to mitigate customer issues or are they just ignoring the complaints? Is the company staff overworked and underpaid or simply exhausted and have no energy to perform work well and take care of customer's orders, services, or create quality products?

9. Imagine a recruiter is searching for valuable candidate and that 'perfect' candidate comes across some negative social media posts about the way the company does business? Recruiters might be fighting a losing battle convincing the potential new hire to come on board with a 'loser company' (unless the job is to fix the company image!). Recruiters need to work hand-in-hand with marketing and PR to ensure job applicants see a positive side of the business and the result is the business is an 'employer of choice.'

10. Job seekers need to pay attention and perform due diligence about the company for whom they wish to work. Companies who want to retain a positive image for not only their customers, but to attract and retain future employees, need to conduct themselves in a responsive and positive manner so there's no reason for 'unhappy' employees or clients to post negative commentary.

RESUME FARMING
FOR JOB SEEKERS

The Mission – ensure your resume is seen by as many hiring managers, recruiters, placement specialists, and headhunters as possible.

The Tool – resume farming – casting the seeds into the field to see what comes up and what inquiries are harvested.

The Goal – to submit multiple resumes to (a) general resume databases, (b) company resume databases, and (c) apply to specific jobs posted within a company's recruiting sites or other public job boards (e.g., state employment commission agencies).

Some job seekers feel quality trumps quantity. Don't hold back because you are afraid recruiters may be talking to each other. Recruiters are proprietary about their resume database and will avoid sharing their 'finds' with external headhunters. Sometimes when job seekers post their resume to job, and never hear back from the company. The job postings may actually be fake. Recruiters in many industries have several philosophies and methodologies, but the objective is to have as many resumes in their company or personal 'arsenal' (database) as possible, so they 'farm' for resumes for as many of the company's job descriptions and categories as possible. Since there is no penalty for posting a job opening and then closing it, recruiters DO post for (a) jobs that internal management feel may be needed in near future / far future based on the company's most recent or long-term strategic growth, (b) as a 'feeler' to see what type of candidates are available that may meet unique qualifications, and (c) to ensure EEOC and AAP compliance by publicly posting a job opening for a job that the company is actually wanting to fill with an internal candidate, but the company policy is to 'announce' the job opening to document they are open to all diverse candidates.

1.   Recruiters and headhunters are 'farming' for as many resumes in their proprietary database(s) as they can. Whenever a new job opens, the recruiter will have a pool of applicants in which to search for the minimum of job skills. Even if you don't have the full set of required job skills for applying for a specific job, *do* upload your resume into the general database for *future* consideration for other positions.

2.   Do not apply for 'all the job openings' in a company database - this reeks of desperation, and the recruiter may permanently blackball the applicant for being a 'pain.' Recruiters are required to decline every applicant for a legal reason if not qualified, and if a candidate applies for all the jobs open, this creates more work for the recruiter. Rather upload your resume

into the general database.

3.   Resume Farming works for the recruiter.
Recruiters will hoard resumes for a long
period of time. Regardless of whether you,
the job seeker, started applying for a job last
week or last year, recruiters may hang on to
resumes based on the possibility that a job
will open that can attract job seekers that
may have a resume in the database from
years ago. The author was a senior
recruiter in a defense company using an
Automatic Tracking System (ATS) resume
database with about 3,000 resumes initially
– two and a half years later, there was over
130K resumes. This enabling identification
and contacting of mass job seekers via
notifications to all past job seekers with
keywords in their resume in a 'new job
notification' communication (email). This
resulted in at least 1-2 interested passive
and active job seekers to return
correspondence and a placement rate of
under 2 weeks per job requisition.

4.   Job seekers are advised to upload their
resume (resume seeding) into as many
proprietary 'resume farms' as possible, so
more eyeballs will see their resumes as well
as qualifications and skills sets. If the
company only allows uploads if the resume
is attached to a 'job requisition,' then look
for the job that most closely fits the seeker's
skills to get the resume 'into' the database –
upload the resume into the database
anyway. Better to be in the database …

than not. Just because you may be disqualified for the position you applied for, won't mean the resume will be dumped. Now it's in the general resume population!

5.   Post to the 'big boy' resume databases and update often. This includes: (a) Monster.com, (b) Indeed.com, and (c) CareerBuilder. These resume databases are filled with millions of resumes – some going back as far as three-to-five years (although the sites claim all their resumes are 'fresh,' they keep older resumes in the database to bulk up the numbers). Recruiters for mid-size to larger companies have subscriptions to search for keywords and specific types of resumes (e.g., government contracting companies may have a higher-level paid subscription to search for resumes with security clearances). These subscribers also 'download' resumes of interest into their own proprietary databases to review later for potential jobs down the road. Some job seekers are shy about posting on the resume databases – only recruiters can search for and find the resumes. Your boss won't be able to see you job searching in those databases, unless s/he as a recruiters subscription (very expensive).

6.   Don't ignore smaller niche resume databases to load your resume into – including your state employment commission's job board. Military job seekers can focus on applying their resume

to database websites that target the military, and/or those in the civilian world or government agencies (e.g., ClearedJobs.net), as well as targeting a federal government job via the USAJobs.gov website that is used by federal agency recruiters.

7.   The trick to making your resume work harder in the 'big boy' resume databases is to 'update' the resume monthly (minimum every 45 days). Those systems check to see if the resume has been updated, edited, or changed daily. Those resumes where the job seeker 'updated' the uploaded resume will move towards the top of the 'fresh' queue. Do actually update or edit the resume – even if it means adding a new blank line at the end of the last page or an extra space after a period on a bullet.

8.   Load your resume into LinkedIn. Too many job seekers are told to use LinkedIn as a job search tool, but fail to ramp up their profile with juicy keywords and job descriptions. Fill in all the blanks, take advantage of sections you can fill in with data – especially the skill sets section (used by LinkedIn as the primary search engine look-see). Ensure that your 'open to contact by recruiters' button is toggle on so those placement specialists can reach out to you for any job interest.

9.   Look for organizations that perform RSS feeds to recruiters and headhunters – *free*

of charge – as a non-profit job assist. Some military-service veteran's organizations will collect digital resumes from job seekers and push those resumes out via RSS subscription feeds to thousands of recipients … from hiring managers to headhunters. These organizations may encourage vets to subscribe to the organization's news feeds of open positions posted by recruiters. One such example is the NortonNet group (centered in the 'beltway' in the Northern Virginia geographic area). Norton Net started a few decades ago to help military veterans with military, DoD, or government clearances to share their resumes with recruiters and headhunters in the civilian sector looking to fill government contract positions.

10.   Be wary of resume services that charge a fee to push out your resume. Some entities will charge the job seeker between $25-$100 to 'distribute' the resume to their list of recruiters and headhunters. The job seeker really doesn't know where the resume is being pushed, or how many times, or what time of day or week. The distribution entity won't show you, the job seeker, what the emails are or may not cc: you on the list going out. Be leery and do a lot of research before taking that route.

REVIEWING THE JOB ANNOUNCEMENT

"I was told to copy the job description online to ensure keywords were in my resume …" is something the author often hears from resume clients. Job seekers copy and paste 'everything' from the online announcement. They can't understand why there is never any follow-up or response.

Copying and pasting the original job description into a resume won't help job seekers.

Job seekers need to describe 'how' their specific task or responsibilities in their current or past positions matches the job description's mandatory experience requirements. This wording showcases an ability to interpret, analyze, and write to satisfy the recruiter's need for documented capabilities. Recruiters can read between the lines for skills, experience, and education via those keywords describing the experience.

1.   When recruiters see 'copy & paste' resumes, they recognize and reject the resume. Recruiters want to read applicant job accomplishments, task capabilities, and achievements … written uniquely to a job seeker's specific background, skills, and experience. They don't want copy and

paste content – which shows the job seeker has no capability to create or interpret.

2. Job seekers can analyze the important words from an open position announcement by scrutinizing the job requisition for general and specific requirements sections. Ignore the benefits and company description. Target the 'must have' qualifications for clues to keywords recruiters are seeking. For example, the job requisition "Budget Analyst" (posted on usajobs.gov) notes:

a) Assist in work to be accomplished; communicate assignments, problems to be solved, issues, and deadlines.

b) Coach team in selection and application of appropriate problem-solving methods and techniques; resolve employees complaints.

c) Maintain program and administrative reference materials, project files / relevant documents; prepare reports; maintain records of accomplishments / administrative information.

d) Represent the team for the purpose of obtaining resources; securing needed information or decisions from the supervisor on major work problems / issues.

e) Represent team findings and recommendations in meetings; deal with issues that have an impact on the team's objectives, work products and/or tasks.

f) Research a wide range of qualitative and quantitative methods to identify, assess, analyze and improve team effectiveness, efficiency, and work products.

3. Most descriptions have a generalized job section and a specific requirements or job tasks section. These descriptions can be in the generalized description:

a. "Assisted in work" could equate to a team member assigned specific workload assignments to research, analyze, identify, and implement solutions to problems, methods, and technical issues.

b. "Represent the team" can be interpreted as presenting reports on specific topics to a group.

c. "Maintain program and administrative reference materials" could equate to a document-database librarian or database maintenance tech with software skills, and alphabetical- and numeric-filing capabilities, and ability to recognize documents 'classes.'

d. "Prepare reports and maintain records" of work accomplishments equates to filing documents in a manual or in digital format (e.g., create electronic files on a server or

SharePoint website in a logical,
organized manner.

e.   "Research qualitative and
quantitative" equates to an ability to
ask questions, perform statistical
analysis, and possibly conduct Lean
Six Sigma studies or process
improvements to work tasking,
production (lowered man-hours),
recommending automation
processes for work-task processing,
and improving customer service
timing and services.

f.   "Resolve simple complaints" could
equate to 'being a people person'
(please don't use that cliché' term!)
able to provide diplomatic workplace resolutions fair to all parties.

What is missing in the 'general' job
description? Anything and everything
related to the real job's tasks and
responsibilities, including: financials,
accounts receivables or accounts payables,
budget oversight, monetary or financial
analysis.

4.   Now review the *'must-have'* job description
details:

a)   "Knowledge of budget concepts,
process, financial coding structure
and the interrelationships among
appropriations

b)   interpret budgetary aspects of laws,
        regulations, policies, procedures and
        provide guidance

c)   interpret / apply budget instructions,
        administrative memoranda, and
        regulatory guidelines from
        procedural, technical standpoint

d)   analyze and relate financial data to
        work plans, business plans,
        Strategic Plans, and organizational
        accomplishments

The above job description bullets in the
'help wanted' notice notes *specific keywords*
the job applicant must ensure is describing
past and current experience in their own
resume to catch the eye of the recruiter.

5.   Target the mandated job skill requirements
        and write about tasks accomplished related
        directly to that experience using the
        keywords.

        a. "Knowledge of budget concepts,
            process, financial coding structure and
            the interrelationships among
            appropriations" means … describe the
            accounting system (name brand
            software) and the line item coding,
            accounts receivables / accounts
            payable, budget appropriations (funding)
            and funding designations (to / from
            business units) and obtaining approvals
            for expenditures.

        b. The section noting: "interpret budgetary
            aspects of laws, regulations, policies,

procedures, and provide guidance" means … detailing knowledge of Generally Accepted Accounting Practices (GAAP), and experience as a Subject Matter Expert (SME) on Internal Revenue Service (IRS) law, regulatory compliance (including Sarbanes-Oxley; SOX), and internal company policies and procedures related to taxes, budgeting, finances, and accounting to advise peers and management.

c. The ability to "analyze and relate financial data to work plans, business plans, Strategic Plans …" … means data research, analysis, auditing, and compiling reports to share in group presentations.

6. The remainder of the job description are more 'generic' capabilities.

a. ability to "communicate orally and in writing; make presentations clearly

b. manage time, balance priorities, and work under tight timeframes and conditions

c. use of computer for word processing, spreadsheets, graphics, and communications programs

d. use of analytical and problem-solving techniques

e. use of automated financial systems" can easily be interpreted as strong work capabilities discussed in the same bullets explaining specific skill requirements.

7.   Copying and pasting the original job
      description won't help job seekers.
      Describe 'how' a specific task or
      responsibility matches the job description's
      mandatory experience requirements to
      showcase an ability to interpret, analyze,
      and write to satisfy the recruiter's need for
      documented capabilities. Recruiters can
      read between the lines for skills,
      experience, and education via those
      keywords describing the experience.

8.   Check for keywords in the job description
      and ensure those are inside the resume you
      are going to submit to be considered. If you
      review a batch of job descriptions
      advertising for the same type of position
      (bookkeeper, accountant, financial auditor,
      banking professional), you can start
      catching on to the repeated words in each
      of the descriptions. Now the trick is not to
      simply list the words at the top of the
      resume in a bulleted skills list, but to
      actually write descriptions of the tasks and
      responsibilities in current and past jobs what
      use those keywords in phrases and
      sentences. Using the keywords in phrases
      increases what is called long-tailed phrases
      for Search Engine Optimization (SEO) to
      increases the 'catch' in queries by recruiters
      using search engines to find those
      keywords in the applicant pool.

9.   Recruiters are looking for job applicants that
      can understand the job descriptions itself,

have matching skills and capabilities in their own resumes, but the resumes have write ups of achievements that are directly associated with those keywords and skill sets. For instance, a recruiter looking for a tax auditor will definitely get excited to read this bullet in a job description:

"audited accounts receivables for 325 clients accounting systems, catching an average of 15 data entry mistakes per client, resulting in corrections and resolutions positive affecting tax returns for higher tax refunds (averaging $300 per client higher than initially estimated)"

10. Don't use jargon or cliché words in a resume. Don't over-generalize the job descriptions, either.

   a. Words and phrases often used in performance evaluations are subjective and are 'emotional opinions' that really don't document specific achievements (e.g., passion, commitment, team player, super interpersonal skills, works independently, detail oriented, and great people person).
   b. Avoid buzzwords used by recruiters in job descriptions or verbiage that would only be used by industry workers. For example, program managers (PMPs) like to use the popular term – stakeholder – but that equates everyone in the company, CEOs to mailroom clerks, vendors, and clients. No one in

any job or company performs tasks, responsibilities, or weekly chores that affects every single one of these 'stakeholders' so it's best to actually pinpoint 'who' the task directly affected.

c. Avoid the use of the word "I" in the resume – recruiters already know it's all about the job seeker.

d. Don't overuse high-level or too over-generalized wording in a resume. The resume content becomes vague and unreadable. The wording sounds awesome at first glance – but after another review – the recruiter really has no clue what the applicant does on a daily basis. In the example below, there is no indication of what type of issues, what type of research, how many, how large, or what type of transactions, or what type of business or business units. There is no indication of types of products, systems, or services in what type of operations environment.

- Research, analyze, identify, and resolve day-to-day issues, research, initialization, and execution of transactions for multiple business sites and/or larger business units
- Design, develop, and implementation of products, systems and services in an operations environment

SCAM JOB
ANNOUNCEMENTS

Online job boards are used by people (scammers and con artists) posing as recruiters or companies looking to hire. It is important to be cautious as to what follow-up you provide to inquiring entities when you are shopping for your next employer of choice. Follow these tips to avoid fake or scam job postings to keep your time, money, and identity safe.

'Phishing' scams target job seeker's personal identify information to appropriate user-names and passwords to steal from bank accounts or set up accounts in the victim's names. Once obtained, birth dates, social security numbers, addresses, and a change of address form sent to the post office, allows the scammers to set up multiple charge accounts, charge them to the limit, and get the 'stolen' merchandise on the street for a fraction of the retail value. Once scammers have a bank account number, if the account owner's passwords are weak, it can take only a few minutes to go into the account and drain it dry.

Another scam is the "Let me send you an advance check for your salary." Once received, the victim deposits it at the ATM, but gets an urgent message the sender overpaid and needs the victim to wire half the money back immediately or send a gift card. The next day after the money has been refunded from the victim's account or mailed at the post offer, the victim finds out the check they deposited was fake and their own checks start bouncing.

1.   Avoid postings sounding too good to be true. A job offering a $100,000 salary logically will require education (formal degrees), years of experience, industry skill sets, knowledge in specific fields of study, and as well as a minimum of at least five-years of experience in a unique (or translatable) industry or field. Job posts which have no skills or experience required – especially if paired with an exorbitant salary – are likely to be scams.

2.   Real hiring companies do not post salary information. There are several reasons for this practice:

        a.   The recruiter or hiring manager wants to hire the most qualified candidate at the lowest salary possible within the company's compensation plan to avoid huge overhead expenses in labor and payroll. Most companies with compensation plans have a low- and a high-end for salary ranges for each job description to use as a guide for EEO and AAP purposes, as well as to avoid litigation for prejudicial hiring practices. The salary range in the compensation plan is based on education, years of experience, and other factors (e.g., holding or obtaining a security clearance for government contracting employees). If the company advertises a salary range, every applicant will ask for the highest range, regardless of qualifications, leaving no salary negotiation room for the hiring company. Some companies may note minimum salary negotiations start at and then state a low-ball figure (one can safely assume the *maximum* salary figure will be no more than 10% of the lowest advertised salary figure).

b. The company won't advertise compensation, because the competition will use that data to offer new hires or current staff a little bit more to retain employees or hire from a limited labor pool in a geographic area.

3. Job advertisements that promise 'perfect' hours, salary, and benefits may seem worth investigating – but look for potential fraud. If the job truly was perfect, the company would not need to advertise – word-of-mouth would spread the news like wildfire. Everybody in the neighborhood would be lined up to apply for the position (possibly none of them will be qualified). Can you imagine the local corner store putting out an ad for a register clerk paying $50 an hour?

The store would have to close operations because so many people will be interrupting business to apply for the job.

4. Avoid job postings requiring a fee (upfront, at hire, or after hire). Legitimate recruiters are paid by employers ... *not* by potential job candidates.

    a. If a job posting requires you to pay a fee to submit a resume or introduce you to an employer for an interview, it is likely a scam. Some 'pay-to-play' businesses scan local company ads for jobs you can find yourself if you put the effort into it; these services market themselves as serving 'niche job market.'

    b. Avoid job postings requiring purchase of a start-up kit. These are usually multi-level marketing companies - usually Ponzi schemes. All the folks able to rise to the top of the pyramid make money, but the entry-level workers on the bottom usually make less than minimum wage once their work hours are tallied.

    c. Another scam is a requirement to pay for training materials or web training seminars. A legitimate company will not require you to pay for your own training. Logically – a company investing in a new hire needs that employee to start generating results or revenue from day one and hire candidates already trained or with experience.

5. Job postings or e-mails asking for personal data including a job seeker's birth date, social security number, or mother's maiden name are likely identity scams. When a job candidate is hired, there is normally an official 'offer letter of employment' sent to the job seeker. Until the offer letter and conditions are accepted, signed, and returned to the company, the company has no legal right to personal data. Once legitimately hired, new employees will be asked for social security number (for health and welfare benefits, and tax withholding), birth date (for the I-9 form; ensuring work eligibility in the country where hired), and asked to volunteer information for the company's Equal Employment Opportunity and Affirmative Action Plan reporting to the federal government.

6. Companies in some industries coordinate and liaise with the larger resume database entities (e.g., Monster, CareerBuilder, and Indeed) to obtain e-mails from newly uploaded resumes with specific (filtered) keywords (e.g., insurance, finance, health) so the hiring companies can contact job seekers en masse (tens of thousands at a time).

    a. The introduction e-mail message

may start off with "you have the perfect qualifications to be one of our newest … (job title)." These mass e-mails work for well for the companies and those job seekers who are interested in applying for positions selling financial services and products, health insurance sales, and other positions. This method is used predominantly in industries where the employee turnover is horrendous (tenure lasting less than three months) or the industry is growing so fast the companies' can't hire fast enough.

b. Some e-mails come in – supposedly from an employer, recruiter, or job board – claiming the sender found the job seeker's resume on a resume sites or company website. (If you don't remember applying, you likely didn't). Some scammers claim to be from well-known company names (who's brand or logo you may recognize). The scam starts with a request for personal data for a pre-employment credit check to complete an application. Scammers ask for data to steal your identity – birth date, social security number, bank account numbers, and bank names.

c. Check the e-mail address. Some clever scammers will create 'spoofed' e-mail addresses with special software (you look at the e-mail and it shows as BankerBob@BankOfAmerica.com; once you click on the e-mail, the address shows as Buck.ES@HackedUniversity.edu (a student's account has been hacked). Legitimate recruiters will have company-related e-mails, such as Robert.Bate@UniverseBank.com. With the advent of new e-mail and website identifiers, legitimate e-mail addresses could also end in .org, .net, and/or .gov.

7. Since the cost is zero to create a fake profile on any social media, fake websites are another platform scammers use. If you click on a social media page and find very little content (or loads of great jobs, but nothing else), the scammer is trying to entice viewers to click on links to 'phish' personal data or to load a 'Trojan Horse' (malware) on your computer. LinkedIn is one platform that users trust as a professional business platform, but fake LinkedIn Profiles can be initiated and used to post fake or scam opportunities in LinkedIn Groups. Twitter makes it easy to post a shortened URL (bit.ly or ow.ly) from scammers and you have no idea where those short links go. Look for the verified badge (where available) on social media and scrutinize the profile is genuine before taking action. Search for the employer or

recruiter names in your favorite Internet browser. If a social media account has under 200-300 followers, be cautious, especially if the employer name claimed is well-known.

8. Scams on legitimate job boards do happen. You recognize the huge job board (resume database) or your favorite professional association's 'career center' page. The job board is legitimate – but – the job may be a scam. If you are skeptical that a job posted on a legitimate site looks a little 'off' or 'suspicious' – check the URL. You may have mistyped the URL and accidentally get to a fake site. Scammers will set up a misleading and almost identical website to the intended site to phish for data. (One example, the URL WhiteHouse.com leads the computer user to a porn site, forcing the official USA government's White House website to obtain a WhiteHouse.gov website URL.)

9. It only costs about five bucks a month to obtain a new URL. It is easy to create fake job boards, employer websites, and recruiter websites. If the URL obtained is clever enough they can come close to the real company's name, it could be hard to spot. The website may look phenomenal and very professional (from purchased website templates). Job boards may have the name of the real company inside the URL, but in the incorrect spot or order: 'googlejobs.com' (fake site) versus

'careers.google.com' (legitimate site). Fake job postings look convincingly real, so job seekers apply and 'register' with basic personal information. Job seekers get on a roll answering the legitimate questions and don't stop when asked for private (and illegitimate) data for 'pre-screening' purposes. Scammers are clever in explaining why they need the personal data, e.g., a personal bank account number to deposit paychecks.

10.   Another job site the author advises every job seeker to be super, extra, careful when job shopping is the 'For Sale' sites (e.g., Craig's List). There are horror stories where eager job seekers agree to meet with potential employers in shady locations and unpopulated areas only to find themselves robbed, raped, or murdered. Some employers who do post legitimate jobs on these sites, but if they have a website already, why post to Craig's List? Legitimate employers also have the option to post real jobs on state employment agency job boards for free.

USING LINKEDIN TO
TURN ON A JOB SEARCH

Many people considering joining (or already an active member of) LinkedIn believe the social media platform is (just) a recruiting site. Although its foundation is as a Business-to-Business (B2) application where business professionals can connect and server each other – it has become a very powerful search engine for qualified candidates for job search and employee placement. It is recommended to have a professional business level profile on LinkedIn (you can switch back and forth from free to paid on a monthly basis, but you may as well purchase the annual subscription for about $200 annually)>

Profile members can indicate on their profile where they are active or passive job seekers, as well as explore career opportunities on the job tab. In the very near future (Oct. – Dec. 2019), LinkedIn will also allow an option for your profile to be open to Premium Subscriber Recruiters (those placement professionals paying for a $500+ monthly for a LinkedIn subscription to perform higher functioning searches; so they are serious headhunters), or to publicly show your interest in job opportunities to everyone.

Using LinkedIn to turn on either a job search or indicate one is open to job inquiries is relatively simple. There is some pre-work one needs to get completed on your profile before you 'turn on' the jobs tab and open to work functions. Once those are completed, you are ready to turn on the option for recruiter inquiries.

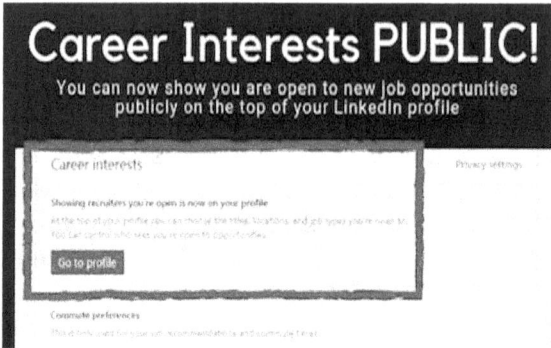

Career Interests PUBLIC!

You can now show you are open to new job opportunities publicly on the top of your LinkedIn profile

1.   Open your profile in LinkedIn and look for your profile picture to click on the Settings and Privacy sub-menu.

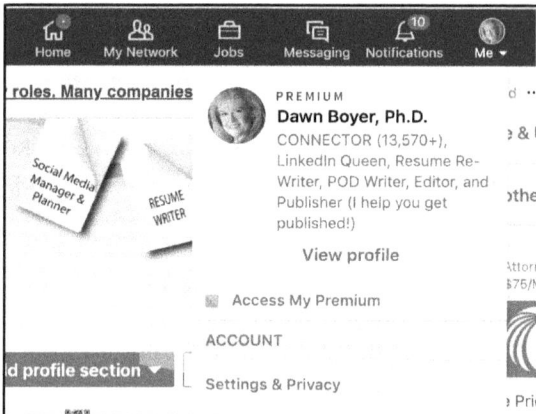

2. Click on the Edit Public Profile so you can update your 'Vanity Plate' URL. Then click on the 'change' link (highlighted in yellow here), then click on the tiny pencil next to the URL for your profile name.

3. You want to use as close to your full legal name as possible. Some folks may have common names – John Smith – so use something that distinguishes this name for all the others with the same name. JohnBSmithPhD or JohnSmith_Virginia.

Back to LinkedIn.com

✐ Edit your custom URL

5. Personalize the URL for your profile.

www.linkedin.com/in/dawnboyer ✐

☰ Edit Content

This is your public profile. To edit its sections, update your profile.

> Edit contents

4. Now you have a professional Vanity Plate URL, use this on ALL your resume, job search, or sharing of your profile to folks looking for more about you. Click on the "Back to LinkedIn.com" link.

5. Now to turn on the job search capabilities for your profile and to indicate you are open for recruiters and hiring managers to reach out to contact you for job discussions.

6. Go back to the Settings and Privacy sub-menu. Click on the Privacy Tab, then scroll down to the Job Seeking Preferences sub-header and click on the "Let recruiters know you're open to opportunities" section, click on 'change' then toggle the "no" to "yes."

Account	Privacy	Ads	Communications

social, economic and workplace research

Choose whether we can make some of your data available to trusted services
for policy and academic research

**How others see your profile and
network information**

**How others see your LinkedIn
activity**

Job seeking preferences

How LinkedIn uses your data

Job seeking preferences

Blocking and hiding

Job application settings   Change

Choose what information LinkedIn saves when you submit a job application.

Let recruiters know you're open to opportunities   Change

Share that you're open and appear in recruiter searches matching your career   On
interests

Signal your interest to recruiters at companies you have   Change
created job alerts for   No

This will be applied for companies that you have created job alerts for.

Sharing your profile when you click apply   Change

Choose if you want to share your full profile with the job poster when you're   No
taken off LinkedIn after clicking apply

Stored job applicant accounts   Change

Manage which third party job applicant accounts are stored on LinkedIn.

Let recruiters know you're open to opportunities   Close

Share that you're open and appear in recruiter searches matching your career   Yes
interests

We take steps not to show your current company that you're open, but can't
guarantee complete privacy. Learn more

Yes ⬤ ✓ Saved

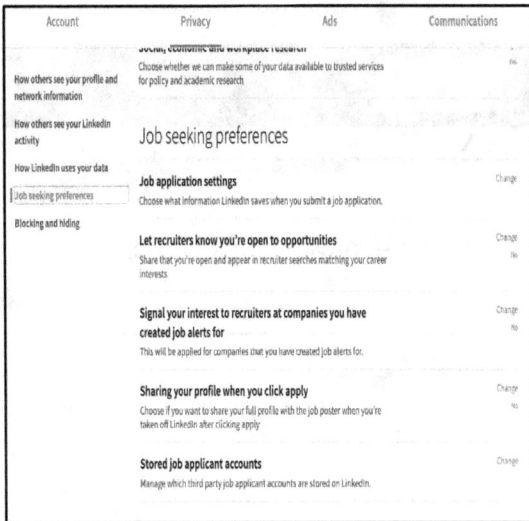

7. Now click on the Home button to go back to
    the landing pages for your profile (news
    feed will show in the middle), and look for
    the "Jobs" icon / tab at the top, middle side
    of your screen. Clicking on that will take
    you to the Jobs Page, where you can
    search for keywords and job titles, as well
    as geographic locations where you prefer to
    work.

For Experienced CEOs Only - **$500/hr Advisory roles. Many companies are seeking Paid Business Advisors...** Ad ...

Initial screen with blank search fields …

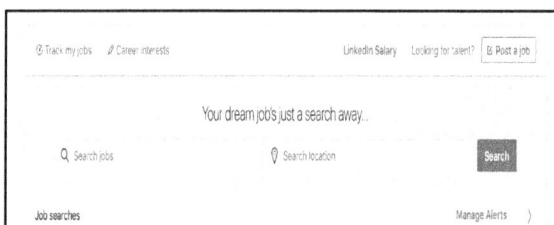

Screen with fields entered for specific keywords and locations …

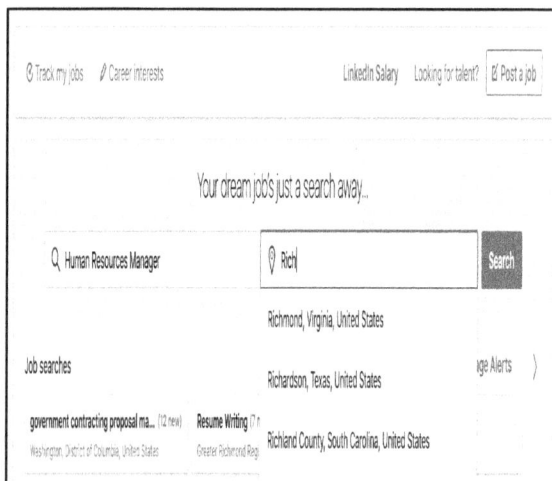

8.   Possible jobs will pop up as a sorted list,
and job seekers can actually adjust the
filters for the job search.

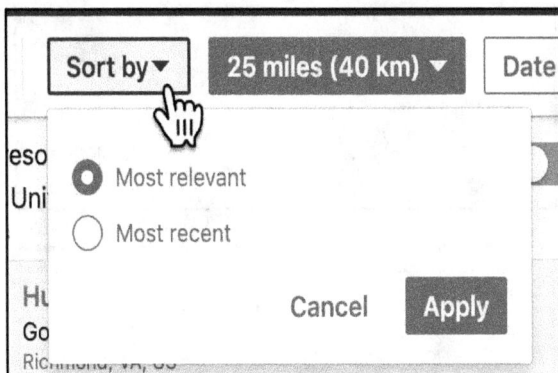

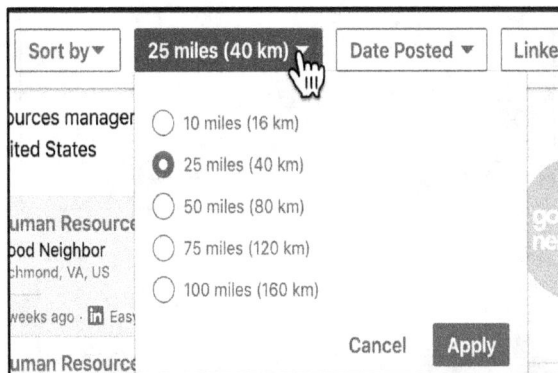

Date Posted ▼   **LinkedIn Features** ▼   C

○ Past 24 hours **(6)**

○ Past Week **(46)**

○ Past Month **(126)**

● Any Time **(166)**

Cancel   **Apply**

LinkedIn Features ▼   **Company** ▼   Exp

☐ In Your Network **(2)**

☐ Easy Apply **(3)**

☐ Under 10 Applicants **(147)**

Cancel   **Apply**

| Company ▼ | Experience l ⟩ | All filters |

Add a company   ⚲

☐ PwC (2)

☐ Aleris (1)

☐ Good Neighbor (1)

☐ averhealth (3)

☐ AdvanSix (3)

Cancel   **Apply**

| Experience Level ▼ | All filters |

☐ Internship (5)

☐ Entry level (42)

☐ Associate (61)

☐ Mid-Senior level (34)

☐ Director (7)

☐ Executive (3)

Cancel   **Apply**

9.   You can use this search to set up a Job
      Alert for similar job titles that pop up fitting
      the filter parameters you have set.

Human resources manager in Richmond, Virginia, United States

166 results

Job Alert Off

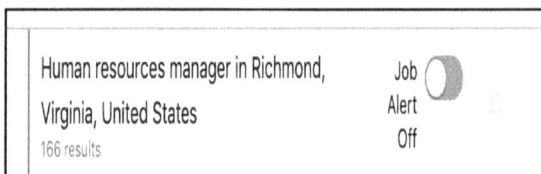

10. Toggle 'on' the job alert, and it will use the job filter options you just used to find an ideal career position for you to be notified for all jobs within your geographic radius until you turn the filter off again based on your preference for daily or weekly notices and method of communication.

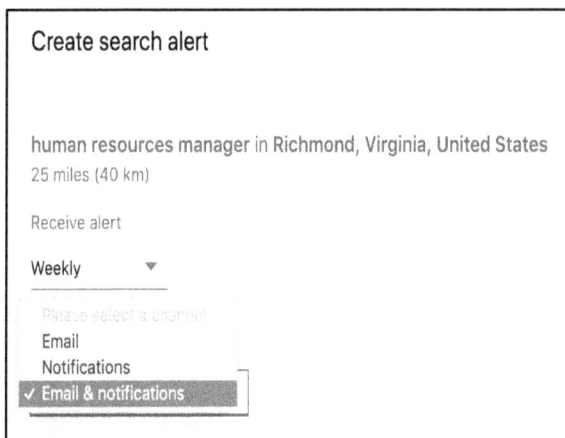

Create search alert

human resources manager in Richmond, Virginia, United States
25 miles (40 km)

Receive alert

Weekly ▼

Please select a channel
Email
Notifications
✓ Email & notifications

REFERENCES

OBTAINING REFERENCES

Job seekers are sometimes uncomfortable about asking for references (this is the same for business owners and entrepreneurs, also) and are not always sure where or who to ask for a professional reference. The place to start … when finding and listing professional references are in a place of strength … at your current job before you start work.

References do not always have to be professional or career-related. You can ask for references from non-profit entities with whom you provided volunteer 'work.' In some cases, friends or distant relatives can provide 'character' references, if they are unable to address work-related instances.

Essentially, no company should call any references from any job applicant until after the interview and an offer letter of employment is issued, with the codicil or caveat that the offer of employment is based on successful and acceptable background and reference checks.

1.   Reference lists should be short in length but have specific information to provide to future employers. It is important to have both phone and email addresses in references because it's easier for the human resources department to send out emails and get

'written responses' for documentation for the employee file versus having to handwrite and transcribe their notes. If the hiring company employs a third-party background check vendor, the vendor reps will likely call the reference directly, so ensure the phone is a cell number the reference consistently uses.

    a. Full Name and Job Title: John B. Cable, Ph.D., Professor of English

    b. Company / Organization: Virginia Commonwealth University

    c. Contact Phone Number: (XXX) XXX-XXXX

    d. Contact Email: NameName@myemail.com

    e. Type of referral: Professional (or Personal)

2. References are always required for government services (GS) resumes, which are added to the very end of the GS resume. The GS should have at least three professional references and at least one personal reference – or – a fourth professional reference.

3. A private sector resumes (commercial) should *never* have references listed on the resume. The reason for this is that a reference list could potential be mishandled

by the hiring company (calling references before the offer of employment is made) or recruiters could potentially use the list to find more job candidates to consider for the job for which you just applied. Type a list of the references to carry with you to an interview and then if the hiring manager indicates they wish to consider you further for the position, they may ask for references they can call. At this point, the job candidate can indicate which references can be called before the offer letter and which they would prefer to keep off the radar until after the offer letter is issued (e.g., their current employer if they don't want them knowing yet that they were job searching).

4. If you are a business owner and have a Google-based business place, encourage customers to post references for your services there – usually just before you finish the last piece of work for them is a great time to ask, then after work or products are delivered is the second best time to ask. Having business references are great, not only for future job references, but increases positive branding for the company itself. Ensure that you grab those online references (via screen shots or copy and paste the text into a document to use later), along with the customer's name, if known.

5. If you have a profile on LinkedIn, send 'in-mails' to co-workers, supervisors,

managers, or clients to connect. In the request, also ask for a recommendation for your work. These recommendations stay on LinkedIn forever (until recommender either deletes an account or the recommendation). This is a great tool to store recommendations on the cloud because the recipient is unable to 'touch' the recommendation (for compilation). This indicates a true referral. Once the recommendation comes in, the recipient can elect to hide (if it's not that complimentary) or show it (if it is a great review) on their LinkedIn profile.

6.   If you have performed volunteer work at a non-profit, church, or other charitable institution for more than a few hours (e.g., you volunteer regularly for months, for about 5-10 hours weekly), then ask the project manager or head of the institution for a letter of recommendation related to your volunteer work. Leaders from organizations in which you were a member, e.g., Boy Scouts Pack Leader or Eastern Star groups, are great sources to look for recommendations if you don't have many professional referrals to list on the resume.

7.   If you have provided a letter of resignation to your company, ask the human resources department for a 'confirmation of employment' letter, as well as the company policy for letters of recommendation from the company (in general) or specific supervisors. Some company policies

disallow supervisors from being called for references for ex-employees and prefer the future hiring company call the human resources department directly.

8.   Co-workers can also be great references if supervisors are unable (via policy) or unable (via preference) to provide letters of recommendation based on their perspective of working with you, side-by-side. Have them provide a short description of the project(s) you worked together, and what part you played, and how the entire team achieved a goal based on your participation.

9.   Advisors and formal Mentors can be great points of contacts for references. Teachers are potential sources for reference letters. Some professors are inclined to only provide letters of recommendations to students earning a 4.0 average in their class(es). Other instructors are okay with providing the letter of recommendation based on the student's activity in the classroom, but directs the student to write the baseline and then send it to the teacher to edit as they are comfortable. Recently, some higher institutions of learning professors are 'charging' for letters of recommendation. This can be considered professionally unethical. The professor could be overwhelmed with requests (and charging a fee is the best way to deter massive inquiries) if the time they have to spend to write the letters, for students they barely know, takes away from their primary

work. Or, the professor is just financially greedy.

10.   Previous supervising managers can be great references when an employee is transferred to another department. These letters of recommendation can be placed in the personnel file, as well as copy provided to the transferring employee.

RESUME WRITING

LEADERSHIP WORDING IN RESUMES

Are you describing yourself as a Director, Manager, Supervisor, or a Team Lead on your resume? It doesn't matter if you are childcare professional 'supervising' young children, or a nuclear physicist who 'manages' a laboratory of scientists; showcasing your ability to lead is an important tool in your job search.

Most businesses and employers are seeking a solution to a problem; they need a warm body in an empty seat to perform tasks, and complete responsibilities in the job. The more leadership capabilities the new hire has, in performing non-supervised tasking, and/or to increase productivity by encouraging and challenging others to achieve more, the better for the company. Review your resume and look for areas where you did take the leadership role in your current or past employment positions, and ensure they are written to focus on your management skills.

You may be missing out on powerful and descriptive key word skills in your career search resume for job hunting. You may have a functional (non-management) job title on your resume. But, in the company there may have been conducting supervisory tasks. You are not legally required to note only the functional job title on your resume as long as the job-associated title is noted. You can 'forward-slash' add a more descriptive job title afterwards.

1.   Leadership definitions:

    a)   **Director**: a person that directs; one of a group of persons chosen to control or govern the affairs of a company or corporation: a board of directors; in most cases, has oversight to one or more managers who focus on specific business units within the institution.

    b)   **Manager**: a person who has control or direction of an entire or part of an institution, business, or a project or program; a person who manages. A manager may have one or more subordinates who supervise smaller groups of workers.

    c)   **Supervisor:**
    a person who supervises workers or the work done by others; superintendent. A person who oversees a sub-set of a business unit or project.

    d)   **Team Lead / Project Lead:** a person who leads or liaises between other members of a group who may have a set of subject matter expertise all working together to achieve a specific or ongoing goal or a specific set of tasks within a project and may be responsible for reporting stages or team results to management.

2.	It is important to note working in any of these capacities on your resume, because it indicates capabilities of taking direction in an assignment, project, or program and leading others to performing and reaching a strategic goal or for accomplishing project tasking. Indicating on your resume you could manage or direct the workers to achieving the goal in a specific time-period, or accomplish a deliverable within or before the deadline, will provide the metrics to document your capability to achieve strategic goals and tasks.

3.	No matter what your job is in your resume, hiring managers are looking for the answer to following types of questions to find indicators of leadership and experience in management. Adding metrics (numbers) to document the value of those achievements and activities increases the value of your participation in the management / leadership position.

4.	Did you manage or supervise others – if yes, how many, what are/were their functional job titles or responsibilities? It is important that you note what your subordinates did regularly, because the insinuation is that you are able to perform their job tasks (cross-trained) or are able to

cross-train the team to enable the co-
workers to step into their cohort's shoes if
someone is absent or leaves the company.

5. Do you train or mentor (formally or
informally) subordinates or peers? Do you
develop the training curriculum? How often
do you train per topic, to XX of learners per
class, for a total of about ## classes over
XX years, and circa XX total learners
trained? A good supervising manager will
ensure that not only is their team trained
well in their own tasks, add on new skills,
keep up with regulatory compliance, but
also enable the team to take on more tasks
in the future. Supervising managers need
to teach their team members well in the
supervisor's tasks, so eventually the
supervising manager can move up or get
promoted to newer and better positions.
Another value in some companies is safety
and safety training under OSHA regulatory
mandates. Being able to train, provide
safety oversight, and prevent accidents in
the workplace makes a worker valuable.

6. What was the value of the equipment,
contracts, or programs/projects over which
you supervised, managed, or in which you
participated? Every company has assets
and how one manages those assets for the
company can speak well for the employee.
A warehouse supervisor is responsible for
the labor force, but also the products and
goods stored in the warehouse, and the
logistics that bring in the merchandise as

well as ship it out to the next destination. One can factor in the value of the merchandise on any given time period to showcase the huge responsibilities of managing such elements.

7. What budget did you oversee (e.g., annually $XXXX)? How did you 'stretch' the budget to meet goals of department or 'company' per se? Whether a job seeker is responsible for the petty cash drawer, supervising several register cashiers at a retail store bringing tens of thousands weekly, or investing millions of dollars to procure assets for the company, managing a budget or funds, and being accountable for every dollar, is a huge management responsibility. Don't be afraid to use the word 'Managed …" on your resume.

8. Where/how did you save money for your employer – or – the employer's client? How much total money did you save? What did you do to accomplish unique jobs/tasks that saved money for your employer or client(s) during tenure? Being able to research, analyze, audit, and identify ways to increase sales or reduce costs in a business is important and useful. There are business consultants who make a living visiting companies to show them how to increase revenue and sales or to reduce overhead costs by eliminating worker hours while increasing productivity. How did you, as the job seeker, going to show how your management skills created wealth for the

company? When elaborating on this,
ensure that metrics are noted – e.g.,
developed and implements three new
revenue funnels, resulting in sales revenue
increases of ~235% over 12 months.

9.   Did you lead a team? If yes, what number of
members of the team and what tasks did
you perform towards the team's goals or
objectives? What was the result of the
completed or accomplished goals for your
company or department – increased sales,
reduced labor hours? What estimated
amount of (project?) work did you / does
your 'team' accomplish daily, weekly,
monthly, quarterly, annually?

10.   What new processes did you instill and what
were results? What was saved (man-hours,
budget money), or what did the processes
increase (productivity)? How did you
personally have a hand in accomplishing
those savings or instilling processes?
Sometimes processes won't increase
revenue or decrease manhours, but they
may improve the capability of the company
to protect itself from litigation or improve
workflow. For instance, one may research,
audit, and identify procedures that are not
following federal compliance for a 'hot topic'
(let's say safety). One can describe how
the research and update of a company
policy alleviated several redundant reporting
actions. For example, the human resources
department added an action step in the
hiring process which documented that each

221 Tiny – But Terrific – 'How To' Tips for Job Searches and Career Improvement (United States, English Version)

new hire was provided a complete internal job description before hire and signed off on their acceptance of the job as written for the personnel file. This prevented potential misunderstanding or possible litigation if employee decided to claim they were not told about job tasks or minimal required responsibilities in that position.

DEGREES VS ON THE JOB
TRAINING – RESUME DESCRIPTION

Formal educational degrees are the result of years of academic study and definitely a formidable achievements. When job candidates claim they have 'the equivalent' of a college degree, that is not currently acceptable practice for wording on resumes. In the distant past (2-3 decades ago), in some industries, this type of statement was acceptable to put on a resume. In today's world (post 2010), when a job description demands a college degree as one of the minimum requirements, the hiring company means an accredited college or university degree.

1. Do not put degree initials or certification initials after your legal name in the top of the resume with three exceptions. The reason for this is the parsing engine that converts the text in your resume over to the SQL relational database in the automatic tracking system (ATS) may not parse the data over into the correct text fields on the back-end. Additionally, one (Drop the Jr., Sr., and III for the same reason – unless your dad or son are searching for a job in the same field at the same time as you.) The exceptions are Doctoral degrees (including legal) and Professional Engineers) as noted in the examples below.

a) Dawn D. Boyer, Ph.D. (doctoral degree, D.Ed., D.B.A. etc.)

b) Melody Magnum, P.E. (professional engineer)

c) John B. Smith, J.D. (legal professional with Juris Doctorate)

2. Plug in the dates of the degrees using one of three recommended options. You want to ensure the resume reviewer understands you have (a) completed, (b) are in the process of completing, or (c) stopped your education (to avoid assumptions or implications about completion of a degree).

a) YYYY, Degree, Discipline, Institution, City, ST … (date when the degree was completed)

b) MM/YY – present, Degree, Discipline, Institution, City, ST … (indicating the student started studies for the formal degree on a specific date, but is still attending). One can always add, "Expected graduation: MM/YY."

c) MM/YY – MM/YY, Degree, Discipline, Institution, City, ST … (ensuring that start and stop dates are related to attendance tenure when a student has not finished the coursework nor graduated yet.

3. In describing formal degrees on the resume
    – spell out acronyms. Some degree initials
    may be similar to other educational
    institutions or the recruiter or hiring manager
    may not be familiar with the acronyms.
    Some colleges and universities may have
    different degree titles than the academic
    field standard to uniquely identify their
    institution's conveyed degrees.

    a) BFA = Bachelor of Fine Art (and add
        on the specific discipline, e.g.,
        Graphic Illustration, Music, or
        Dance.

    b) BA = Bachelor of Art, Major in
        (what?), Minor in (what)

    c) Ph.D. = Doctorate of Philosophy
        (this designated degree is usually
        related to an industry field with a
        dissertation study submitted for
        research)

    d) D.Ed. = Doctorate of Education

    e) M.S. = Master of Science

    f) M.B.A. = Masters of Business
        Administration

4. Schools with academic accreditation will
    have proof of the accreditation. Accrediting
    organizations are mostly 'regional' with a
    few 'national' organizations. The

accrediting review boards audit and research schools' strategic goals, degree programs, and curriculum for between 1-5 years. The accrediting institution has designated educational accreditation status (similar to a job performance evaluation). These accrediting organizations are recognized by the Council of Higher Education Accreditation (CHEA) and affirm standards and processes of the accrediting organization are consistent with the academic quality, improvement and accountability expectations established by CHEA, including the eligibility standard the majority of institutions or programs each accredits are degree-granting.

National Accrediting Organizations (as of 2019)

- Accrediting Commission of Career Schools and Colleges (ACCSC)
- Accrediting Council for Continuing Education and Training (ACCET)
- Accrediting Council for Independent Colleges and Schools (ACICS)
- Association for Biblical Higher Education (ABHE)
- Association of Advanced Rabbinical and Talmudic Schools (AARTS)
- Council on Occupational Education (COE)
- Distance Education Accrediting Commission (DEAC)

- National Accrediting Commission of Career Arts and Sciences (NACCAS)
- Transnational Association of Christian Colleges and Schools (TRACS)

Regional Accrediting Organizations (as of 2019)

- Accrediting Commission for Community and Junior Colleges (ACCJC) Western Association of Schools and Colleges
- Higher Learning Commission (HLC)
- Middle States Commission on Higher Education (MSCHE)
- New England Commission of Higher Education (NECHE)
- Northwest Commission on Colleges and Universities (NWCCU)
- Southern Association of Colleges and Schools Commission on Colleges (SACSCOC)
- WASC Senior College and University Commission (WSCUC)

Most recruiters are savvy to which schools are accredited. When they review resumes and see non-accredited schools on the education list, then they will likely reject the applicant.

Unfortunately, some schools claim to be accredited. When students attempt to transfer credits earned to other accredited schools, they find out their classes are not eligible under accreditation standards. One example was the ECPI school, who before 1991 was not recognized as having the accreditation to confer formal academic degrees. Students who graduated from ECPI before 1991, which is when the school achieved their academic accreditation, could return to ECPI to complete some additional 'accredited' classes, enabling them to graduate – again – after 1991 with an accredited degree.

5.   Between the formal degrees and the non-degree training (short duration training certifications), there may be 'post-graduate' certifications. It is perfectly acceptable to put these certifications inside the formal degree section between or the most recent education because these are normally conferred through accredited colleges and universities, thus they are 'formal' institution education, albeit not official degrees. Examples of post-grad certifications are noted below, including from outside the USA with accreditation board noted).

a)   11/99, Post-Graduate Diploma (Certificate), Dams & Reservoirs Engineering, University of Technology, Baghdad, Iraq (Accreditation Board for Engineering and Technology (ABET) accredited)

b)   2017 – 2022, Postgraduate Teaching License Pre-K-8, ODU,

Darden School of Education,
Norfolk, VA

6. If the job seeker is 'fresh out of college' (or as folks in the far east call, 'Freshers'), and the resume doesn't have much work experience, it is advised to list the degree in the top of the resume (per example below). Otherwise, formal degrees, certifications, and training should be listed in the bottom of the resume because work experience is more vital to share with recruiters. On the flip side, to avoid any age bias against an older worker, do not put the date of the college degree if it is not within the last 10 years. If the degree was conveyed within the last 10, do note the date. The date of the degree may only be relative if it indicates that the job seeker has more valuably recent field experience and knowledge. Recruiters may assume the job seeker is younger because of 'more recent' college degree.

EXPERIENCE SUMMARY

- 1 year, Scientist and Lab Manager (genetics and bio-data; lab studies)
- 4 peer-reviewed scientific publications
- Bachelor of Science, Zoology, Virginia Polytechnic Institute, Blacksburg, VA

7. Is an online degree more or less valuable than a brick-and-mortar school degree? The biggest concern for recruiters is whether the online school (and degree) is

accredited. The online degree does *not* have less value from an on-line school than a brick-and-mortar school. Even brick-and-mortar schools offer 'hybrid' classes, where students are taught via online meeting software or international satellite feeds. That students are not sitting in the class does not lesson the learning achieved from the school versus those with 'virtual' attendance. Online degree recipients may actually provide the employer with a more computer-savvy employee, more creative ability to resolve and solve diverse problems, and an internal drive to stick to a schedule for a goal.

8. Certifications and non-degree training showcase the job candidate is a (continuous) adult learner and open to new training to increase job skills and capabilities. Job seekers often believe employers will hire and train the new hire to the full skills sets to perform a job. About 98% of companies advertising for a job candidate does not have the time to train a new employee more than settling them into their new position. The company will not send a new hire to training – and more likely can't afford the training – that is why they are hiring employees with the already built in skill sets! If the job applicant continues to receive turn-downs for positions for which they are qualified, it may be time to upgrade their training and certifications or enroll in an accredited degree program.

9.   List certifications, even if not directly
      relevant to the job seeker's career path,
      (perhaps they took grant-writing class, but
      are a CEO of a for-profit company). The
      diversity of the learning may spark an
      impression the job seeker is open to life-
      long learning (they don't let knowledge age
      or stagnate).

10.   A degree in a discipline does not entitle any
      graduate to walk into a management
      position immediately after graduation. The
      field may be oversaturated with eligible
      workers (e.g., the Human Resources field) –
      or – such a niche job there isn't a demand.
      This means new (fresher) workers may
      have to work up the ranks from a junior
      management position or work in another
      field or industry until a niche job opens.
      Sometimes, it is acceptable to take the
      lower paying or ranking position if it gains a
      learning experience.

LISTING TECHNICAL
SKILLS IN A RESUME

One of the hardest decisions to make is where and how to list your soft, hard, and technical skills in a resume so the list will attract the recruiter's eye quickly, and entice them to continue reading. In some cases, the list may be associated with an information technologist listing the languages, applications, platforms, and certifications they have worked on or achieved. In other cases, it may be embedded in the general types of jobs that the job seeker has held over the last 10-15 years in a 'years of experience' listing.

1.   Where, what, and how long the list should be dictated by the type of position to which the job seeker is applying the resume. If the job seeker is anything except an IT technologist or computer scientist, they may want to concentrate on listing their general job titles in broad industries.

2.   A military service veteran with years of military experience and security or police background may list their years of experience in the following example with their one-line Objective, followed by their experience in number of years. Notice the industries (fields) listed broadly in parentheses after the general job titles):

Objective: Security Specialist / Manager / Director

Experience Summary:

- 20 years, US Air Force, Master Sergeant, Honorable Discharge: 01/15
- 10 years, Operations Management Security / Anti-Threat Management (military, security)
- 8 years, Teaching, Training, Instruction (military, security)
- 5 year, Technical Systems Management (installation, maintenance, operations, training)
- 10 months, Project Manager / Logistics (inventory, warehouse, transportation)

(resume body)

3.　　A graphic artist who has had some college courses, loads of self-taught experience in some graphic applications, but is overloaded with years of low-level customer service representative and retail jobs, can format the resume to showcase the graphic art skills at the top of the resume.

These can be listed in alpha order or grouped by types.

OBJECTIVE: Graphics & Digital Artist

Technical / Computer Skills

- Adobe Photoshop CC
- Blender
- Unity
- 3DCoat
- SketchUp
- Wondershare Filmora
- Hard-Surface, High- and Low-poly models
- Organic Models
- Modo
- Maya
- ZBrush
- Substance Painter / Designer
- Mari (3D Texture)
- Houdini

(resume body)

4.   A job seeker who is not only diving into a new career field, has a military background, and entrepreneurial experience, will showcase skill sets directly relevant to future job applications as a computer scientist.

OBJECTIVE: Computer Scientist, Software Engineer

EXPERIENCE SUMMARY

- 20+ years, Computer Programmer, Web

Developer, Database Developer, Software Hobbyist
- 20+ years, US Navy, Electronics Technician / EOD, Chief, Honorable Discharge: 04/00
- 10+ years, Business Owner, Entrepreneur (service industry)
- 5 years, Curriculum Development / Training (military NEC 5332)
- Security Clearance: DoD, TS / SCI / CNWDI (last adjudicated: MM/YY; expires: MM/YY)

HARDWARE / SOFTWARE / TECHNICAL / COMPUTER

- Adobe Creative Suite: Illustrator
- Android Studio
- Artificial Intelligence (AI)
- C / C++
- CSS
- DRUPAL CMS
- GIMP
- GitHub
- Google Firebase
- HTML
- JAVA / JAVA Script
- Knowledge Discovery (Big-Data)
- LabView (NILabView)
- MySQL
- Oracle DBMS
- Pascal
- PHP
- Python
- QT Creator
- SQL

- UNIX (LINUX)

  (resume body)

5. The following skills listing on a resume may be the best layout for a person who has followed a military spouse during three-year stints in each location, but hasn't been able to develop a long-term stable position on one company or employer. This skills and years of experience list showcases the educational degree, then years of positions using interpersonal / soft skills, and her diverse work experience in her target, as well as associated fields.

   OBJECTIVE: Licensed Social Worker

   EXPERIENCE SUMMARY

- Bachelor of Science, Applied Behavioral Science
- 7+ years, Restaurant Worker (retail food services)
- 2 years, Mental Health Worker / Case Manager (social services)
- 2 years, Transaction Coordinator (real estate)
- 8 months, Teacher / Instructor (English)

   (resume body)

6.   Those interested in getting into the
academic realm of teaching in virtual,
online, or brick-and-mortar schools may
have to format their curriculum vitae in
showcasing the following elements at the
top and the first page, starting with their
Teaching Philosophy, with the general list of
years of experience following:

STATEMENT OF TEACHING PHILOSOPHY

As someone who has had a successful
professional career and a vast dedication to
lifelong learning, I now strive to be the best
educator I can be to give back to society
and to pass along … (etc.)

EXPERIENCE SUMMARY

- 20+ years, Data Center and Lab
  Deployment (Fortune 500 Companies)
- 15+ years, Data Center Management
- 13+ years, Project, Portfolio and
  Program Management
- 12 years, Senior IT Manager (Private,
  Public; Film Industry)
- 8+ years, IT Staff Management
- 7 years, System Engineer (Pharma
  Industry)

(resume body)

If the instructor is teaching information technology, this list would be directly underneath their Experience (years of) Summary listing to showcase what IT skills they are offering. But if they are seeking to teach non-IT topics, but want to emphasize what technical skills they have in their background, they would list these tech-skills at the end of the resume / curriculum vitae, after the training courses (taken) section. Note the IT skill sets are broken into types of skills in general listed in alpha order (not necessarily level of experience).

(resume body)

SUBJECT MATTER EXPERTISE

- Data Center Operations: Rack, Power, Cable, Patch Plan Management
- Database Engineering: Oracle, MySQL, Cassandra, Hadoop
- Disaster Recovery / Asset Recovery
- Machine Learning
- Network Engineering: DC Core, Gateway, Switch, Firewall, WAF, VPN
- Procurement: Bill of Materials, Purchase Requisition, Approval, Delivery, and Receipt
- Project, Portfolio Management: Local, Global- and Internet-Scale Infrastructure
- Security: PCI, PII, SOX Compliance, Tiered Architecture (Web, App, Database)
- Systems Engineering: iOS, Linux,

Solaris, AIX, NAS/SAN/RAID/JBOD

7.   This resume owner is driving his job search towards project and program manager, so has his years of skills and experience at the top of the resume that is focusing on industry specific types of general jobs (work experience). To avoid being pigeon-holed as an IT tech person, they have listed their industry-related hard skills at the bottom of the resume.

EXPERIENCE SUMMARY

- 9 years, Production Manager, Lighting / SFX Technician (hospitality, concert, business events)
- 5 years, Producer/Videographer (video capture, editing)
- 4 years, Executive Project, Program, Portfolio Management
- 2 years, SME Consultant –Drones (pilot, manufacturing, start-up investments)
- Project Management Professional (PMP)

(resume body)

HARDWARE / SOFTWARE / TECHNICAL / COMPUTER

- Apple Motion
- Final Cut Pro
- Adobe Creative Suite

- Adobe Acrobat DC
- Onshape
- Tinkercad
- Pronterface
- Cura
- Anycubic Kossel (built/tuned 3D printer)
- 3DR hardware and software
- DJI hardware and software
- FRSky Taranis X9D+ QX7 (programming / modification)
- Arduino (firmware) modifying and flashing
- MWOSD Configurator
- PID tuning
- Betaflight, Cleanflight, KISS GUI
- Blender
- Grand MA lighting console (programming)
- Akai MIDI controller mapping; Resolume and Pangolin

8. Sometimes a job seeker has been in the same 'type' of job for decades, but still needs to list years of experience and to showcase their skills. The list may not be 'long,' but short and succinct gets the point across. In this resume, the experience is listed at the top, and the skills sets are added to the 'short' list near the bottom of the resume, which also includes recognition and awards.

   OBJECTIVE: Logistics Manager

EXPERIENCE SUMMARY

- 20 years, US Army, Sergeant, Honorable Discharge: 01/10
- 19+ years, Project Manager / Technical Supervisor (UAV, Military, Government Contracting)
- Clearance: DoD, Secret (last adjudicated: 01/01, expires: 01/11)

(resume body)

TECHNICAL / COMPUTER / RECOGNITION / AWARDS

- Catalogue Ordering Logistic Tracking System (COLTS)
- SIPRnet
- MS Office: Word, Excel, PowerPoint, Publisher, Outlook
- 10/09, Commendation, (OIF), Fort Stewart, GA
- Armed Forces Expeditionary Medal
- Army Achievement Medal
- Army Commendation Medal
- Iraq Campaign Medal

9.   In some cases, the resume may require certain information in designated areas based on the (future employer) company-required resume layouts. This is still a good opportunity to showcase skills and capabilities.

OBJECTIVE: Program Analyst, Project Manager, Director of Compliance, Business Development

EXPERIENCE SUMMARY

- 20+ years, Senior Project / Program Management
- 16 years, Trustee / Company Director
- 10 years, United States Army, E-4, Legal Specialist, Honorable Discharge

PROFESSIONAL CAREER SKILLS

- Trustee / Project Management Financial
- Business Transactions / Advisor and Legal Subject Matter Expertise (SME)
- Veteran's Health Benefits SME and Advisor

10. Sometimes a job seeker may have a huge set of diverse employment experience and needs to showcase that diversity. If too long, the list needs to be edited to avoid overwhelming the recruiters with too many foci. In the case below – the experiences that may not necessarily be directly relevant to the target position (military, HR management, textbook reviewer) could potentially be eliminated for brevity, depending upon what position the job seeker is targeting and skills related to non-career relevant technology can be

eliminated (e.g., school Course
Management Systems).

EXPERIENCE SUMMARY

- 20 years, Radiology Technologist (RT)
- 19 years, Computed Tomography
  Technologist (CT)
- 14 years, Magnetic Resonance Imaging
  Technologist (MR)
- 11 years, Director Radiology
  Management (healthcare)
- 6 years, Professor (radiology & political
  science, business)
- 5 years, Reviewer / Author (academic,
  textbooks, medical journals, blogs)
- 4 years, Certified Radiology
  Administrator (CRA)
- 3 years, United States Army, Sergeant
  (E5) Honorable Discharge: 11/03
- 2 years, Senior Competent Professional
  (SCP), Society of Human Resources
  Management

(resume body)

COMPUTER / PLATFORMS / AWARDS / RECOGNITION

- Blackboard (CRM)
- LEO (CRM)
- Moodle (CRM)
- WebCT (CRM)
- MS Office: Word, Excel, PowerPoint

WHAT NOT TO
INCLUDE IN A RESUME

There are elements eager job seekers want to place inside a resume, but the content is not practical, or the data is illegal for hiring managers or recruiters to ask. It may not be best to add that information. First time resume writers search for templates on the Internet to use in their job search and believe these templates could be helpful. Resumes need to be simple, 'Plain Jane' in layout and text formatting. There should not be a bevy of bells and whistles to impede the processing of the resume's information in the automatic tracking system (ATS) used by the hiring company in parsing the data to the SQL database. Following are some tips on what not to use or include in your resume.

1. Photos can be unfairly positive or negative as well as potentially promote bias and prejudice in hiring practices. Some countries (e.g., Eastern India, Africa) demand photos on hiring resumes, but in the United States, it is illegal to use 'looks' as a hiring qualification in most jobs. If a company wishes to hire a cute little young thing for a front desk receptionist position, a recruiter may intentionally look for a candidate's photo (Internet search, LinkedIn profile, Facebook page) to see if the

applicant is a young, slim, pretty, and blonde (euphemistically known as the 'front office look'). This would be an unfair hiring practice. All applicants who apply for a publicly posted open position must have the 'best qualifications' for the position that are 'work-related' – not 'looks' related. (Exceptions to this rule would be fashion models, actors and actresses, or news-show hosts and pundits - those seeking employment based on their unique 'look' or physical characteristics – in addition to their experience or skills sets.)

2. Icons, symbols, and graphics should be avoided – mostly because those graphic elements in the resume could 'muck up' the parsing of the data into the Automatic Tracking System (ATS) database. If the resume owner uses cute iconic symbols, e.g., a tiny envelope picture to indicate an email address or an old-fashioned rotary-dial to indicate a telephone, those may be dumped on the other side of the firewall as non-text characters. Adding certification graphics can result in the same issues. For instance, the green circle with the abbreviation CISM in the center logo, indicating a Certified Information Security Manager is 'overkill' on the resume. Simply write out the words behind the date it was conveyed and leave off the graphics (example below).

•   MM/YY, Certification, Certified Information Security Manager

(CISM), Issuing Organization Name, City, ST

3. Tables can also result in scrambling of terms when used to list elements within a resume. The absolute best formatting to use when one wants to show a long list but to use white space on the resume from left to right sides is to highlight the list and then format that information into 'columns.'

One may want to list a set of information technology-based skills, but listing it in one column creates a huge white space on the right hand side of the sheet. Putting the list in a table will make it neater and use the white space better. The parsing engine may not like the table and re-un-scramble the list back into the one-line column.

Initial List:

- MySQL
- Oracle DBMS
- Pascal
- PCs (Window-based)
- PHP
- Python
- QT Creator
- SQL
- UNIX (LINUX)

List of terms in a table:

MySQL	PCs (Window-based)	QT Creator
Oracle DBMS	PHP	SQL
Pascal	Python	UNIX (LINUX)

List of terms formatted into three columns
(formatting menu: "Format," "Columns," "3"):

MySQL	PCs (Window-based)	QT Creator
Oracle DBMS	PHP	SQL
Pascal	Python	UNIX (LINUX)

4. Text Boxes are 'data content' boxes 'locked' into a unique location within the document. The ATS may consider the text boxes as a graphic, and will delete the content – or push the content to the bottom of the resulting text-based resume. The best practice is to avoid using the text boxes and learn to format the text within the word document's layout. (Centering, justification, columns, bullets, numbers, and paragraph indent formatting are basic, and all job seekers *should know* how to format the document for these elements!)

5. LinkedIn Profile URLs (at the top of the resume) can confuse the parsing engine. It's best to create a 'Vanity Plate' LinkedIn profile, as well as place this URL link down inside the Technical section of the job seeker's resume. If the LinkedIn profile URL is near the top or in the Point of Contact information, the parsing engine may

accidently put that URL into the email text box versus the job seeker's legitimate email address (the author has seen this in ATS software).

The job seeker should decide whether adding in the LinkedIn profile URL is redundant if the recruiter is already holding the resume in their hand. There are rumors some recruiters will compare resumes to LinkedIn profiles for 'differing' information, indicating potential 'fibbing' on either, and dismissing candidates where the information on the resume doesn't exactly match their LinkedIn profile. It's best to leave the LinkedIn profile URL off the resume altogether to avoid either the email confusion or the content comparison.

6.   Labels are redundant. If anyone sees (###) XXX-XXXX, they are surely going to interpret that as a phone number, so why label it? If a recruiter sees "Name@email.com" – they understand it is an e-mail address, so why label it?

7.   Birthdates and social security numbers can be used for identity theft. If job searching due to unemployment, the last thing needed is identity thieves stealing your data and cleaning out what little is in the bank account. Your age is no one's business, so unless the publicly posted job position is age relevant to the position (child model, between four and six years old), then one's birthdate is not vital on a resume. It is

acceptable, once one is hired, to provide this data for employment verification via the e-Verify system (I-9 form), filing employment taxes, and to enroll for benefits.

8. EEOC protected information should not be on a resume. The U.S. Equal Employment Opportunity Commission (EEOC) enforces federal laws that make it illegal to discriminate against a job applicant or an employee because of the person's (a) race, (b) color, (c) religion, (d) sex (including pregnancy, gender identity, and sexual orientation), (e) national origin, (f) age (40 or older), (g) disability or (h) genetic information. Thus none of this self-identifying information should be listed anywhere on the resume to avoid the impropriety of the recruiters even knowing this information.

9. Hobbies unrelated to a professional career waste a lot of white space. A model train hobbyist would only need to mention this pastime if they were seeking to build miniature sets for a Hollywood movie. Skiing on the weekends is a great sport for health or winning marathons is notable for building physical stamina and strength, but have no bearing on one's ability to write program code for software.

10. References should not be listed on private sector resumes. Do not provide references until requested. While this is not prevalent, some recruiters use reference lists to 'troll'

for more candidates for open positions. The candidate may not be 'strong' enough, so calling the candidate's references could provide more applicants with even stronger skills and experience. Note: one exception would be a government services (GS) resume, in which professional references must be listed or the resume may be considered 'incomplete.'

RESUME GAPS – ADDRESSING
THE WORKFORCE ABSENCE

Workers may have an absence from the workforce to explain in their resume. Layoffs, reductions in force, terminations for cause, worker's compensation absences, or a leave of absence to care for family members (maternity, paternity leave) or even for an acute physical illness. There is a prevalence of older citizens developing Alzheimer's and other physical illnesses that a family member may have to leave the workforce to care for the family member, then there is the struggle to get back into the workplace after months or years of absence.

Regardless of the reason, resumes with rather large gaps (three months or more) raise eyebrows and promote questions – "What were you doing in this time gap?" – and job seekers feel obliged to provide 'too much' information in some cases. The easiest thing to do it provide a short summary explanation for the absence, and in some cases, a job seeker can word that gap in career on the resume in a positive manner to actually redirect the absence inquiry. The following examples will show how to wordsmith gaps in the resume to redirect the attention of recruiters.

1.   Maternity or Paternity Leave / Stay At Home Mom / Dad: Home Manager. When you

take time off to get pregnant, have a baby, and raise your child before putting them into childcare, those months or years of time off can get 'awkward' to explain when you are aiming for that high-paying executive position. While this job is hard to do, it is also hard to explain it without using patronizing terms. Use these business terms to ensure the absence is explained in business terms.

06/14 – present, Home Manager, Private Client, Round Hill, VA

- Managed / monitored household, including scheduling of appointments, balancing / accounting for monthly budget expenses, and oversight of minors

2. Job Search: Decided current job wasn't working and dropped to pursue more focused search on desired industry / field. To explain the absence from work or simply a longer than expected job search – simply note the dates and the activities in the shortest number of words possible on one line. Job seekers can explain more in the interview if asked why it took so long. (Reasonable answers: (a) the economy (e.g., 2008-2010 market crash and recession), (b) niche market skills with few jobs in local area to explore, or (c) salary expectations.)

03/19 – 07/19, Job Search Activities

3. Student: Sometimes a worker gets laid off
    and in the realization there is no work to be
    had easily because of lack of education or
    job skills or lack of work in the current
    economy, the worker may decide to go back
    to school. While the student loans may add
    up, at least the job seeker is doing
    something productive in their work gap. If
    the student can add in a part-time job to the
    resume, the recruiter can see that the job
    seeker didn't let that time go to waste.

    12/18 – present, Full-Time Doctoral
    Student, Old Dominion University, Norfolk,
    VA

    09/10 – 05/11, Full-Time Student,
    Tidewater Community College, Portsmouth,
    VA

4. Volunteer: Just because you didn't get paid
    doesn't mean it's not work. In some cases,
    volunteers work harder and have more
    responsibilities than paid workers. List the
    'volunteer job title' and then define the 'job'
    tasks and responsibilities.

    05/11 – 06/11, Volunteer / Customer
       Service Representative
    Hope House Thrift Shop Foundation,
       Norfolk, VA

    -   Provided customer service / department
        support as sales associate and cashier;
        greeted and assisted ~20 customers

(daily); rang up sales of ~$30 per sale, managed register for cash, ATM, credit sales, refunds, and exchanges; managed merchandise organization, displays, and housekeeping of goods by organizing, shelving, and moving merchandise according to supervisor's tasking

5.   Internship / Retraining: refocusing job skills on new field / industry or gaining additional skills; completing training webinars or seminars to learn about potential or related work / knowledge skills. Some workers may be nearing retirement and want to reduce the heavy load of job responsibilities, but they don't want to stop working, either. If the job seeker is trying to switch careers, sometimes taking a lower-level position will help them gain valuable insight into the field or industry. Students who graduate (or about to graduate) can use internships to build their resume as well as learn new skills. In some states, law clerks must serve internships for 1-2 years after the bar exam is passed before they can 'practice' law.

MM/YY – MM/YY, Court Clerk Internship, Honorable Judge Judy, Hollywood, CA

- Filed, organized, and prioritized court cases for judge (daily)
- Ensured bailiff's are scheduled for court cases

6.   Family Business: called to help family out in

biz during hard times. When a family business is in trouble due to top management's failing health or age, a younger family member may need to step in temporarily to manage or work in the business. Because it's a small business, this is an opportunity to 'enhance' the job seeker's career history by 'puffing' up the job title (not lying, just puffing), and writing a description that elevates the value of the actual job and responsibilities. A daughter, who's mom sells beads part-time online steps into the picture until mom can recover from surgery can use this opportunity to really showcase their management and business operations skills in the resume description (sample following).

MM/YY – MM/YY, Vice President of Marketing and Operations

- Interim manager for social media and brand marketing for small family business while owner recuperates from acute illness
- Performs logistics management for packing and shipping merchandise, with products valued between $XXX and $XX,XXX
- Perform bookkeeping, inventory tracking and auditing, and quarterly tax determinations and submissions

7.   Part-Time Jobs in Lieu of Career Track to find your passion. If the job seeker is working one or multiple jobs to pay for the

bills while searching for that 'perfect' position, they don't necessarily have to list those burger-flipping or newspaper-delivery jobs on the resume. One line, worded in sample below, will indicate the job seeker was working, but just not in their career field. This should be sufficient to indicate they were sitting at home, watching soap operas and eating chips all day.

Occasionally people will save up to travel for long periods before going back to work. Everyone has read stories about a person who sells everything they own to then travel around the globe for months or years at time. (If you started a blog and posted regularly, do provide the URL in the activity bullet – who knows? – you could become a travel writer!)

MM/YY – MM/YY, Non-Career Relevant Employment

MM/YY – MM/YY, Travel (UK, Scotland, Ireland, Spain, France, and Italy)

8. Home Health Care Worker: With the increase in elderly cases of Alzheimer's, more and more younger family members are being forced to take time out of their career to care for their loved ones. Additionally, sometimes a family member may have an acute health issue (e.g., terminal cancer, auto accident, Wounded Warrior – service disabled veteran). When a worker has to pull out of their career track

to caretake, it could become a full-time job to manage the patient. There are several ways to list this work gap. The resume owner can either provide generally specific bullet to explain the situation, or provide generally vague (and privatized) information about the activity in that time period.

2015 – 2019, Caregiver, Veterans Affairs, Sacramento, CA

- Provide home health care to Wounded Warrior, including oversight and scheduling of medical appointments and mental health care

04/16 – 09/16, Home Health Care Manager, Private Client, Richmond, VA

09/15 – 07/16, Home Manager, Private Client, Chicago, IL

- Provided personal health and home management services to private client

9.   Acute Illness / Medical Conditions: medical 'emergency' with complete resolution of issues. Sometimes the job seeker has a medical work-stoppage, medical treatments, physical therapy, or mental or addiction crisis that forces them to stop working. Anything health-related is Health Insurance Portability and Accountability Act (HIPAA) protected and privileged information that recruiters and hiring managers cannot ask about legally. But providing a one-liner that

explains the work gap of more than 3-6 months can

MM/YY – MM/YY, Recovery period (vehicle accident)

MM/YY – MM/YY, Work Sabbatical to Recover from Surgery

10. Prison: There are folks who have lost career momentum because of jail or prison time. There is no way around it, and leaving that gap on the resume without any explanation forces an uncomfortable moment in the interview. There are industries and fields where convicted felons are not, and cannot, be considered (e.g., banking, finance, government contracting) for position, but there are plenty of other career positions that allow convicted (and rehabilitated) workers a chance at a new beginning. Some prisons have started changing their names to be more 'low-key' so when prisoners get out, they can list the place name on their resume without it becoming a red flag. Alternatively, the job seeker can list vaguer wording on the resume.

MM/YY – MM/YY, Rehabilitation, City Holding Center, Richmond, VA

- *Obtained job training in welding and construction, as well as undergo social rehabilitation to repay debt to society*

MM/YY – MM/YY, Non-Career Relevant Employment / Activities

03/19 – 07/19, Job Search Activities

RESUME KEYWORDS
AND LANGUAGE

The absolute most important thing to worry about in a resume is the language. I am not talking about dirty words, but instead referring to 'clean language' free from clichés, filler words, and full-blown conversations. Resumes are 'teasers' to recruiters – and should have just enough information in them to showcase the job seeker is a 'doer' that gets things accomplished, but also documents how well the job seeker did that unique job via documentable achievements. In some sections, the wording should be specific, while in other sections, the wording should be generalized to prevent cubby-holing.

1. The resume should be laid out in a simple and 'Plain Jane' layout, but also wording should be on a sixth-grade reading level. No one wants to struggle through reading a resume using 'high-falutin' words only a Ph.D. can interpret. Making the language too difficult to read implies pomposity.

2. At the top of the resume underneath the point of contact information should be an "OBJECTIVE: (job title sought)" on one line. Not that awful subjective summary paragraph (B.S.) recruiters hate and roll

their eyes at when they see it. Instead, keep it simple with a bulleted list of years of general industry experience you have to offer the future employer to capture their attention and interest on your background to encourage them to keep reading, e.g., (below):

- XX years, Human Resources Manager (Commercial and Government Defense Contracting Industry)
- XX years, Senior Project Manager, Senior Program Manager (Manufacturing)
- XX years, Supervision and Team Lead (Quality Assurance and Process Improvement)

3. The Objective Statement should be one line and simply state what 'general' job title the job seeker is applying for. It should not be a request for the company to do something for you. "I want to work for a progressive company that allows me the opportunity to obtain training and promotional opportunities to gain job knowledge, skills, and abilities to further my career. I am a wonderful people person, and eagerly take in new tasks, and learn things quickly."

4. Keep subjective wording out of the resume. Subjective language is mostly about soft skills and one can't document those in a resume – these must be demonstrated in person. Theoretically and realistically – you

can't 'leverage' soft skills on a resume. You can note you are a people person on the resume, but that is subjective; recruiters aren't interested in reading 'I am wonderful' descriptions. They are more interested in documentable (provable) and objective information on a resume, including accomplishments and achievements and what the job seeker physically did on a regular basis.   Soft skills are desirable personality and subjective manners in which (and how) a job seeker is able to operate within an environment, especially within a working environment in which the new hire is striving to 'fit into' the people, including personality traits, mannerisms that match those around them (socially), and their body language that makes others comfortable around them (the job seeker).

5.　　A professional resume is not always built with practical aspects, viewpoint, or dimensions. The author has seen some 'so-called professional' resumes that were absolutely gorgeous in their layout and format. The wording and content are too vague and general … there is no real description or real understanding as to what the resume owner did on a weekly or monthly basis in their job tasks and responsibilities, nor any documentable achievements.

6.　　Dump the buzzwords and cliché language. The term, "stakeholder" is a term used by folks in PMP training, but refers to *everyone*

from the CEO to the mailroom clerk and
stockholders, as well as all the company
vendors and the customers. No one person
is responsible for or to *all* stakeholders in a
company. If one completes a task, then a
specific set of persons (coworkers,
supervisors, or clients) will benefit, and they
can take the results of the completed task to
perform higher level task to a strategically-
met organizational goal.

7.   Purge the filler, weak, and passive words.
        These are primarily 'weak' and 'passive'
        verbs starters that need to be exchanged
        out with more assertive and powerful action
        verbs. The words 'the' and 'that' are two of
        the most overused words in the English
        language. If you write a sentences
        including those words, 95% of the time you
        can remove those – no one will know the
        difference. Some other examples of filler or
        weak wording would be:

        •   In order to …
        •   was picked to be trained for …
        •   In support of …
        •   served under …
        •   was promoted to …
        •   was picked for … out of X candidates
        •   was identified to …

        What to substitute? More action oriented
        words that imply you DID something …

        •   to …
        •   provided training to …

- completed tasks for project XYZ …
- supervised ABC in absence of (boss's title) …
- Provided Subject Matter Expertise advice as designated specialist for …
- Leveraged SME knowledge to provide …
- Completed updates for …

8. Keep the bullets' wording concise, rich, start with an action verb, and delete all the subjective language; provide 'results' descriptions and metrics where the results were documentable. Even jobs that are considered 'low-level' can be enriched with added metrics to showcase just how hard someone worked and the documentable results of their labor. For example – a dinner waitress:

- Covered six tables, seating 4-6 guests, with each table flipped at least twice during shift for a total of circa 60 guests during dinner shift of 4-5 hours
- Responsible for menu suggestions and sales, with an average of $28 per head, for an approximate value of $1,680 of food sales, and circa $600 in bar sales, for an average of $2200-$2600 of sales revenue generated per shift

No matter how high-level or low-level your job responsibilities, providing metrics will import to the resume reader the accomplishments reached to prove how dedicated and hard working the job seeker is – at least on paper.

9.   Reduce the amount of wording in each
bullet and avoid blocks of conversation.
Start the bullet with an action verb and get
straight to the point, and eliminate the
'conversational rambling' to get your point
across simply and fast. The following
example is one from a payroll specialist that
ambled all over the place to get the point
across:

- Administered payroll activities related to
  unionized, non-union, and Government
  workers to ensure adherence to payroll
  deadlines and maintaining HRMS/HRIS
  system. Performed Audits Internally
  within employees' records. Maintained
  vacation calendar, work with accounting
  to assisted in forecasting, Integrated
  Human Resources with knowledge, and
  communications skills. Ensure proper
  use of confidential information and
  analysis.

The rewritten piece, which starts with the
action verbs, and tells the 'meat' of the job
is worded more succinctly and uses metrics
to stress the importance of her
accomplishments:

- Administered weekly payroll activities
  related to unionized, non-union, and
  government workers to ensure
  adherence to payroll deadlines with
  values at ~$300K per payroll, for ~300

employees
- Maintained HRMS/HRIS system data including employees' vacation schedules and paid time off (PTO) accumulations
- Performed internal audits within employees' records annually on ~300 records resulting in corrections of ~10% of records' missing information

10. Ensure industry and job-related 'keywords' are in the job description itself. If the job seeker is an accountant, use industry terms: Accounts Payable, Accounts Receivable, Invoices, Billing, GAAP (Generally Accepted Accounting Principles), and other relatable words and terms throughout the entire resume. List the types of applications used in the job – Peachtree, QuickBooks, and other accounting or bookkeeping software.

If the job seeker is a Project or Program Manager, they need to use words such as Lean (Lean Six Sigma), manufacturing, and process-improvement. If the job seeker is a human resources practitioner, they need to use key terms such as personnel, staff, benefits, compensation, time-scheduling / time-keeping, succession planning, recruiting, EEO, AAP, and other key terms related to the job.

Don't rely on acronyms – spell out the acronym the first time it is used in the resume to ensure that the reader knows exactly what the term refers to: Equal

Employment Opportunity (EEO) and Affirmative Action Plan (AAP) are two terms for the human resources and personnel management field.

MAKING A RESUME 'AUTOMATIC TRACKING SYSTEM' (ATS) FRIENDLY

The author worked as a recruiter in human resources over ten years and used many automatic tracking systems (ATS) for resume storage and applicant tracking. The author identified many issues inside the resumes that were submitted by job applicants and this list identifies many do's and don'ts to ensure the job seeker's resume uploads smoothly, transcribes cleanly, and comes out on the other side of the firewall as readable, and still in a functionally performing format for layout.

1.   Do all your resume writing and submitting in a Microsoft Word document file. It is imperative you use the same software processing programs that most recruiters, hiring managers, and human resources personnel will be using in their offices. The ATS may not be able to convert your Open Office or Google docs-based resume, thus you may never hear back from your resume posting because the document is unreadable. Do not convert your Word document to a PDF. While some systems encourage uploading of PDF files, those files are not editable, thus sometimes they may convert over strangely (content all askew) on the other side of the firewall in

the 'text-based' version that recruiters and hiring managers may be viewing.

2.   Use 'normal' font and font sizes. Arial is plain, and Times New Roman with serifs is OK, but sometimes hard on the eyes. Use between 10.5 (minimum) and 12 point (maximum) sized font. Keep in mind, when you hand your resume over to a middle-aged hiring or recruiting manager at a job fair, they may need reading glasses and are having a hard time reading that teeny, tiny font – it's exhausting and it's too easy to move to the next job candidate who used larger text font. Avoid fancy fonts, differing fonts (e.g., using Cooper, Arial Rounded, and Times New Roman all in one resume).

3.   Avoid writing a long subjective, boring paragraph at the top of the resume. Insert the header word 'Objective' – then JUST the job title afterwards – all on one line.

4.   Summarize your 'general' (NOT specific) jobs in a years of experience list at the top of the resume, e.g., 5 years, Supervisory Management, 10 years, Technical Analyst (military, federal government). The example below summarizes over 20 years of various and multiple positions within four career tracks and, yes, some overlapped in years of experience:

EXPERIENCE SUMMARY

- 14 years, Professional Consultant /
  Trainer (Leadership / Professional
  Development)
- 13 years, Information Technology
  Supervisor / Manager Information
  Systems (MIS)
- 11 years, CEO, Professional Trainer
  (Corporate Leadership / Personal
  Development)
- 2 years, Information Technology
  Software Tester and Technician
  (Financial Industry)

5. Avoid – as in 'avoid like the plague' – online
    resume templates. These templates are
    constructed using tables and word / text
    boxes, and some are beautiful, but they are
    just not practical. Once these beautifully
    laid out resumes are loaded into an ATS,
    the parsing system starts converting the
    word document to a text document and
    parses the data into data fields in the SQL
    database. Cheap ATS platforms may not
    parse the data over perfectly and your
    resume will turn into an unreadable mess on
    the other side of the firewall. Recruiters do
    not have time cleaning up these resumes.
    You can model the placement of the
    information on the online resume templates
    by using simple text and formatting in Word,
    but do not insert your data into these
    templates. (Additionally, you do not know
    what may be 'attached' to these templates

you are downloading – including malware,
Trojan horses, and other computer
viruses!).

6.   Leave a reasonable margin around all four
sides of the resume. A generous margin
would be one inch, but the minimum should
be .8 of one inch. A margin of .25 (one
quarter of an inch) is unsustainable and
won't print properly if the recruiter wants a
hard copy. If the resume has to go over that
third or fourth page, that is OK. You can
actually decrease the line height for your
content by going to paragraph, line spacing,
and clicking on 'Exactly' then 1-2 points
taller than the actual letter font (e.g., 10.5
point Arial font, with 11.5 point line height)
which will condense the resume content, but
still allow readability.

7.   Everyone already knows that (XXX) XXX-
XXXX is a telephone number, so you don't
need to label these elements. Same for the
email address. Avoid the up and down line
"|" between elements – the parsing engine
could mistake that for a capital "I" or a lower
case (el) "l" or even a Roman Numeral one
"I."   Don't use cute little icons, either. The
symbol for a telephone is cute, but the
parsing engine won't know what to do with it
and may stick in into the bottom of the text
resume on the other side of the firewall.

8.   Do not put information in the header or
footer of the resume. Parsing engines will
toss out content in those areas. You may

be the most highly qualified candidate for the position, but when the recruiter is trying to find your name, phone number, email, or address, it's nowhere to be found because the system dumped that content. Put your point of contact (POC) information at the top of the resume, page one, and then open up the File, Properties, Summary menus, and type in your Full Name, Email Address (permanent), and your Phone Number in the "Author" text box. The worse-case scenario, the recruiter can attempt to find your information there if your POC is missing from the top of the visible pages.

9. Don't write your job descriptions with full sentences. Start with an Action Verb, then describe what was completed, or achieved, then leave off any periods at the end. You are not writing regular sentences, you are listing bullets of accomplishments, thus periods are not required. Keep the descriptions as tight and short as possible.

10. List all your technical skills – especially if you are in the technology or information technology field. Those job seekers who have a short list of technology skills and knowledge or experience with industry-related software or hardware should list those at the *bottom* of their resume. Job seekers who are IT-technicians or computer scientists should list all their IT-knowledge at the *top* of the resume, immediately under their list of years of experience. Samples are noted below, and the skills can be listed

in alpha order or by types:

Non-IT Person, listing tech skills towards
bottom of resume:

CAREER TRAINING / CERTIFICATIONS

- 2014 – present, Coaching Certification, International Coach Certification Academy, Psy Tech, Inc.
- 2005, Life and Business Coaching, School of Coaching Mastery, St. Louis, MO
- Life Coach Courses, Inner Life Skills (ILS), Boulevard Witkoppen, Fourways
- 2004, Certificate, American Seminar Leader Association (CSL), Pasadena, CA
- 2004, Business Management Training Program, Workshop in Business Opportunities, Inc., New York, NY
- 2000, Certificate, Conference on Directing, Controlling and Managing Projects, Skillpath, Mission, Kansas
- 2000, Certificate, Managing Your Success, Deloitte & Touche LLP, New York, NY

HARDWARE / SOFTWARE / TECHNICAL / COMPUTER

- HTML/JavaScript (Front end)
- Java (Business Logic – using Oracle Application Server JWeb Cartridge)
- MS Office: Word, Excel, PowerPoint, Outlook

- Oracle / Oracle 8i / Oracle Application Server
- Web-based (thin client)
- Website Development, Programming

The job candidate who is seeking a position
in the computer field should showcase their
IT-related skills at the top of their resume.

Computer Scientist, Information Technology
Specialist:

OBJECTIVE: Computer Scientist, Software Engineer

EXPERIENCE SUMMARY

- 20+ years, Computer Programmer, Web Developer, Database Developer, Software Hobbyist
- 20+ years, US Navy, Electronics Technician / EOD, Chief, Honorable Discharge: 12/03
- 14+ years, Business Owner, Entrepreneur (service industry)
- 3 years, Curriculum Development / Training (military NEC 5332)
- Security Clearance: DoD, TS / SCI / CNWDI (as US Navy EOD tech; *expired*: 2005)
- Work Preference: Central / Northern Virginia (open to telecommute)

HARDWARE / SOFTWARE / TECHNICAL / COMPUTER

(experience in each ranges from hands-on use to basic familiarity, including self-taught applications)

- Adobe Creative Suite: Illustrator
- Android Studio
- Apple Operating Systems
- Apple / Mac Computers
- Artificial Intelligence (AI)
- C / C++
- CSS
- Drupal CMS (v.7; v.8)
- GIMP
- GitHub
- Google Firebase
- HTML
- Java / Java Script
- Knowledge Discovery (Big-Data)
- LabView (NI-LabView)
- MS Office: Word, Excel, PowerPoint, Outlook
- MS Office: Access
- MySQL
- Oracle DBMS
- Pascal
- PCs (Window-based)
- PHP
- Python
- QT Creator
- SIPRnet / NIPRnet
- SQL
- UNIX (LINUX)

HOW FAR BACK AND
HOW MUCH JOB HISTORY

A well-written resume provides a 'teaser' of your capabilities to future employers. It does not provide a life history (unless you are in academics and are submitting a curriculum vitae). You want to provide just enough information to showcase not only what you have achieved and accomplished, but what you are capable of doing in future career positions. Too many 'older' workers are so eager to provide information they overwhelm the recruiter. Or, job seekers are attempting to make their resume look like a C-suite executive when they are not seeking that position nor are they qualified.

It is not necessary to go back to the very beginning of your work history on your resume. Most recruiters want to see the more recent and relevant experience on a job seeker's resume.

1. Know the difference between a bio (one page intro), a resume (2-4 page job history for 10-15 years of experience), and a Curriculum Vitae (Latin for life-story) which can run 20-30 pages long (academic institution job search). When you are seeking a position in the private sector, you will submit a resume. If you are invited to present or talk to a congregation, you

provide a bio to be read as your
introduction. If you are applying for
positions at colleges or universities, then
you would provide the longer curriculum
vitae for consideration. Another type of
resume is the United States-based
government services resume (often called
GS), which can be longer than standard
resume because each job description
requires a fully-loaded header with
addresses, supervisor's names and phone
numbers, and salary or security clearance
information, which stretches the length
exponentially.

2.   Writing a resumes to only one or two pages
defeats the purpose of providing rich and
key vital words relevant to the job seeker's
skills and experience. Job seekers keeping
resumes down to a bio (one page) or two-
page resumes hurt themselves by not
spelling out a more diverse employment
history. The more content and vital
keywords in a resume, the better and faster
a candidate can be found - even if their
resume is four pages long. Regardless of
what career counselors advise, 2-3 pages is
OK in some cases where the job seeker has
extensive knowledge, skills, and
employment history directly relevant to the
career path and job requisition.

3.   Jobs (work history) should be listed in
backwards chronological order for at least
10-15 years backwards in history. Full job
description(s) should be loaded using every

available character space in each job, with
MM/YY dates, and bulleted descriptions of
accomplishments and achievements so
readers can determine the profile owner's
'capabilities' from that online and summary.
Never *note* more than 20 years of 'anything'
on your resume; if you take a college
degree date and the 30 years of
employment, a recruiter can add up and
figure out you are over 50 years of age.
Instead, if you have been in the military for
35 years, then note a 'ceiling #' of years
then add a plus sign: "20+ years in the US
Navy."

4.   What is the "rule of thumb" in terms of what
to include? If you have been in the job
market for over a decade, the rule-of-thumb
for years of experience is normally 10-15
years of experience. If you have had only
one job in the last 10-15 years, then it's 'ok'
to go to 20 years of experience if the
previous job has relevant and diverse
experience to share. If you have had only
one employer, the job seeker should break
out job titles to show progression and
promotions or transfers to emphasize how
diverse a range of job responsibilities they
had over the years.

5.   Don't go back more than 10-15 years in
your job history … employers are only
interested in your more recent job skills,
knowledge, and abilities. Unless you are
fresh into the career and the job market or
have only a few scraps of employment

history, then write about anything that feels like work experience to expand your resume (e.g., childcare [babysitting], house cleaning [for relatives], church activities, and hamburger flipping).

6.   If you have only had one job in the last 15 years use volunteer experience to round out your versatility. One job seeker didn't have much 'real world' paid job experience, but had over 10 years of experience assisting his church in audio-visual communications (speakers, recording, lights) and was able to leverage that volunteer activity of about 10 hours a week into a new job.

7.   If your college degree is not within the last 15 years, then don't add a date of graduation, but if it is within the last 15, DO note the date. Recruiters may assume (avoiding the age bias) the job seeker is younger because of 'more recent' college degree. Do remember to add in college course titles in the degree information because those course titles may lend themselves to search engine optimization based on career-related keywords.

8.   How do you handle those earlier years of employment with non-relevant jobs? If the jobs were NOT relevant to current job search / career, you can actually 'place-hold' the period of time to show you were doing something, but no need to explain it fully and recruiters will understand. For example:

01/14 – 12/17, Cashier, Hardee's Fast
Food, San Clemente, CA
would best be written as:

01/14 - 12/17, Non-Career Related
Employment

9. You can explain 'gaps' in job history by
    creatively wordsmithing the resume to
    explain the gaps in any manner that sounds
    respectable and feasible. Some examples:

(Home-based homemaker, wife, mom)

MM/YY - MM/YY, Home Manager (or Home
Health Manager)
Private Client, City, State

- 1-2 bullets explaining in general what a
  mom normally does - scheduling, care
  taking, childcare, budgeting, purchases
  etc.
- 1-2 bullets explaining caring for a private
  patient, including doctor's transportation,
  scheduling, medications, home
  management, etc.

(you were unemployed)

MM/YY - MM/YY, Non-related career
activities

(insinuating one was busy, but not working
on the career choice job at the moment)

(you were looking for work, but busy with volunteer work at the time, also)

MM/YY - MM/YY, Volunteer
Non-Profit Organization's Name, City, State

- 1-2 bullets explaining in general what volunteer tasking or activities that indicates the work the job seeker was performing

10. Does a job candidate have to submit salary history details? The GS resumes do require (mandate) salary information, but avoid providing any salary history either directly into a private sector resume or in an interview. Ask the recruiter for the relevance of the salary information (in some states, it is illegal to ask for that information).

You could note that asking for your past salary could be indicative that your future employer may not think you are currently worth the competitive salary for the position being considered at this point in your career. Ask the recruiter if they can supply the job's salary range and you can then assure them you are doing so to avoid wasting their valuable time in recruiting you if the range is not within your expectations.

If they can only offer the baseline (minimum) range, then you can quickly perform a calculation as to whether a 10-20% range would reasonably be their top

offer for baseline salary and decide to
continue the conversation.

HOW TO WRITE A COVER LETTER

Job seekers have trepidations about writing a cover letter. What to write about? How many details should I add in? What elements are going to be repetitious to the resume? How do I phrase the cover letter – formally, informally, semi-formally? Do I need to tailor the tone of the letter for each job application?

1. Write the cover letter in the same tone for a job in any case - focus on positive aspects of the job you just came out of and what you have to offer to the company as a future employee.

2. Are cover letters required for every job application? No. Many companies won't care about cover letters, and recruiters are aware cover letters may not necessarily be written by the applicant (hired out). Other cover letters are 'boilerplate' templates and won't provide any vital information the resume doesn't already cover. Statistically, job seekers may come across less than 10% of jobs which require a cover letter. Have one on hand, just in case. If the cover letter is NOT requested then do NOT force the additional material on the hiring managers - provide the cover letters ONLY

if requested.

3.   You won't know whether to take a certain
        tone, unless you are intimate with the
        environment and type of company
        employees. Job seekers may not be privy to
        that information from 'cold' applications.
        Take the high road, and create a letter that
        come across as formal job application
        notice. Never stoop to casual street-talk or
        bar-level friendly conversational tones - that
        sets the incorrect mood for the entire
        conversation.

4.   At the top of the formally (formatted
        business) cover letter, there should be the
        date, then the full company name and
        address, with an Attention: (general job title)
        line under the company name for whom the
        letter is intended. Then skip a line and write
        the formal greeting:

        a) Dear Sir or Madam:
        b) Dear Human Resources
            Representative:
        c) Dear Hiring Manager:

5.   There should be only three paragraphs and
        one page to relay vital information recruiters
        and hiring managers may want to see, other
        than the grammar, punctuation, and spelling
        within the letter itself.

6.   Paragraph One: where did you, the job
        seeker, find the information about the job?
        Human resources will want that data to

continue to market to a market demographic. Why do you want to come to work for the company? (Not a general BS answer, either!) Mention the company logo, motto, website simple summary, or strategic business goals that actually interests you and attracted your attention. Mention whether you actually know anyone who works in the company who may have referred you (and may be able to earn a referral fee).

7. Paragraph Two: can mentions something - anything - NOT already mentioned in your resume (e.g., "I am the volunteer President of the local XYZ programming club, with 200 members, who run competitions in computer software programming for local colleges and universities to mentor and guide students in the IT field towards careers in STEM."). The subjective language that doesn't belong in the resume can be used in the cover letter itself (e.g., "The awesome service members in my glorious platoon, thinks my leadership 'rocks'.") You are looking to convey, and present, great content related to leadership, strong people-skills, training skills, and computer (technology) experience, over and above what is mentioned already in the resume.

8. Paragraph Three is the Point of Contact (POC) paragraph: this paragraph should include text to this affect: "I am available for telephonic or face-to-face interviews, Mon-

Fri, 8:00 a.m. to 9:00 p.m., and/or anytime weekends before 9:00 p.m. You may reach me via my (cell) phone number (###) XXX-XXXX or correspond via my email at: email@email.com." Ensure your availability for the exact times you are open to chatting, or communicating via Skype, online chats, or emails are mentioned. Some recruiters work on weekends when they are more likely to reach job seekers (off hours for most folks).

9. Will applying to a job out-of-state hurt your chances of getting the job? If so, how can you compensate? If you have amazing skill sets and experience and are willing to move – let the hiring company know. If you mention in a cover letter you are looking to transfer – *or* – are already moving to a new geographic area, then recruiters understand you are not necessarily seeking compensation for relocation. This puts you on equal footing with other job applicants (your competition) in the area. You can mention a willingness to meet via telephonic interviews (Skype) to save them (and you) costs of traveling to meet face-to-face.

10. The cover letter should be on ONE Page - no more.

FORMATTING A
PROFESSIONAL RESUME

Concentrating solely on formatting a professional resume (versus a Bio, C.V., or a government resume), the following layout is recommended with each element as noted below. Note each section may have sub-headers, also.

1. Point of Contact Information: Full name, City, State, and Zip, as well as cell phone number and email address. Leave out the street address on private sector resumes because the recruiters do not need that information and you don't want them to pre-judge you if they think you live in the 'wrong section' of the city. City and State provides the recruiters the information needed to determine if you are in the local area to the job site or need to be considered for any potential re-location fees.

   FirstName MI. Last Name
   Manhattan, New York 12345
   (XXX) XXX-XXX
   MyEmailAddress@myemail.com

2. Objective: This should be one line with states what type of job you are applying for in general or specific terms. This should not be a huge paragraph of subjective language

asking what the company can do for you.

OBJECTIVE: Human Resources Manager

OBJECTIVE: Director or Vice President of Sales

OBJECTIVE: Territory Sales Manager

3. Years of Experience: Should be the section at the top of the resume that the recruiters will look at first. This will provide general years of experience metrics that showcase the field or industry of your career history. This section does not include education – only work history or years of experience in specific skills or field. No matter how many years' history of experience, top off your experience at 20 years to avoid age bias for job consideration. (If you have more than 20 years of experience, then note "20+" years.) Note that Education is not mentioned in this experience list. A few specific degrees or certifications, e.g., Doctorate Degree in (field), Engineering Degree (P.E.), or Medical Doctor (M.D. degree from XYZ University) can be mentioned on one line in this list if directly related to job for which the applicant is applying.

EXPERIENCE SUMMARY:

- 20+ years, Retail Management Customer Service / Logistics, Warehousing, and Shipping
- 12 years, Public Health / Microbiology

Researcher (microbiology laboratory)
- 12 years, Instructor / Curriculum Development (Secondary Education Mathematics)

EXPERIENCE SUMMARY:

- 7 years, Firearms / Ammunition Handling (retail sales; police equipment)
- 4 years, Sheriff's Deputy / Police Officer (local city, county)
- 1.5 years, Security / Police Management (training, supervision)

EXPERIENCE SUMMARY

- 20+ years, Classroom Teacher (5th-8th grade & 11th-12th grade)
- 16 years, Director of Instructional Technology
- 15 years, United States Navy, E5 / Intelligence Specialist, Hon. Dis: 03/93
- 3 years, Instructional Technology Specialist (Military, Private, Public Schools)
- 2 years, United States Naval Reserve, E5 / Intelligence Specialist

4. Backwards Chronology of Job History – 10-15 years. This is the meat of the resume. Provide the dates, the job title, and the company name, city, and state for whom you worked. Underneath the job title header, provide between 3-10 (maximum) bullets highlighting the major job

responsibilities and achievement, using as many metrics as possible to describe how well one performed in the job. Crunch the wording as tightly as possible to keep the bullets short. Any bullets going over four lines may be too long.

12/10 – present, Leasing Consultant / Assistant Manager
Real Property Assets Management, Alexandria, VA

- Manage, coordinate, and train a five-member leasing team to manage, monitor, and maintain a billion-dollar asset (two high-rise apartments) and assisted in managing (name of properties) and leasing consultant at (name of properties) to generate leasing income and maintain compliance with Virginia Housing Development Authority (VHDA)
- Performed human resources taskings, including recruiting, interviewing, hiring, and training two sales lease consultants, responsible for increasing occupancy, resulting in baseline of 64% to increase of 89% within seven months
- Etc.

09/08 – 12/10, Radio Personality / Reporter / Newscaster
WXXX 89.9 FM, Radford, VA

- Researched potential news or feature

stories; presented local news and feature reports in the 'public radio style' on both local and national news programs including: National news programs: Fox News Talk, MSNBC, CNN, CNBC

- Investigated, wrote, and produced investigative and human-interest circa 3-8 stories daily; combined video, audio and graphics to effectively convey each story
- Etc.

This list will go back approximately 10-15 years.

5. Education (formal degrees): This refers to Associates, Bachelor's, Master's, and Doctoral degrees from accredited universities and schools. Any degrees from non-accredited schools need to be listed under the training section. Adding in course titles that may be directly associated with the career field increases search engine optimization (SEO) for the resume in resume databases. If there are only some college courses, then list the dates of attendance (MM/YY-MM/YY); and for completed degrees only note the graduation month and year. If the job seeker has no college education, then list Diploma, Name of High School, City, and State. If you had a spectacular Grade Point Average (GPA), then by all means brag about it here. (Anything below 3.0, avoid the GPA mention.)

FORMAL EDUCATION:

- 05/14, **Juris Doctor, Law**, James Madison School of Law, Washington, DC; GPA: 3.68; *Courses: Legal Writing, Contracts, Torts, Property, Professional Responsibility, Intellectual Property, Intellectual Property & Competition Law, Civil Procedure, Constitutional Law, Law Review, Criminal Law, Criminal Procedure, Evidence, Copyright Law, Corporations, Telecommunications Law, Community Property, Client Interviewing & Counseling, Wills, Trusts*
- 08/02, **Master of Science, Mechanical Engineering,** Virginia Commonwealth University, Richmond, VA; GPA: 3.48; *Thesis; Opposed-Flow Flame Spread in Cylindrical Geometry; Courses: Gas Dynamics, Convection Heat Transfer, Engineering Design – Analytical Methods, Combustion,*
- 06/98, **Bachelor of Science, Mechanical Engineering,** University of California at Santa Barbara, Santa Barbara, CA; *Courses: Chemistry, Physics, Differential Equations, Statics, Circuits & Electronics, Linear Algebra, Advanced Calculus, Strength of Materials, Engineering Mechanics, Thermo-Science, Engineering Economic Analysis, Marine Technology, Fluid Mechanics, Design, Materials*

6. Training (webinars, seminars, conference

training, certifications): This list provides a valuable set of keywords and terms to be 'caught' in the recruiters search. All that is needed is the date of completion, the title of the certificate or course (no course numbers are needed), the presenting organization, city, and state. This list can go back 10-15 years, also.

CAREER TRAINING / CERTIFICATIONS:

- 2006, Certification (Patent Attorney), United States Patent and Trademark Office: Registration # XX,XXX
- 2014, State Bar of the Commonwealth of Virginia: Bar # XXX,XXX
- 1998, Commonwealth of Virginia State Licensed Professional Engineer: Mechanical Engineering # XX,XXX (expires / renewal scheduled for 2020)

Naval / Military Training

- 03/19, Engineering Duty Officer School Sr., Engineering Duty Officer School, San Diego, CA
- 01/18, Naval Sea Systems Command Drydocking Course, US DoN, San Diego, CA

7.   Technical knowledge: Employers want to know what technology skills future employees may have – to either hit the ground running or with the ability to train other employees (or even clients) in the use of computer-based technology. Providing a list of technology the job seeker has worked

with, touched, or is even familiar with adds to the value of the job seeker's skill sets. The more technically skilled a job seeker is, the more potential value in enabling the company's future strategic goals and objectives.

HARDWARE / SOFTWARE / TECHNICAL / COMPUTER

- Adobe Creative Suite: Illustrator
- Anycubic Kossel (built/tuned 3D printer)
- Apple Motion
- KISS
- GUI
- Blender
- C / C++
- CSS
- Cura
- DJI hardware and software
- DRUPAL CMS (v.7; v.8)
- Final Cut Pro
- FRSky Taranis X9D+ QX7 (programming / modification)
- GIMP
- GitHub
- HTML
- JAVA / JAVA Script
- Kolor Suite
- MWOSD Configurator
- Onshape
- SIPRnet / NIPRnet
- SOLIDWORKS
- TinkerCad

- G Suite: Drive, Docs, Calendar, Slides, Sheets, Analytics
- Open Office (Apple): Pages and Numbers
- MS Office: Word, Excel, PowerPoint, Outlook, Access, Project

8. Presentations (training to others), Conferences, Publications: Being able to teach others in job-related skills, or new skills (see bullet above), enables employers to save money by assigning instruction to current employees with skills. Or, presenting at conferences (academic field) imparts that the presenter is a subject matter expert (SME) in something. Additionally, having published – whether in a local newspaper or an international journal or as an expert in an advice column adds importance to the job seeker's education or background as someone with advice that others value.

PRESENTATIONS / CONFERENCES / WHITE PAPERS / PUBLICATIONS:

- 2017, Presenter, South Carolina Educational Technology Annual Conference, Greenville and Charleston, SC: The Two Sides of EdTech: Essentials of Collaboration and Communication between the Instructional and Support Sides of Educational Technology Presenter, Northwest Evaluation Association Annual Fusion

Conference, Charlotte, NC
- 2015, Presenter, South Carolina Association for School Administrators Annual Innovative Ideas Conference, Myrtle Beach, SC: Make Personalized Learning a Reality by Creating a Blended Environment

9. Patents, Languages, Awards, Recognition: These are minor achievements in comparison to the job descriptions, but indicate the job seeker was good enough in their career position to warrant extraordinary recognition for work or service above the minimum standards of the job.

RECOGNITION / AWARDS

- 07/14, Recognition Award, TSA, Houston, TX
- 2007, Certificate of Appreciation, H-5 site Manager, Tal'Afar, Iraq
- Good Conduct Medal
- Joint Service Commendation Medal
- National Defense Service Medal
- Navy Achievement Medal
- Overseas Service Ribbon (2)

10. Volunteer, Community, Trade Organizations: Showcases diversity of background and experience and could also showcase some additional 'work experience' – regardless of salary.

VOLUNTEER / COMMUNITY SERVICE /

TRADE ORGANIZATIONS

- 01/16 – present, Board Member, Learning Forward SC, Columbia, SC
- 2010 – 2017, Student Scholar Mentor, Citizen Scholars, Spartanburg, SC

HOW AND WHY TO AVOID
LYING ON YOUR RESUME

Everyone hates a liar. Lying equates to cheating. Lying engenders mis-trust, negates otherwise excellent communications, and destroys relationships. Why lie on your resume and destroy potential good-will before you are even employed? Essentially - no one should lie on their resume. Period. If recruiters and companies (HR Departments) find out you have lied about anything on your resume, there is an exponentially high percentage you will be fired for cause and that firing / termination will not look good on your resume or for future employers.

1.   While lying is not illegal – applying for a position that requires security clearances based on lies about your activities or work history could be a fire-able offense when you have lied on your resume (or even security clearance application). If the government finds out you are attempting to gain access to classified materials pertinent to the safety of the USA, then yes, you could potentially be arrested and prosecuted for (attempted) spying.

2.   No … not everyone is 'doing it' (lying on their resume). When companies have access to third-party background checking

vendors and social media is so rampant out on the Internet, just a few minutes of research and normally find out just about anything about a person. MOST folks are savvy enough to know if they lie on their resume, they WILL get caught.

3.   In most recent years (after 2010), some recruiters and hiring managers are adamant the applicant's resume match the applicant's LinkedIn profile verbiage *exactly*. In their mind, mismatches or different information otherwise indicates 'lying.' If you change your profile on LinkedIn, be sure to update your resume for needed edits.

4.   It is illegal to ask a job candidate their age. You should not lie about your age, but you can 'disguise' your age. If you dress well, carry yourself well, have well-done makeup, don't have obvious age-related silver or gray hair, and are able to stand straight and walk without stumbling (related to age) recruiters will find it hard to guess your age. Most folks in their 60's can easily look in their 40's if they take care of themselves and their health.

5.   Is information on your resume an outright lie – or is it puffed up to sound more important? You are allowed to 'bombast' in a resume, as long as the puffery is not overextended to the point of non-believability.

        Bombast (noun): high-sounding language with little meaning, used to impress people;

"the bombast of gung-ho militarism";
synonyms: bluster, pomposity, ranting, rant,
nonsense, empty talk, humbug, wind,
blather, claptrap. (dictionary.com)

6.   The author has stressed adding metrics to
resumes to showcase the job seeker's
capabilities. There are opportunities where
one can 'stretch' the metrics (puffery)
without lying. If you are a dinner waitress
that works 40+ hours a week or during the
'in-season' (e.g., beach resort), but work
slows down to about 15-20 hours during the
'off-season,' then provide metrics for the
busy times. An example: '…wait on five
tables (lunch/dinner), with at least two
flipped parties per table, with an average
dinner tab of $230 and average bar tab of
$35 per table, with totals of between $2,200
to $4,000 in revenue per 8-hour shift.' You
are describing the busy season and not
including averages from the slow season,
so you are definitely telling the truth, but
also not lying simply because you omitted a
seasonal differentiation.

7.   An example of puffery, without outright
lying, could be that the job seeker worked
for a Fortune 500 company – but, they
actually worked for a sub-division of the
main business unit's subsidiary, and as part
of their job, coordinated project, policies,
and procedures with management at the
high-level division. Thus an implication of
'HQ's experience.' This isn't outright lying;
it's puffing up the relationship within the

realm of believability.

8. If you noted a fact or metric on the resume, e.g., a mistake in the years employed at past employers (typing a 11 versus a 12 for the year or month), that typo is most likely forgivable. *Be* absolutely horrified a typo indicated a missed detail or implied your experience was more than reality if caught by a company representative.

9. Lying on a resume doesn't hurt only the fired employee – it could spell disaster for the company, and could possibly entail litigation. The author worked for a large government contractor as a human resources manager and was tasked with analyzing education on all the employees within the company for government contracting proposals. The goal was to verify every single formal degree indicated on resumes by current employees. What came out of the investigation was astounding. The company had four large business units, and of those four units, about 10% of all employees (4,500 at the time!) in each unit had 'implied' (lied) about completing formal college degrees, or 'equivalents.' There is no 'equivalent' to a college degree – either you took formal classes from an accredited college or university and graduated with a degree – or you didn't. Equivalency doesn't count in federal government contracting contracts. In some cases, the government contract did not require a degree and the 'lucky-to-still-

have-a-job' employees corrected their resume. After allowing employees the opportunity to 'correct' resumes, about 10% of the remaining employees were unable to prove claimed degrees. Those employees lied on their resume (and some continued to lie – 'my diploma was destroyed in a fire' or 'the college no longer exists, so I can't provide transcripts'). The company had two issues – ethics violations (lying) and potential loss of government contracts (or lawsuits) for not having qualified employees working on each contract (some valued in the millions of dollars annually). The company terminated the remaining employees for lying on their resumes (including a business unit VP). It still hurt the company (lost revenues for time-charging employees, plus the cost to recruit and replace), and with an internal ethics failure. After that, human resources checked all hired employees' resumes for formal educational degrees, including asking for college transcripts or copies of original diplomas.

10. If you get fired after lying on your resume – you will have to come up with a pretty darn good excuse to future employers as to why you were let go so suddenly after months or years of stellar performance. It is best to come clean in the most positive light possible. 'When I was hired, I was told by the hiring manager to indicate 'X years of experience equitable to college courses' to qualify for a government contract. Naively I

wrote 'equal to' a college degree, along with the few years I attended some college courses. Unfortunately, the company audited personnel resumes and demanded proof of graduation and I didn't have it, thus was terminated for untrue information on my job application and resume.'

AVOIDING FILLER AND PASSIVE WORDS IN YOUR RESUME BY SUBSTITUTING ACTION VERBS

Some job seekers start each bullet in their resumes with "I." They don't understand the entire resume is about them, thus the word "I" is unnecessary. Resume writers also think they should write a complete sentence for each bullet highlighting their accomplishments. The resume is a 'teaser' document and should be written as tightly as possible, concise, to the point, and by deleting filler words or phrases.

Most job seekers are not familiar or comfortable with formal writing, thus interject 'conversational' wording into their resumes. Resumes with superfluous words or written in informal conversational sentences make the content longer than necessary and too wordy.

1. Avoid writing job task bullets using weak, passive phrasing. For instance, "Was picked to serve as leader ...," indicates something was *done to them*, versus the job seeker actively *doing something*. In military appraisals, the term "Selected for" is used often. This is passively written. As written, it means they may have been selected for something ... but doesn't prove they actually did it. The job seeker wants to

firmly equate and establish their role and that role's tasks and responsibilities. The bullet should have stated, "Supervised a team of six, tasked with project ABC, resulting in XYZ" which is a much stronger, actively written statement with a strong action verb at the beginning.

2. Replace vague, weak, or overused buzzwords with stronger action verbs or nouns. One of the buzzwords used often is 'stakeholder' (originating in the Professional Project Manager (PMP) certification training), which is too close to meaning and parallel to 'stockholder.' (The company may be private, thus have no stockholders, per se.) It's best to avoid confusion. Stakeholder means 'everyone' related to any particular entity – employees, management staff, customers, and vendors. Rarely, if ever, is any one person responsible for a task or responsibility that directly affects 'everyone.' Best practice is to use specific terms as to whom benefited directly from a particular achieved task or job responsibility, e.g., personnel, team members, co-workers, or peers. These are clearer and more appropriate descriptors.

3. Nothing is more off-putting to a recruiter than a resume filled with subjective terms. "People person," "Excellently performed," "Superbly managed," and "Excelled at…" are subjective descriptions. These are based on personal opinions or emotions, which can't be documented or proven.

Never use subjective words in a resume. The alternative is to show, not tell about your accomplishments and back those up with metrics. "Performed audit on warehouse inventory, resulting in 100% match with inventory database on a quarterly basis." This statement *shows* (documentable) 'excellence' versus *telling* about it.

4. The words 'the' and 'that' are the most overused words in the English language - drop those and in most cases the sentence still reads well. Most folks reading the content will never know those words are missing, because they will 'psychologically' add them back in while reading.

5. Eliminate the word 'all' from your resume. No human being can be responsible for 'all' of anything. There is always a co-worker who can perform your job when you are on vacation or on meal-break or equal team-members to take up the slack. Instead, metricize the task you are describing – "Answered ~125 calls daily as customer service representative."

6. Using military speak ("in an effort to support," "in order to," "as ordered" - or passive language "was chosen to" in their descriptions. This is prevalent in the military services and used often in military performance evaluations. These are used in an effort to beef up a service person's performance records with subjective

language to make the service person look
good.

7. "References provided upon request" is
    already assumed; why waste valuable white
    space? Don't bother writing this on the
    resume.

8. Avoid useless filler phrases or clichés. It's
    part of the conversational language, and so
    many folks use the terms with they talk to
    others, they don't realize the phrase can be
    shorter or eliminated. Some phrases are
    unnecessarily long or passively written.
    Some examples to consider converting:

    In order to … convert to = to …
    was picked to be trained for … convert to =
    completed training …
    In support of … convert to = Supervised …
    served under … convert to = Completed
    tasking for …
    was promoted to … convert to = Managed
    team of …
    was picked for (*) of X candidates convert to
    = Led project for …
    was identified to … convert to =
    Responsible for completing …

9. Other filler words that may be used in a
    resume, which need to be either eliminated,
    quantified, and/or explained in more
    objective detail are:

    a great deal of
    absolute

entirety
a number of
at the same time
just
majority
many / much
neatly
numerous
over time
over the years
seemingly
several / slightly
throughout time
though obvious
very / very much
undoubtedly

10. Volunteer work – keep it simple. Just state the dates, the role (volunteer, board of directors), the organization, city, and state. If recruiters are curious, they can ask for further details on the job seeker's role. Don't write a huge paragraph in a conversational tone about what the fundraising was for and how much or what was achieved. If you spent more than 20-30 hours volunteering, then push that volunteer 'work' description up inside your job description listing as 'real work' – even if unpaid.

METRICS TO BUILD
CAPABILITY BELIEVABILITY

Metrics (noun): a method of measuring something, or the results obtained from this. "The report provides various metrics at the class and method level."

Recruiters are very interested in 'results' – in other words – what did the job seeker achieve and accomplish. For example, what was improved, what revenue increased, what productivity was increased, and/or what overhead or man-power was reduced? The best thing a job seeker can add to their resume after ensuring vital key skills words and phrases are in the resume are quantitative descriptors (revenue earned, revenues increased, and manpower or overhead reduced). The metrics can tell a story about you, the job seeker, and your capabilities for future jobs based on what tasks and responsibilities you had and have completed in past and current jobs.

Metrics are numbers the resume owner showcases on a resume to 'demonstrate' their achievement and accomplishments in provable metrics (e.g., increased sales by $XX or XX% in 14 months; decreased labor man-hours by XX% by implementing (ABC), resolved XXX trouble-tickets daily with an average of 3.75 mins per resolution).

Adding metrics (numbers) to document the value of those achievements and activities increases the value of your participation in supervisory or management and leadership positions. It is important to provide 'results' descriptions and metrics where the results were documentable, because metrics define and document the degree of the achievements. Metrics 'show, not tell' about your capabilities for future employers.

Metrics can also be a qualitative list, including lists of tasks completed relative to a single responsibility. An example a lawyer could use: Participate in first- and second-level team of six performing document review, privilege review, Quality Control (QC), and redactions for personal identifiable information (PII) using Relativity. Metrics not only include numbers but *lists* of identifiable elements (e.g., oversight of $1.5M worth of laboratory equipment, including Bunsen burners, glassware, culture cabinets, HEPA-filter extractors, etc.).

1.   Show how you performed successfully by talking about the results of those efforts. You want to indicate your work ethics and success in your past and current jobs by demonstrating what and how much you achieved. Using numbers gives recruiters a comparative context to judge what was accomplished. Metrics should be in not only the current employer's job description, but also past job descriptions to showcase a 'history' of achievements, backed by the documentable numbers.

2.   The more metrics (numbers) in a resume
        that can 'show, not tell' what the
        achievements were – in measurable units –
        the better. The numbers 'showcase' the
        skills a resume owner has without actually
        saying, "I am wonderful, hire me and I'm
        witty, too!" Even wait staff can note how
        many tables, what his/her per table average
        for sales were during their shift, the average
        bar tab per customer, and cash register
        duties on their resume.

3.   Military resumes tend to carry over 'military-
        speak' to the civilian world resumes, but
        metrics are universal. A showcase example
        of a military veteran resume's metrics would
        be, ""built a (XYZ) unit that saved over $40K
        in overhead costs for the military
        command," "researched, analyzed,
        identified, and obtained requisition
        permission to install (ABC) software,
        reducing man-hours by XX hours weekly,"
        and "increased productivity by XX% over
        two-year period." Military service members
        tend to perform a lot of analysis and
        logistics, also. Mention what projects
        (number) were analyzed, and the results of
        the analysis was disseminated to XX
        commanders in XYZ commands, resulting in
        intel analysis shared with XXX battalions in
        the war theater. Another example would be
        "supervised maintenance of XX military
        vehicles, ranging from ~XX HUMVEES to
        ~XX personnel carriers and transport trucks
        between XX bases in (Camp name),

Afghanistan."

4.   Business development or salespersons can showcase achievements via metrics by noting, e.g., "increased sales revenue 435% in last three fiscal years (FY07-FY10) by adding XYZ to product line ..." Additionally, mentioning the territories serviced, the number of territory subordinates managed, and the average sales per territory may be important metrics for resume descriptions.

5.   If the job seeker is in retail, then include metrics indicating ability to work in a busy retail environment, including answering the following questions:

    a.   What numbers of customers were served during each X-hour shift?

    b.   What was the average sales for each customer coming through the checkout line, serving about ## clients hourly or per shift?

    c.   How close to the penny did you come when you closed out your register at the end of shift daily (e.g., 100% cash drawer amounts for cash, checks, and credit card purchases daily)?

    d.   What amount of merchandise did you set up or shelve per shift (e.g., XX tons of incoming household goods per month)?

    e.   What amount of personal sales did you make for retail environments selling large ticket items (e.g., sold approximately four king size

mattresses weekly, ranging from
$XXXX to $XXXX for an average of
$XXXX in monthly sales).

f. What was the square footage of the
store in which the job seeker was
responsible for shelving and
organizing merchandise?

6. Job seekers for C-suite positions can
document accomplishments by listing
overall company metrics, e.g., revenues or
profits earned, revenues increased by
percentages, and/or manpower or overhead
reduced through specific efforts. What were
the total number of personnel oversight?
What job titles were directly managed and
were their accomplishments (with metrics)
under the executive's leadership? Did they
oversee any acquisitions, mergers, or
interact with legal counsel on liability issues
or lawsuits against other entities? Were
they involved in company patents,
trademark registrations, or did they manage
overseas employees in how many
countries?

7. Information technology field workers, as well
as online customer service representatives,
can report metrics, also. How many help-
desk tickets did you resolve in XX-hour shift,
ranging from (what minor) issues to (what
major) issues, with an average time of 5.75
minutes per ticket. How many system
conversions were completed, over XX
months, from legacy software to new,
updated applications? How many banking

customers were assisted per hour, ranging from bank account inquiries to resolving credit issues, with 99.9% resolutions within three minutes or funneling higher-level issues to next tier for resolving? What type of cyber-protection applications were installed, monitored, or managed during tenure and how many cyber-attacks were prevented over XX months?

8. Health care industry workers should ensure vital medical and healthcare skills are loaded into the resume - phlebotomy, patient meds, triage, and specialized skill sets such as operating room surgical assistance. The job seeker should also note how often these skills were used with bona fide metrics, e.g., perform surgical assistance circa six times daily from minor surgery (tonsillectomy) to major surgery (heart valve replacements), three times a week, for the last XX years. How many patients were seen on a daily basis? What type of patient care ranges and activities were provided to the general patient population?

9. Teachers, professors, and adjunct professors in the academic field should be highlighting metrics related to number of students taught per class or per semester (school session) for each topic taught. What were the student's achievements or positive outcomes? For example, "taught 25 students, ages 10-11, to Standards of Learning for state of (name), resulting in

98% of class meeting or exceeding SOL test score minimums, contributing towards 97% overall school achievements scoring." What curriculum design and/or daily lesson planning was achieved for how many courses or classes? Additionally, those who have taught as adjunct professors should copy and paste the course descriptions into their curriculum vitae to showcase the classes as a qualitative metric.

10. Job seekers can also describe metrics for tasks that were not primary job responsibilities, including mentoring and training peers and co-workers. "Trained approximately 15 co-workers after transitioning from legacy application to updated cloud-based service software, twice monthly for four months" or "trained/mentored X sales staff on productivity, resulting in X% decrease in service claims over XX months."

BEATING THE AUTOMATED
TRACKING SYSTEM (ATS) -
GETTING PAST THE FIREWALL

In the recruiting world today, job seekers need to understand the technology that is used in the Automatic Tracking Systems (ATS) resume databases. The resume owner may spend too much time on making the resume pretty - thinking that would get the attention of recruiters. Recruiters don't search for 'pretty' in their databases - they perform Boolean Searches in the SQL database (within the ATS), to find 'keywords' and 'key phrases' within the content.

The search engine in the ATS acts just like a 'Google search.' The machine looks for the most occurrences of those keywords or phrases in the applicant pool for that job or their entire resume database (including online databases, e.g., Indeed, Monster). The applicant with those keywords mentioned the most times are driven to the top of the results queue. This has worked this simply throughout the last 20+ years that ATS platform applications and relational database systems have been around.

The following are tips and facts to review to plan how to get your resume through the upload, into the system, and past the 'firewall' set up for qualified candidates. The author was in HR for 24+ years, and a Senior Recruiter for 11+ years and used multiple ATS software packages. This involved cleaning up multiple resumes who were submitted through the ATS after job seekers believed 'the pretty' design would make their resume stand out by adding loads of graphics, icons, and graphic formatting.

The ATS system's primary goal is to save the resume in two forms: 1) the original document, and 2) parsed data into a SQL database which funnels content into text boxes to a 'text-based' file. Even the ATS systems with highly-functioning parsing engine are not able to grab all the resume content and parse the text into the correct boxes. (One example of 'bad parsing' is when job seekers add LinkedIn URLs to the top of their resume which results in the parsing engine accidentally plugging the URL into the SQL data cell for the email. The results are job seekers may never get that inquiry email message about a new job because a URL is in the box for the email messages. More vital tips are listed below.

1.   The resume must be written and laid out in a 'plain-Jane' presentation and format for the ATS' parsing machine to transfer all the wording over into text boxes used for the Boolean Searches inside the ATS' SQL database. A simple resume with clean lines, one font (Arial or Times New Roman, 10-12 point height) in an easy to read size, with no colors, lines, or borders, and no icons or graphics, is the best format versus 'fancy' resumes. Once the original resume is uploaded to resume databases, the document is converted to a plain text for key

word searches (as well as the original retained), so fancy designs are a waste of time. The author highly recommends resumes be uploaded in Word document format versus a pdf file. Stop trying to make the resume look like a 'work of art.' Recruiters might not see the original resumes once uploaded into the ATS. Original resumes get parsed over to Boolean searchable SQL databases and converted to text files - recruiters will never see the 'pretty.'

2. ATS systems are set up for each job posted to ask specific questions for the required minimum experience, skill sets, and/or security clearances - which weeds out about 80% of the applicants who naively believe if they 'just got in front of a hiring manager, they could talk the HM into hiring them without the minimum qualifications with their eagerness to learn.' Companies don't want to train new hires. They want folks ready to hit the ground running. Recruiters use ATS platforms with pre-qualification questions, of which some answers are vital to meet the minimum requirements or get to the next step of qualifications. In some government contracting industries, security clearance levels were vital job qualifications. The ATS could include questions to ask the job seekers if they had the 'minimum' number of years of experience required by the federal contract and their security level and when the clearance was last adjudicated (for freshness or staleness). Job-related

questions - answered 'correctly' – will funnel applicants to the next level of review.

3. Forget about keeping the resume to two pages - that cheats the job seeker when 'lazy' recruiters don't want to read through a third or fourth page. With today's digital uploads for resumes, it is acceptable to have 3-4 pages - especially if the job seekers experience is rich. Resumes nowadays can run between 2 to 4 pages for the private sector, and can run between 3 to 20 pages for a Government Services (GS) resume. The best thing a job seeker can do it ensure that vital key skills words AND phrases are in the resume, include metrics ($ earned, revenues increased, manpower or overhead reduced, etc.).

4. Do NOT use a template pulled off the Internet - those use word text boxes which gum up the parsing engine in the ATS resume databases. It is highly advisable to avoid any type of templates. The templates often use word text boxes or tables to guide the users into putting specific data in certain places in a resume for formatting. Unfortunately, those word text boxes cannot be read easily by the parsing machine pushing the data into a SQL database. The data in the templated resume may be dumped (deleted) because the parsing machine doesn't know what to do with data. You can pull a template off the Internet then use it as a reference guide for placing your information inside a plain word document.

5. Headers and footers are often deleted in many ATS applications; do not put your point of contact (POC) information in the header section of a word document. You may have outstanding experience and qualify for an interview, but the ATS has trashed your POC information so recruiters can't contact you!

6. It's not 'getting the attention' of the recruiter that fails a job seeker. Wording is a factor, too. If you describe your job in flowery, subjective terms, but really don't describe the 'meat' or weekly tasks and responsibilities of what you do or did in your current or past achievements, there is no room for the objective descriptions. Pretend you are trying to tell a 12-year-old kid what you do for a living when you word your resume. Recruiters don't want to waste brain cells to decipher 'buzz-words' and 'tech-speak' – so keep it simple. If the resume sounds like a Ph.D. talking high-level words and vague terminology, then you have failed in proving you are good at communicating using simple language and objective wording for your job descriptions.

7. Keywords and skill words are critical in resumes for Boolean Searches in candidate pools for specific job requisitions within the job applicants or the ATS software database. At the bottom of the last page of the resume, applicants should list, in alpha order, their key skills and phrases recruiters

will more likely look for in Boolean Searches
within the applicant pool. This provides
additional 'word counts' for the Boolean
search engine in the ATS holding the pool
of resumes, as well as provides a snapshot
of key skills in the resume that doesn't take
up valuable 'white space' at the top of the
resume. This set of keywords provides an
increased chance against the competition to
be found based on the queries in the
applicant pool or the entire resume
database for job seekers. (See example
below.)

*KEY & TRANSFERABLE SKILL
WORDS*: analysis, banking,
Business Administration, business
service improvements, Customer
Service, decision-making,
deliverables, deposits, employees,
evaluations, financial advisor,
Human Resources, leadership,
Manager, mentored, operations,
performance evaluations,
procedures, professional
development, project manager,
Quality Assurance, scheduling,
senior management, Supervisor,
Team Leader / Team Manager,
tracking, training

8.   Don't write a horribly subjective and lengthy
     'Objective' statement at the top of the
     resume - the only thing that should be in the
     Objective (one line) is the job title you are
     seeking.

9. Regardless of what the ATS, company, or recruiters ask for – submit a MS Word document format. PDFs are unable to be edited for proposals for quotes to federal contracts. Not all companies have an Adobe license to convert pdf files to Word documents. Conversions often includes page breaks at the bottom of the word document pages. Most companies use MS Office software. If you create a resume in Open Office, or Google Docs, the ATS may not be able to read it. Recruiters don't have time to download new software to read your resume. Open Office and Google allows the file to be 'exported' as a MS 'compatible' file document.

10. If the recruiters have NOT asked a job candidate for something, then the job candidate should NOT supply it, including references. Offering references could work against the job seeker (recruiters could find candidates from a references list!). Job seekers sending extra materials causes stress to recruiters. The recruiters want to be able to complete a search in the ATS system, either on the applicant pool OR the entire database, and view the resume (regardless of length) that come up at the top of results queue. Extra documents, reference letters, and piles of certifications should be kept separate. The job seeker can offer them - if asked for - at the time of the interview or as part of the hiring process, but NOT before.

KEEP YOUR RESUME
UPDATED AND DYNAMIC

Are you an active job seeker or a passive job seeker? Whether you are content in your current job, a passive job-seeker (open to discuss any opportunity that comes along) in your career, or sweating bullets for that next job because of termination or eminent layoffs, it is critical in keeping your resume updated. The resume should have work-related accomplishments and achievements, as well as metrics that showcase the importance of your work. When you update your resume monthly, you have created an easy-to-reach reminder of what you achieved annually for performance appraisals and evaluations (think of it as a professional diary).

Workers in any industry should have a professionally-written baseline resume to update regularly. Recording work activity in a resume ensures the job seeker can be a passive job seeker year round, but an active job candidate at a moment's notice. This enables reminders to your boss on work-related achievements for annual work performance evaluations and enable documentation for unique accomplishments or goals achieved and document training, certifications, and/or formal degrees completed.

'Never say never' to opportunity.

Regardless of how long you have been in your current job, if something comes along that is more your passion, at the right salary level. regardless of whether you have been with the current company six weeks or six years, you want to be ready with an updated resume. Even though the author has been in a consulting business for 10 years, the curriculum vitae is added to constantly. You never know when a job offer comes along from someone you just met at a conference, a chance encounter at a client's office, or at a party.

Passive Job Seeker: One who is currently content in the employment position they are in, but understands their employer may not have promotional opportunities or the ability to increase salary and compensation options. While the current job has a comfort level, the job seeker may have their resume 'out there' floating around, but is not actively applying the resume to publicly posted job requisitions for consideration as an 'active' applicant for any particular position. A passive job seeker will have an open mind if a 'too good not to follow-up inquiry' comes along or a full-time student who is sharpening up their knowledge and skills in advance of active job search activities.

Active Job Seeker: One who is actively applying for jobs and performing networking activities to seek a new career position at the earliest possible hiring date. This includes searching for open position online, making cold-calls to companies seeking information on (as yet) unpublished positions in the near future, or

1.   Keep a baseline copy of your resume stored

on a cloud-server that you can reach, access, or pull down to your computer, update, then re-store back on the cloud. This enables you to have access to it constantly via the Internet, from work, home, or traveling at a moment's notice if the opportunity for a new career opportunity presents itself.

2. Post your updated resume in major resume databases (public, Monster.com, CareerBuilder.com, Indeed.com, Corporate Gray, etc.) as well as on private servers. When you update your resume on these resume databases, your resume will instantly be 'moved' up in the results queue as a 'fresh' resume in their system. This may result in more recruiters reaching out to you because of the freshness of the resume.

3. Passive job shopping should start at least six months in advance of any active (or dire) need (whether a student or out in the real world). Establish a professional resume (or have one written) that focuses on accomplishments and achievements, and loaded with any metrics defining and documenting the degree of achievements. Gather references from teachers, co-workers (from part-time or other jobs), supervisors, and/or community leaders to have those letters on hand for future employers. Once the resume is completed (circa 4-5 months out), post that document online on the major job and resume

databases to see what, if any, nibbles start coming through. Continue to add to the resume or 'reposting' it (monthly) to 'refresh' it in the system (tricks the system into thinking you have loaded an updated resume) to keep it high in the rankings for 'newness.'

4. Actively look for job requisitions publicly posted by companies in the career industry in which seeking a new position, and watch their own company for promotional opportunities. What is most important about watching these job openings is to cull specific tasks and responsibilities to possible include on a resume, where warranted. For example, you may be a dinner waitress, but additionally be responsible for the cash register at end-of-shift, in which you tally receipts and compile reports to the home office. You should include a 'bookkeeping' tasks bullet on the resume with metrics (e.g., averages of cash or assets for which you are responsible).

5. Actively network with friends, family, tactfully and under the radar with their co-workers or peers in the industry, and/or with potential new employers via their clients. A passive or active job seeker should ensure available paid or unpaid time off to use for those last minute interview appointments as well as be available before and after work, during lunch, and on weekends for meeting with hiring managers.

6. You should start job searching as soon as you start your new job – you should always be in passive job search mode. Sometimes that new job you started last month has not quite lived up to the advertised promises, or you realized why the last three employees in this job quickly exited after only a few months each tenure. There is no shame in realizing that the job is not a good fit with your skills, career, or environmental needs and you need to exit quickly and professionally.

7. Set up job alerts – regardless of whether you are in an active or passive job search. Sometimes recruiters catch up to job seekers just a 'little too late.' The author once accepted a job as a high-level manager, and four weeks later was sought out by a recruiter for a very lucrative career position, but had already 'settled' in and decided to stay. WHY is this good (to have kept the job alerts)? You can conversationally chat with the recruiter to find out inside information about the company, the salary range you might have qualified for, what type of perks the company offers employees in those positions, and other information you may not have been able to ask about in actual job negotiations.

8. Keep a folder of all of your best work so you can easily add it to your portfolio. An artist's portfolio is great if you are a graphic or performing artist, but a portfolio is not

something a recruiter shopping for candidates in a non-artistic field will ask for. What they want to see are examples of projects and programs one has managed. In some cases that information is proprietary to the company (current employer), so not ethical to show to recruiters in a portfolio. What recruiters want to know is how you saved a project, what you did to increase profits, what you did to decrease overhead or man-hours, what technology you used to increase productivity (you really can't add those examples in a 'portfolio' per se). So, write about it in your resume as you update it.

9.   Update your resume with each new added skill. You should treat your resume as if it were a performance evaluation you have to present to your boss every month to be judged on what you did right in the job to keep the job. Every month, you should add major accomplishments and achievements, and what those meant in results to your employer - increased revenue, decreased overhead costs, increased productivity, new clients, training of peers and/or coworkers so they can do their job better. What have you done that is not in your job description that was a positive thing for your company / employer, and how did they gain by your industriousness? If you do this monthly, then annually, you have an updated resume for your current job, and you won't have to struggle to remember everything you did at the end of the year.

10.   Passive job seekers should always be
        seeking additional education, training, and
        certifications on anything and everything to
        increase skills sets, education, and
        capabilities. Use YouTube free tutorial
        videos to learn how to increase ability to use
        MS Office or other software applications. If
        you are government contractor or
        government employee, search out the DAU
        (Defense Acquisition University) for free
        classes. University Massive Open Online
        Courses (MOOC) allow you to 'audit' a
        course for free. Subscribe to online training
        site (e.g., Lynda.com) for software learning
        modules you think could be useful in a
        future position or a totally new career path.
        (LinkedIn owns Lynda now and a paid
        LinkedIn subscription gets you access to
        Lynda.com for free). Check local city's adult
        education offerings for computer classes,
        accounting packages (e.g., QuickBooks).
        Some local businesses offer free training
        (Jackson Hewett / Liberty Tax offers free tax
        classes). Do not stop learning or you lose
        your ability to learn job skills when they are
        on the horizon.   Don't be scared of
        computers. Educate yourself on software
        and hardware. Microsoft Office Word and
        Excel are vital business software – learn to
        format the word document, type memos,
        letters, and potentially contracts; know how
        to plug in Excel formulas and use multiple
        tabs and links to process data. Learn any
        accounting software - even if you don't
        become an expert - at least be able to

identify debit and credit columns, tax-deductible expenses, overhead expenses, and non-tax-deductibles.

BIO, RESUME, CV, GS:
WHAT'S THE DIFFERENCE?

A resume is a document that provides a history of employment experience to potential employers to consider applicants for a job.

Resume / résumé; North American (noun): a brief account of a person's education, qualifications, and previous experience, typically sent with a job application. synonyms: CV, life history, biography, details; curriculum vitae; vita, bio "a few Saturdays in a veterinary hospital might look great on her résumé"; a summary. "I gave him a quick résumé of events"; synonyms: synopsis, abstract, outline, summarization, summation; abridgment, digest, abbreviation, survey, overview, review, sketch; wrap-up; headnote, brief; rare conspectus, summa, epitome, compendium "this is a brief résumé of the problems" (dictionary.com)

What is the difference between the different types of 'resumes' accepted for consideration for employment purposes in the United States?

Descriptions of each type of resume:

1. **Bio**

A one page length document that is used to 'introduce' a speaker to a group, or for networking purposes; used to introduce someone to a speech audience, or to gain interest in a c-Suite candidate who is a passive job seeker that has been asked to share a 'little something' about themselves. A bio is not normally used as or considered a full resume for job consideration.

2. **Resume**

A document on standard-sized paper, with between 2-4 pages of bulleted job achievements and accomplishments that showcases the job applicant's capabilities; a resume is considered a 'commercial' or 'private sector' resume, of which 10-15 years of employment history is sufficient to determine current skills and past experience for employment possibilities. If a job seeker is 'new' (considered a 'fresher' in some countries) to the world in job experience, usually two pages would be sufficient, but someone with 20-30 years of career history could viably run a resume for up to four pages, depending upon how much amazing experience in projects, operations, revenues generated, supervisory and staff management of staff experience the job applicant can define.

3. **Curriculum Vitae (CV)**

Curriculum Vitae is Latin for "life story." A CV is used in the academic community to showcase the entire teaching and professional history of the academic, including publications,

conferences, quorums, and technical skills. In the
academic job search for instructors, adjunct or
associate professors, or tenured professors, then
the CV could go as far back as 15-20 years,
especially if that experience includes teaching,
instruction, training, and other educational-related
information about their experience. Most
universities and colleges need to know ALL about a
job seeker who is apply for lecturer, adjunct
professor, associate or tenured professor positions,
including not only a teaching philosophy, but also
educational experience, professional (non-
academic) experience, and conferences,
publications, and elaborations upon their technical
skills for using classroom management software,
any certifications, and any volunteer activities. This
information provides the institution of higher
learning the abilities to differentiate between a
multitude of candidates who may all be qualified to
teach a particular subject, but have a rich and
diverse background in many industries, as well as
in the teaching field.

4. Government Services (GS) Resume

In the United States, if one wishes to work
directly for an agency or entity that is considered a
federal government employer, the resume and
application is considered for government services -
USA Federal jobs. This resume has similarities to
the CV in possible length, but also has additional
(and personal) details required by the hiring
institution such as supervisor's names, phone
numbers, and salary information. The hiring
managers are looking for the longer resumes and
work history and experience could go back 20-25

years,. To avoid any age bias, it is suggested to eliminate dates, salary, and other private information for jobs and experience older than 15-20 years, to avoid any potential ageism bias. The length of a GS resume is open to longer than four pages because the header information required in the resume could feasibly take up 1/3 of the page for each job experience or title. Thus resumes running over 10 pages are 'forgiven' for length due to the amount of information required in each.

5. Best sizes or lengths for resumes

   a) A BIO is only one page
   b) A resume can run 2-4 pages (max)
   c) A CV can run 20-30 pages - many academic institutions want to see ALL the academic experience, as well as business experience and skill sets
   d) A GS resume can run 10-15 pages

6. Is there any other type of resumes that are practical for job shopping?

Again - it depends upon what type of job one is applying for. Many executives use a one page 'bio' simply to get the attention of a placement specialist, while most traditional job seekers use a resume (1-4 pages), and academics use Curriculum Vitae's, which could run between 3-30 pages.

If you are outside the artistic realm, I would advise sticking to the traditional resume format. But, If you are in an 'art industry' (graphic artist, musician, performing artist), then creative resumes may be just the ticket.

A graphic artist may design a brochure that is actually their resume, but when a recruiter pulls it out of an envelope, the brochure opens into a tri-fold document with colorful images and content laid out in an artistic spread. Most performance artists – singer, musician, theatre background and/or actor/actress would likely have a visual portfolio created for future recruiters (or casting directors) to view via websites that hold a collection of works (e.g., Behance.com) or the artist's personal website. But they still need a 'normal' resume to load into resume databases to official applications via the company human resources processes and legal channels.

7. Should I use fancy paper to print out my resume?

We are past the days of typing up a resume or printing it out on paper anymore. Most, if not all businesses nowadays prefer or require all job applications with accompanying resumes to be posted online in either their company proprietary resume databases or they obtain the resumes via licensed searches from the commercial resumes databases (e.g., Monster.com, Indeed.com, CareerBuilder.com).

8. Will I get more attention to my experience, skills, and resume if I mail the resume to prospective employers?

No. You will only annoy the recruiters or cause them more work. All resumes are now required by most companies to be posted for 'official applications' via the Internet and online websites. The reason for this is if a job applicant applies to a posted (public) position, then the company is required to track that resume as an official application. If the resume is manual, then that causes clerical work. If the applicant applies online, then the process is automated, and all the information is input to the tracking database by the applicant. This takes a load off the shoulders of the recruiting staff.

9. Should I use colored text, borders or photos / graphics in my resume to get more attention?

No. Avoid using those elements in ANY form of resume. If you use text boxes, borders, tables, graphics, and other 'fancy' elements in the resume it will 'gum up' the Automatic Tracking System (ATS) that feeds the resumes via parsing into the SQL database. Content inside text boxes may be dropped, border may be deleted, and graphics will be pushed to the end of the resume on the other side of the firewall. The text formatted resume on the other side of the firewall could get pretty ugly. It's best to have just straight text for all the content inside the resume.

10. Do resumes have to be in PDF file format?

Some companies have directions to load PDF file resumes, but it's actually better to load Word document-based resumes. Do NOT use alternative word processing software such as Open Office or Google docs – the resulting document file

may not be able to be opened in the ATS platform.
The resume databases are set up to read and
process MS Office Word documents (or worst case
PDFs).

ELEMENTS OF A
PERFECT COVER LETTER

Cover letter (noun): a letter sent with, and explaining the contents of, another document or a parcel of goods. "remember to include a cover letter when mailing out your prospectus" A cover letter is submitted with a job application and resume explaining the applicant's credentials and interest in the open position. (dictionary.com)

1)   Are cover letters still needed? Are cover letters gauche and passé?

From the most recent statistics the author is aware of, less than 10-15% of employers seek cover letters. Cover letters are quick 'quizzes' to see if the job seeker can logically write a complete sentence if the job has any requirements for writing memos, letters, and other correspondence. Cover letters are not passé per se; it just depends upon the job opening and what future employers want to see from applicants before the interview.

The employer may want to see if the job seeker can put together a decent letter (memo, write policy, etc.), and the cover letter provides a way to at least show potential employees if one can write. Yes, it's a good idea to at least keep a well-worded 'semi-template' on hand with the vital details for contact to the job seeker in case a job requisition asks for one.

2)   Why is writing a cover letter important?

It makes up for a resume that can't stand alone. Your resume should be effective if unaccompanied by a cover letter. A resume may need a little persuasive help – so a cover letter can make up for low-strength resumes. A strong cover letter - not the resume – could potentially instigate a callback.

3)   What's your attitude towards cover letters? Are they essential to your decision-making process? Which do you read first - a resume or a cover letter?

As a recruiter for over 20 years, the author paid little attention to cover letters – usually loaded with subjective content. The only value would be for two factors:

a) If the job required a lot of writing and there was a need to review the applicant's writing style to ensure it matched professionalism and quality assurance; this only works if the cover letter was 100% guaranteed to be written by the job applicant. Cover letters could be written by third parties, so a recruiter using a cover letter to judge writing skills takes a gamble.

b) Recordkeeping of the job applicant being referred by an already existing employee that was deserving or earning a referral fee.

4) What are the best ways to create an amazing cover letter to get that interview?

Below are elements to include in a well-written cover letter.

+++++++++++++++++++

Header = date, recipient's name (or To HR Manager or Hiring Manager), company name, address, city, state. zip

First paragraph = tell the recipient where you found the job opening or if you heard of the job via an employee who has passed the resume on to the hiring manager or HR department. This assists HR in tracking sources for future marketing decisions, as well as documents employee referrals if the company offers referral fees / awards.

Second paragraph = tell the recipient something related to one's skills sets, but NOT the same information already noted in the resume - new and fresh insight to the experience and skills sets elaborated upon in the cover letter where there wasn't room to chat about it in the resume due to limiting the number of pages (four or under).

Third paragraph = vital point of contact information, encouraging recruiters to call for a telephonic interview (first) to chat about the job and parameters (before spending time and gas for a face-to-face). Document the hours of availability for phone calls (seven days a week, between the hours of XX:XX a.m. and XX:XX p.m.), at (###) ###-####, or you can be reached at your email address at ZYZYYZ@myemaildotcom.

Respectfully: Followed by Full Legal Name, (NO Address), (if you have a graphic file with your signature, you can add that into the letter, but otherwise, not necessary) and
Enclosure / Attachment: Professional Resume

++++++++++++++++++

5)   What is best format and software to use?

Keep the resume and the cover letter in MS Word Document file format. MS software is used universally, thus the HR or Hiring Manager won't have to deal with Open Office, Google Docs, or other software to open the file.

6)   How do you phrase or write your cover letter?

As you would if you were writing a cover letter for a job in any case - focus on positive aspects of the job you just came out of and what you offered to the company.

When one is submitting a resume to an academic department for French, English, or Literature, there is a presumption that it would be best to use the accents in the words where applicable (resumé vs resume), but outside of that venue, hiring managers may not care as to whether the word has accent marks or not if showcased in a cover letter.

7) In general, how do you get the tone of your cover letter just right?

Try to avoid the tone of the letter from becoming a 'Hey buddy, how are ya, I need a job, can you help me out there friend?" type of tone to a more desirable and professional writing style, "I understand you are looking for a candidate for a job opening to resolve a problem or some pain your company is feeling because the spot is empty or doesn't have a competent incumbent?"

8) When sending in a resume, for a middle-management position, without a cover letter prohibition, one should always include a cover letter.

If the cover letter is NOT requested then do NOT force one on recruiters or placement specialists - provide them ONLY what they request or require … and no more.

9) Will applying to a job out-of-state hurt your chances of getting the job? If so, how can you compensate for that or explain that in the cover letter or resume?

If you mention in a cover letter you are

looking to transfer - or - are already moving to a new geographic area, then recruiters know you may not need to be compensated for the move, thus you are on equal footing with others who are already in the area. You should also mention you would be willing to meetings via telephonic interviews initially to save them (and you) costs of traveling to meet face-to-face.

10) How do you tailor the tone of your cover letter based on the job/company you're applying to?

You won't know whether to take a certain tone, unless you are intimate with the environment and type of employees the company has, and most folks may not be privy to that information from cold applications. Take the high road, and create a letter that come across at least as semi-formal (standing on the fence, to be safe). Never stoop to casual street-talk or bar-level friendly conversational tones - that sets the incorrect mood for the entire conversation.

CREATING YOUR FIRST RESUME –
ELEMENTS TO INCLUDE

1)   What is the importance of a good resume?

To provide a 'teaser' of your capabilities to future employers. NOT a life history (unless you are in academics – then you should be writing a Curriculum Vitae [Latin for life story]). You want enough information to showcase not only what you have achieved and accomplished, but what you are capable of doing in future career positions. And hint at greater things, but not get too down in the weeds with details.

2)   What are the elements of a complete resume (contact info, objective, experience, education, skills, awards, and volunteer experience)?

There are three major types of resumes per se: 1) the Curriculum Vitae (CV) used for career search by academics and college professors, 2) the Government Services (GS) used for applications to jobs in the federal (USA) government with elements of salary, supervisors' names, and other personal information required, and 3) a private sector Resume (commercial resume) for non-government or non-academic career job searches. The following sample shows the sections for Private Sector / Commercial Resume elements to be included.

+++++++++++++++++++++

FirstName MI. Last Name
City, Street, 5-digit zip
Cell Phone Number
Email Address

Job Objective - ONE LINE with as few words as possible with the Job Title you are seeking (*NOT* a subjective paragraph of 'BS' run-on, grandiose verbiage)

Years of Experience:

XX years, (general type of career position, e.g., Accountant)
XX years, Bookkeeper
XX years, AP/AR Administrator

Professional Experience (Backwards chronology)

MM/YY - present, Job Title
Company Name, City, ST

2-5 bullets explaining primary duties of position and any specific, metric-based accomplishments

repeat for 10-15 years of experience

Education (formal degrees first)
YYYY, Degree, Discipline, School Name, City, ST
(Spell out the degree - so BFA should be written
out Bachelor of Fine Art)

Training / Certifications
YYYY, Certification, Name, Training Organization,
City, ST

**Languages, Patents, Volunteer Work, Trade
Organizations**
Spanish - proficient
MM/YY - present, Volunteer, Name of Organization

++++++++++++++++++++++

3)   How Many Pages Should Your Resume
      Be?

      While many 'old-school' career guidance
      counselors still recommend two pages or
      less, that advice is pretty much old news in
      the 21st Century. If a job seeker has an
      amazing set of experience and skill sets, I
      tell my resume clients that up to four pages
      is acceptable. Three is comfortable. One to
      two pages may cheat the job seekers with
      the low quantity of data.

4)   Do You Need to Include References?

      Absolutely NOT on a resume. Provide the
      interviewing managers a list of references if
      they ask for them at the end of the
      interview. Do not send or offer references
      before meeting with any company

representatives. I have heard of recruiters who use the references lists from job candidates to troll for additional candidates for the same position or use the names to try to fill other vacancies. Your references didn't sign up for that type of contact.

5) What Should Your Resume Not Include?

EEOC-protected information - sex / gender, political references, birthdate, family information, no photos, or religious preferences should be mentioned (any mentions of membership in political clubs or activist organizations should be avoided). While recruiters and hiring managers are not legally able to ask if one is a citizen, with the flux of immigrants and green card holders seeking work in the USA, one can 'offer' information on passport or green-card status at the end of the resume, which answers the question recruiters are not allowed to ask.

6) How to Customize Your Resume for the Job You're Applying For (Did the job posting ask for specific things to add to your resume, for starters?)

Actually - would advise against writing a resume to *only* one job title. It's better to showcase diversity in one's background by listing work in backwards chronological order. Now if there were two distinct and diverse careers (you were secretary by day; concert pianist at night), then you may wish to divide the backwards chronology of those distinctly separate careers into two section chunks, each labeled for clarification:

Professional Experience (Business Administration)

- list of jobs, with dates and descriptions

Professional Experience (Concert Pianist)

- list of appearances and concerts, with dates, organizers, and sponsors

7) Are there things you should highlight based on the position's job description?)

I would not highlight or bold-face any words in the resume's job descriptions - it is distracting. The recruiters will perform a Boolean Search using Keywords in the Job Applicant pool and look at those resumes where the keywords were included in the resume, so there is no need to bold the font.

8) Are There Resume Templates Readily Available Online?

Yes – hundreds of templates are 'out there' on the Internet. BUT, it is highly advisable to avoid those like the plague. Many use word text boxes to guide the users into putting specific information in certain places in a resume for formatting. It's easy to create a template with word boxes already laid out in aesthetic locations on the document. Unfortunately, those word text boxes can

NOT be read easily by the parsing machine that is funneling the data into a SQL database.

9) Should You Use Templates for Resumes?

No - not as templates per se – but – you can use them to 'model' your own resume in a word processing document. The data in the templated resume may be deleted because the parsing machine doesn't know what to do with it. Also, headers and footers are deleted in many Automatic Tracking Systems; do NOT put your point of contact information in the header section of a word document. You may have some outstanding experience and qualify for an interview, but the ATS has trashed your POC information so recruiters can't contact you!

10) What Are Some Common Resume Mistakes People Make?

a) Job seekers may be using Open Office (free software) and unfortunately, the files they save in this software is NOT open-able by users who do not have that software. It is imperative to write your resume in STANDARDIZED word processing software (MS Office Word is the universal standard). Open Office does allow users to export their resume as a Word-Compatible document.

b) Some job seekers think they have to convert their resume into a PDF. That is not true. It's actually better to keep the resume in a Word-Compatible document because the parsing engine likes it better and can convert the data into the SQL database easier and cleaner.

WHY RECRUITERS WILL
NOT CALL YOU BACK

A typical worker in a human resources department could work between 40 to 60 hours a week – most prevalently because they are short-handed as the HR department is not in income-generating business unit. The HR department is an overhead expense. Because of the lower-numbers of personnel providing services under a 100% overhead funded budget, the staff – including recruiters – are trying to accomplish more in their work hours than otherwise income-producing employees.

Keeping this in mind, job applicants should understand the overwhelming responsibilities of recruiters simply trying to track the applicants resumes and document and record those applications in response to federally mandated documentation for affirmative action plans and EEOC compliance. In addition, many recruiters are filling up their day performing first interviews with job candidates that are immediately qualified, providing additional testing, and performing as panel members for face-to-face interviewing, as well as providing on-boarding services or typing up the offer letters. That is a lot to physical work in an eight-hour day.

When the author was a recruiting for over 10 years, the biggest 'complaint' from job seekers was they "never received response or feedback from companies" to whom they had applied for jobs. While this question begs for ideas to 'thank' job applicants in new and material ways, the stronger way to interact with a job applicant for branding is to treat them courteously, communicate with them - and often throughout the stages of the requisition (open job), and to let them know where they stand in the pecking order of consideration as a viable candidate.

Large corporations may have a huge number of job openings, to the point where a single recruiter may be 'working' as little as 10-15 open positions to as many as 60-70 job requisitions as any given time. If the open position is marketed broadly, there may be as many as 100-200 applicants applying their resume for consideration. That could potentially be the equivalent of 14,000 resumes to review. That would be physically impossible for any single recruiter to read or respond to all of those applicants in a reasonable time period. The logistics is mind-boggling.

When the author worked at a large defense contracting company, with as many as 4,500 employees, there were as many as 300-400 job openings for current and future contract work positions with as many as 300 applicants per position. Think 120,000 resumes of candidates who all wanted a response back to their individual application!

Thank goodness for Applicant Tracking System (ATS) software applications! These software programs help recruiters cull through the massive number of resumes in a much shorter time. In these ATS applications, recruiters can deep dive into a pool of applicants for each position by performing a Boolean search on keywords within the resumes. Those resumes with the most keywords om the resume will pop to the top of the results queue. Reading the top 5-10 resume usually provided a sufficiently qualified candidate for interviews by the hiring manager.

Simply put … there are not enough hours in the day for a recruiter to respond to each and every job applicant for all the positions open within the company's recruiting outreach. In small companies, the recruiter may also wear multiple hats - supervisor, manager, bookkeeper, accountant, etc., and is trying to juggle normal responsibilities with recruiting efforts. They may already be working 50-60 hours a week in their normal tasking, and may not have the administrative help to respond to every applicant's resume postings.

1.   If the company does have an ATS application in use, the recruiters or program supervisor may not have programmed auto-generated responses in the system. Or, the program being used is not capable of generating auto-responses (e.g., "we have received your resume and will notify you if you are deemed qualified"). Unfortunately, the ATS system and the recruiters do not always use the auto-response which notifies the applicants via email that one or more factors related to the job's minimum requirements were or were not reached. When the author was a recruiter, multiple-

auto-responses were used to graciously acknowledge applications, indicate if resume owners were or were not qualified against minimum requirements, and thanked the applicant for their time and effort. The messages also encouraged them to continue to apply for positions within the company that were currently open or to come back and check for new positions as they opened.

2. Sometimes job seekers input their point of contact (POC) information in the header of the resume document. They may be an amazingly qualified candidate, but sometimes the ATS program will 'cut' out (delete) any header or footer information. This results in the recruiter reading the resume, but not being able to contact the submitter because the POC data is missing. To resolve this, put the POC data in the top of the first page, but also open up the "File", "Properties" in the word processing menu and type in the full name, email address, and phone number in the Author text box, so the last-ditch option to identify the job seeker can provide some information.

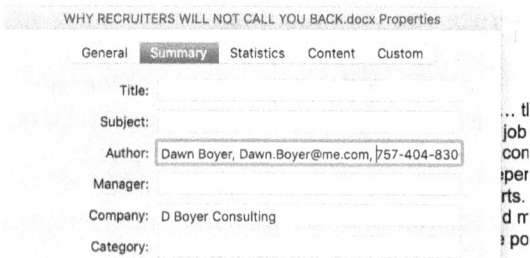

3. Recruiters need to see: Full Name, City, State, Zip, Cell Phone #, and Email address at the top of the resume. If any of this info missing, you may never get calls at all. Recruiters want to know where you live (are you currently in Japan and would have to sell your house to relocate or are you just down the street and within an easy commute to work?). You don't need to include your street address in a private sector resume, but a government services resume does require that information. When the resumes are parsed, the email goes into a text box, and the email is used to generate responses or mass-appeals to potential qualified applicants for future jobs. Don't label the information – an email or phone number is pretty obvious.

4. A resume is NOT a conversation - it's a 'conversation starter.' If you don't provide enough quantitative and quality information – just enough to tease – you won't be called in for an interview. Either you didn't say the right thing (keywords) or you said too much (excruciating details that gave away everything and you came across as someone who would be hard to communicate with because of your verboseness). The resume wording or lack of really good juicy information in their resumes could be simply awful. The author has seen too many resume clients who 'copy and paste' the job description into their resume because job seekers think that

is what the recruiters want. It's not. It hurts the job seeker. Recruiters want a job seeker to study the job description, then relate rich and concise descriptions about how their current and past experience fits the details of the job description.

5.   Never assume a company will hire you and train you. The job seeker may have indicated they would need training to get up to speed for a position. ALWAYs pay attention to the minimum requirements. If you don't have a specific 'must have' - they will not call you on the off-chance you have a great personality and are willing to learn. In any historic tight economy, a new hire must hit the ground running to avoid cost and labor overruns, which eats into company profits.

6.   Someone soliciting an informational interview could be a 'industrial spy' and I would be concerned about bringing in a stranger to chat about what my company is doing - especially on-site where there may be proprietary secrets laying around. If there were a candidate that seemed too good to be true and only wanted an informational interview, versus being seriously interested in working specifically for my company, this would raise a red flag.

7.   Job seekers must initially pass the online, digital screening tests. Because the sheer number of applications for one position sometimes forces recruiters to automate

pre-qualification questions. It may be physically impossible to read all the submitted resumes, so recruiters may use initial screening tests. As a government contractor, the author had to screen applicants for security clearances (sometimes needing Top Secret / SCI or higher). If the applicants passed all the pre-screening questions for where they are open to working (geographic location of work site, active security clearance level, and minimum salary expectations) the applicants could then be moved into a 'qualified candidate pool.' Then the recruiter can use the Boolean search within the applicant pool for keywords that the hiring manager would share 'must be in the resume' to cut the number of qualifying candidates down to a manageable number. If the recruiters are good at public relations, they will use the auto-responses to generate communications about whether a candidate has qualified for next look or has not – unfortunately not all companies have enabled these ATS features.

8. The jobs could be fake. This enables recruiters to 'farm' for resumes for as many of the company's job descriptions and categories as possible in shorter periods of time. There is no legal or ethics penalty for posting a job opening and then closing it. Recruiters post for

    a. (a) jobs that internal management feel may be needed in near or far future based on the company's most recent or long-term strategic growth to see what is 'out there.' Employers may want to survey salaries so they post the job description then ask, "What are your salary requirements?" as an interest; most ATS platforms can be programmed to ask for minimum salary requirements. (Some states are now regulating (Virginia recently) making it illegal to ask for salary history, but that doesn't outlaw asking for salary ranges in applications.)

b. (b) as a 'feeler' to see what type of available candidates may meet unique qualifications, and

c. (c) to ensure EEOC and AAP compliance by publicly posting a job opening for a job that the company is actually wanting to fill with an internal candidate, but the company policy is to publicly 'announce' the job opening to document they are open to diversity candidates. The federal government and private sector companies do this. They have internal written policies towards attracting 'diverse' candidates based on a federally required, in-house, Affirmative Action Plan (AAP) or Equal Employment Opportunity (EEO) compliance. To ensure that an internal candidate is easier to choose (but not a guaranteed choice), the job description will be written to the resume of the internal candidate, then posted for the minimum required number of days, so any / all applicants can see it was publicly posted (thus fulfilling the minimum requirements of the AAP/EEO policy). Usually the post is for 3-5 days, and sometimes targeted for holidays or long weekends when external applicants may not necessarily catch it. The position may be posted at 11:59 p.m. on a Friday, then take it down at 8:01 a.m. on the following Tuesday, so the 'dates' show it was posted for five calendar days to document a five-day minimum. This ensures a limited pool of applicants to review and cull out against the internal 'choice.'

9.   Recruiters have differing philosophies and methodologies, but their primary objective is to have as many resumes in their company licensed or proprietary resume databases as possible. A recruiters job is to 'collect' resumes of qualified candidates. I have had hiring managers in past companies go to job fairs and collect resumes and keep them stashed in their desk drawer for future reference. You have heard the phrase for quilters, "Whomever dies with the most fabric, wins!"? Same goes for recruiters, "Whomever dies with the biggest ('bad-ass') collection of resumes in their resume ATS,

wins!" Recruiters may be looking to create a pool of candidates – especially in the government contracting field. A recruiter could be told the company is pursuing a particular government contract and 'here is the list of job descriptions the contract is seeking.' The recruiter's responsibility is to attract application submissions, to see if there were any matching skills and experience to the potential positions, and if the company decided to pursue the contract, the recruiter would ask permission of the applicants to use their resume as a proposal resume for the contract. This doesn't mean that the company will get the contract or that the applicant will ever be contacted again.

10. Job boards recycle older advertisements or create fake advertisements to make it look like they have more jobs available. The MORE jobs posted, the more the company seems to be coming across to the job applicants as a vibrant and growing company. Older advertisements may be simply a general job description in the company's compensation plan the recruiters use to attract potential applicants. But, just because it's been posted before, doesn't mean it's not valid or 'old' per se.

CONVERTING AN OBJECTIVE STATEMENT
TO A 'YEARS OF EXPERIENCE' LISTING

During the 20th Century, career counselors offered advice on how to write a resume. One of the standardized pieces of advice was to write an 'objective statement' at the top of the resume, indicating the job applicant's strengths and capabilities and any specific or unique piece of information needed to help the recruiter decide to keep reading. Unfortunately, in today's recruiting world, that long-winded paragraph at the top of the resume is now a hindrance in recruiters being able to quickly identify keywords and skills and background – it is just too tedious to read. Job applicants also have a hard time writing about themselves in that paragraph and often turn it into a conversation about what they *want* versus what they *have to offer* future employers.

In the example or a poorly written objective statement – the recruiter doesn't glean what the actual 'objective is' and the language is very subjective. What are 'high levels'? What does 'strong' mean? What are 'tight timeframes'? What is 'judgement'? The use of 'over' and the '+' sign is redundant relative to years of experience.

*Human Resources professional with
over 6+ years industry experience in*

high potential talent strategy, executive assessment and development, succession management, college recruiting, and leadership development program operations. Strong track record of executing projects and processes, amidst tight timeframes with high levels of autonomy, accuracy, and judgment, producing high stakeholder value.

Recruiters are not going to read a huge paragraph of BS that glorifies how you are a 'people person', are superb in 'handling problems,' and can 'use MS Office' (which should be a prerequisite qualification anyway), and that you are 'looking for a company who can train you in management' … yada yada yada. Essentially the objective paragraph is simply too wordy, too subjective, and hard to read quickly.

1.   An Objective statement should be *just that* and nothing else. Stop writing that awful subjective summary paragraph at the top of the resume - which mostly pure B.S.. Recruiters usually hate it and roll their eyes when they see this typical objective statement. All that should be present on one line is:

        OBJECTIVE: (job title sought)

2.   Underneath that Objective, the job seeker should keep it simple silly (KISS) with a bulleted list of years of experience you have

to offer the future employer to capture their attention and provide them immediate info on your background to encourage them to keep reading, e.g., (below). This list provides all the easy to read information a recruiters is seeking in years of experience in general career fields, with some sub-general indicators for types of industry.

- XX years, Human Resources Manager (Commercial and Government Defense Contracting Industry)
- XX years, Senior Project Manager, Senior Program Manager (Manufacturing)
- XX years, Supervision and Team Lead (Quality Assurance and Process Improvement)

3.   Some job seekers feel they should provide personal information in the objective statement. Resume owners should *not* put photos, birth dates, social security numbers, or information about your family, pets, or goals for a future family. These provide information that is EEOC protected. One never knows who will be reading the resume - this data could provide identity thieves a useful tool.

4.   One exception to the rule of adding a descriptive paragraph to a resume is the curriculum vitae. In this type of resume, a Statement of Teaching Philosophy is usually required by the institution of higher learning

for the CV. An example would look like the sample below (shortened for brevity), with the list of years of various teaching and professional-business experience (listed in higher to lower number of years) immediately underneath.

STATEMENT OF TEACHING PHILOSOPHY

As someone who has had a successful professional career and a vast dedication to lifelong learning, I now strive to give back to society and to pass along knowledge so others can better themselves. Seeing people advance in their careers and live to their highest potential is motivating to me and a driving force behind my desire to teach. I believe education has the power to transform a person's life – both in the short- and long-term. My passion is the constant pursuit and sharing of the latest thinking and understanding of our world and human society, especially as applied to organizations. Students should be given the opportunity to challenge themselves to reach their higher potential through measured, competency-based educational standards. Students should be given the tools, resources, and necessary instruction to achieve goals in an environment that facilitates innovation and decisive collaboration. To foster an effective learning environment, I engage

with students frequently, adding value
and perspective to drive interest.

EXPERIENCE SUMMARY

- 19+ years, Data Center and Lab
  Deployment (Fortune 500
  Companies)
- 17+ years, Data Center
  Management
- 15+ years, Project, Portfolio and
  Program Management
- 15 years, Senior IT Manager
  (Private, Public)

5.   A police officer's resume with Objective
     statement and years of experience would
     look somewhat like the following example:

OBJECTIVE: Director of Security

EXPERIENCE SUMMARY

- 12 years, Firearms / Ammunition Handling
  (retail sales; police equipment)
- 7 years, Sheriff's Deputy / Police Officer
  (local city, county)
- 3.5 years, Security / Police Management
  (training, supervision)

6.   A lawyer's resume would look similar to the
      following example:

OBJECTIVE: Deputy Attorney General;
Assistant US Attorney

EXPERIENCE SUMMARY

- (name of state) State Bar License
- 10 years, Attorney at Law (regulatory compliance; quality management, document review)
- 5 years, Pharmaceutical Litigations / HIPAA
- 4 years Foreign Corrupt Practices Act (FCPA)
- 6 months, Department of Justice (DOJ) investigations

7. A job seeker with Change Management and Training experience can write the Objective statement and years of experience similar to this sample:

OBJECTIVE: Test Lead

EXPERIENCE SUMMARY

- 10 years, Training, Education (curriculum design, education, corporate training)
- 9 years, Public Relations (presentations, social media content, communications)
- 7 years, Administration (data maintenance, reporting, environmental research)
- 4 years, Market Research Analyst (target market, customer-service satisfaction)
- 3 years, Project Management (change management)
- 2 years, Systems Testing Manager (bank, financial, IT systems)

8.   A retiring military service-member with management and operations experience can write their objective similar to this sample, including the list of military-associated experience:

OBJECTIVE: Operations Manager

EXPERIENCE SUMMARY

- 20 years United States Air Force, Staff Sergeant/E5, Honorable Discharge: 07/18
- 14 years, Operations Supervisor / Project Manager / Team Leader
- 9 years, Instructor / Training (military; job skills)

9.   Sometimes the job seeker wants to hedge their bets and add more than one job objective on their resume. While this is not perfectly ideal, it is OK to showcase the diversity of the background with more than one Objective as long as it doesn't get too long or list too many job objectives. The best advice? Pick one job objective and then swoop with others depending upon the job the applicant is seeking directly.

OBJECTIVE: Facilities Security Manager

EXPERIENCE SUMMARY

- 20+ years, Linguist (Mandarin Chinese; speaking, reading, and writing)
- 17 years, Business Translator / Contracts

Oversight (international imports/exports)
- 9 years, Intelligence Analysis (federal, military)
- 6 years, Program / Project Manager (intelligence, security, facilities, military)

10. Even if the job seeker has only been in one type of career (e.g., the mortgage- and loan-processing field) for most of their career, the resume owner can still write a 'list' of years of experience for their general career positions.

OBJECTIVE: Auditing and Compliance Manager

EXPERIENCE SUMMARY

- 10+ years, Mortgage Loan Processor and Managing Supervisor
- 10+ years, Quality Assurance / Research Analyst for Mortgage Processing

INTERVIEWS

FILLER (KILLER) WORDS IN INTERVIEWS

Are your 'ums' and 'ahs' and 'ands' killing your interview? The first impression to a potential employer is definitely how you look when you walk in the door – shoulders back, head erect, smart looking in a freshly pressed business suit, shined shoes, hair stylish. You look the part of the job. You earned it.

The second impression for the interview is how you speak and how you present yourself as being 'articulate.' It's amazing how many job candidates walk out of an interview and thought they 'nailed it' by answering all the questions thoroughly and thoughtfully. Days later they receive the rejection email with no real explanation of what it was that tripped them up for serious consideration.

It could be their manner of speaking – literally. Being able to speak clearly, concisely, and it's important to articulate your thoughts well – regardless of whether your education is a high school diploma or a Ph.D. Speak well and get that new job!

1.   Americans hear noise coming at them from media sources – radio, TV, phone, and office chatter almost 24/7. They are unaccustomed to the silence between sentences and tend to avoid that silent gap

with 'filler words.' You have heard them –
"you know," "…and …," or "ums." Some
people psychologically feel if they don't
continue to talk, non-stop, the 'stage' will be
taken from them and the power will be
stripped from them in the conversation.

2.   If you are applying for a sales position, a
figure-head public relations representative
job, or in a career field where fluent speech
is a must, there is no room for filler words.
You know what I'm talking about – the 'you
know' every 4-6 words, the faltering
confidence fillers such as 'um,' 'ah,' or the
ever-present 'and' every three words to fill in
the silence. Some folks use the word 'like'
throughout their conversations.

The author's parents were not happy about
the author's constant use of the words, 'you
know,' as a teen. They started a campaign
to squelch the use of those filler words.
Every time the author used that phrase,
they immediately repeated it back. The
cure took less than a week because it was
so annoying when they mocked the author.
The author used the same trick with her
teens – problem cured (within a few weeks).
You can also have friends keep a clicker
(dog training) or bells nearby – every time
they hear you speak a filler word, they can
'ring' you. Not only will they become
conscious of your use of the filler word(s),
they may become conscious of their own
use and make an effort to avoid fillers, also!

3. It is painful to listen to people who use filler words. If a middle-aged job applicant walks into an interview and recruiters can count the 'ums' and 'ahs' in the dozens or even the hundreds, that's a problem. Recruiters are not going to hire that person, no matter how good the answers are or how thoughtful the responses, or their broad experience – after wading through the um's and ah's. They can't carry out an intelligent conversation with clients if the job seekers need to use conversation crutches.

    Have someone listen to a casual conversation between you and someone else. (Or, turn on a recorder while you talk to someone.) Count how many times you used those filler words. You might be flabbergasted how many times filler words creep into your sentences. If you can't string a well-put-together sentence to sound intelligent, then the impression to the listener is – you aren't.

4. When you are having a conversation with someone, are you listening to what they are actually saying – or – are you forming a response in your head before they finish? Did you talk over the interviewer while they were trying to explain something? Talking 'over' another person's conversation subconsciously implies their contribution to the conversation is not important. This can be an interview killer. Practice listening to folks and don't respond for a few seconds. Use that time to formulate your answer,

then answer each point you heard – even repeating the question so your brain has time to formulate a better answer.

5.   Public speaking classes also help one learn how and what to say, and in many cases, it's not so much you are using the crutch words to fill in the space, you simply haven't prepared your speech or answers and practiced them enough. Practicing your answers to a variety of questions that may be asked in interviews are helpful, as well as memorizing answers to standard inquiries before you arrive at the interview. If you are preparing for an interview, look for common questions asked in interviews and create answers and practice them until they come across naturally.

6.   Don't curse. Talking 'ugly' could come across as an effort to fitting in with the crowd, but it can also leave a nasty impression on those in the room who were testing you out as to how you would react to adverse conditions within a conversation. Just because the hiring or interviewing manager says something 'inappropriate,' doesn't mean it is a green light for the job seeker to respond in kind. Accidents happen – if you spill the coffee or water during the interview, anything coming out your mouth should be simply an apology and then move on with the conversation as if the incident didn't happen.

7. Steer clear from answering any questions related to EEO protected groups. Don't discuss religion or what church you are attending (or not), countries of origin, what gender one identifies with, or how many kids you want to raise or adopt in the next few years. Don't talk politics – no matter how badly you want to respond to something off-hand that the recruiter or hiring manager mentioned. This includes talking about relative matters to union contracts and related matters. You can acknowledge if you are union member if asked, but don't offer opinions on the most recent contract negotiations or whether you are inclined to picket in protest. Stay objective and neutral.

8. Accents happen and they often incite curiosity and potentially 'illegal-to-ask' questions about nationality origins. "Oh, what an interesting accent, where are you from?" Be prepared to either decline to answer or answer in a way that quickly gets past the question without really answering the burning question of where you were born or raised or your citizenship. "I learned to talk from my parents, who were from Senegal and Jamaica, but polished my English here in the states, where I grew up." Or, "Thanks, I grew up in the deep south, so if I say something too heavily accented for understanding, let me know, I will be happy to repeat."

9.   Slow down when you are talking. Most job
        seekers are nervous in interviews, they
        want to put on a polished persona – and
        really get that job. The job seekers may
        start talking too fast, or too loud, from the
        nervousness or passionately excited to be
        there.   Breathe deeply before answering
        each question, pay attention to your speech
        speed and enunciation. It's OK to say –
        "give me a second to think about that," and
        then pause to gather your thoughts and the
        right words to answer questions.

10.   Be prepared with interview questions of
        your own to ask interviewers. Interviews
        are two-way conversations. If at the end of
        the interview you have no questions to ask
        the hiring manager, then you come across
        as not having a real deep interest in the
        position. Prepare by reviewing the job
        description, the company website, research
        as many employees on LinkedIn as you can
        find, and put together a list of questions that
        you want to ask from curiosity or directly job
        relevant to ask of the interviewers.
        Remember, you are searching for your
        'employer of choice' as much as they are
        looking for the 'perfect job candidate.'

BACKGROUND CHECKS
FOR JOB SEARCHES

Job seekers are often worried about two hiring practices – background checks and referral contacts before they are willing to let their current company know they are shopping around for a new position.

1. Background Checks and Referral Contacts: Depending upon what industry you are going to be working in, most employers need to confirm that the applicant whom they have identified as a qualified candidate continues to be qualified by 'checking their story,' so to speak. The issue is liability if the information on paper (resume and company's legal application form) and the interview (discussion and confirmation of experience, skills, and education) are quality assured for correctness and factuality. A company hires a candidate to work on a government contract and the contract requires a Bachelor's degree, and the candidates says "yes, I have the equivalent of a degree" (doesn't exist – you have an accredited school degree – or not). The company could lose the federal contract for non-compliance if the new hire is placed to work in a contract position

without the minimum credentials.   Here is what a job seeker should understand and be prepared for.

a.   Do not add in references or supervisor's name and phone numbers in a private sector resume – that listed can be on a separate paper and provided *only* when asked for at the end of a job consideration interview.

b.   Employers cannot legally or ethically call your references or perform a background check (job history, residence history, credit or finance checks) unless and until the job seeker has reached the stage of having received an offer letter of employment and provides a written signature for the hiring company to place those calls and submit the candidates name to a background check process (or third party vendor, e.g., Lexis-Nexis).

c.   In this litigious society and work environment, when a background check on past employers is done, and references called, most companies direct the human resources department to be the only authorized representative to provide work history confirmation. In essence, they will confirm: Job Title(s), work dates (length of service), and work locations. They will not provide salary data (it could be a market competitor phishing for compensation information). If asked, the human resources department may answer the question, "Is this person eligible for rehire with your company?" In this case, an affirmative answer will be a positive feedback, and a negative answer may intimate there was 'trouble in paradise' – or – it is simply company policy to not allow rehires.

d. While this is not a prevalent action, some recruiters will use reference lists to 'troll' for additional candidates for an open position – even for the position which the candidate has applied. The candidate may not be 'strong' enough, but calling the references could potentially provide additional interested applicants for the position with stronger skills and experience. Hold off on providing reference lists until asked.

2. Make sure your references have provided permission to you in advance for you to offer their names and contact information to potential hiring companies. Nothing can be more awkward than a phone call from a complete stranger about a co-worker from years ago … that the reference may not even remember! Most companies prefer to have the full name, their job titles, the full name of the mutual company in which the job seeker and/or reference worked, as well

as the phone number (with area code) and the email address. The email address allows company hiring managers to send out written requests and inquires, as well as copies of the written authorization to the references documenting permission for them to reach out. Your references should be up-to-date, and professional (supervisors, managers, major clients, co-workers / peers). If you don't have enough 'real work' references, look to volunteer organizations for leadership to provide a telephonic reference. Letterhead references were common in the 20th Century, and are still acceptable, but in this digital age, are easily compiled with enough information to compile a 'fake' letter.

3.   Background checks should be used for valid reasons related directly to performance of job tasks and responsibilities and/or exposure to liability issues via the employer to clients or vice versa. If the employer starts venturing into areas in the background check or asking questions related to non-work-specific topics, stop them by pointing out you need to know what the reasons are for the more extensive research.

4.   Any employer will have potential exposure for business liability (and/or insurance purposes). Making direct phone calls to previous employers may suffice, e.g., (a) a trash truck attendant may not necessarily need a background check - they will not be

exposed specifically to people in working their job;, but (b) a parking lot attendant who parks cars may need to have a background check for petty theft or auto theft.

5. If the company has / needs liability insurance and/or bonding in place, then they may hire a third-party vetting party vendor to perform the background check for local, state, and federal level criminal offenses and prosecution (meaning they have been charged, and found guilty). The onus for payment for this background check is on the hiring entity, not the job seeker. There are a few small businesses who request that job seekers provide copies of their Department of Motor Vehicle (DMV) records, especially if a Department of Transportation (DOT) agency-regulated driver's license is required.

6. If the company deals with client or company finances, then a full-blown background check including financial history and credit check would be prudent for the future employer. If a company is a government contractor, and the employee needs to attain or retain a security clearance, they will be required to submit information about their finances. Someone who is deep in debt or has massive credit issues will be more proportionally tempted to steal, embezzle, or succumb to threats or bribes.

7. If the company deals with state or federal government (government contracting) then

it would be prudent to have the full background check before the offer letter so if the employee needs a security clearance, ANY potential for that clearance being denied will be found in the first round background check. If a job candidate comes from another country or has family living in a 'watch list' country for terrorist activities, then that information will create a red-flag for the adjudication process and may delay the process for anywhere between six months to several years during the investigation.

8.   A company should never perform a background check on any job applicant until the company obtains a 'wet signature' (or digital signature) authorizing the hiring company representative to perform that background check. Authorization paperwork should also be specific which and how much of a background check will be performed and WHY that level of background check will be performed, e.g., a criminal and financial background check will be performed due to the potential of the employee dealing directly with client finances and/or accounting information

9.   The job applicant should be provided the warning that drug testing and/or background checks will be performed inside the written offer letter of employment with the caveat that any offer will be 'contingent' upon the candidate 'passing' the minimum standards for the background check (no felonies, no

convictions, no bankruptcies, no poor credit history, etc.).

10. Job applicants should be told there will be a background check and/or drug testing in the initial interview - not the final interview! This allows the applicants to either back out of the consideration for the position gracefully and avoid wasting of time and energy, or to offer any information and explanations that may not be forthcoming in background checks or may be able to update information that may come back from archival or out-of-date available data (e.g., arrest for drunk driving or DUI, but results were diabetic side effects from new medication or lack of insulin injection, but court records may have not been updated yet).

SPECULATION WORK
& SKILLS TESTING

Job seekers are often worried about two hiring practices – background checks and referral contacts before they are willing to let their current company know they are shopping around for a new position. Job seekers are often leery of providing examples of their work without the work samples (ideas) potentially being 'stolen' or used (with small adjustments or changes) in the company's design efforts without getting paid for the time and materials. In some cases, an applicant will be tested on their work-related skills before the offer letter of employment is issued (e.g., physically being able to lift 50 pounds or drive a forklift truck).

1.   Testing: It is perfectly legal to test a job candidate for specific skills. Many temp agencies will test typing and speed for temporary workers to ensure they can use a computer keyboard with proficiency. Welders may need to show they can perform MIG or TIG welding in tests for sample metals.

2.   Two vehicles to showcase one's work is via Portfolios are via LinkedIn partnership products:

a. Behance (.com) provides a phenomenal platform application to showcase creative artist's work, whether dance, music, fine art, or acting. Providing the URL link to one's portfolio profile will allow not only hiring managers to see your work, but also potential third-party persons interested in hiring for gigs to determine if your work style fits their needs.

b. SlideShare (.com) also provides a platform for managers or instructors (trainers, teachers) to provide presentations on specific subjects. One can provide the URL to the specific slide or a portfolio to guide hiring managers to view specific topics one had researched or provided presentations to groups.

3. Spec Work: In some industries, architecture, advertising, broadcast design, graphic design, and commercial art, for example, the potential employer may ask job applicants or candidates to perform 'spec work' (speculative samples of work for hiring consideration). These professionals are expected to participate in speculative work. The job candidates (or the freelance artists) are the mercy of the hiring company or potential client in this regard. The initial design is not the final product, but is followed by extended financial engagement to refine or execute a design. In communications design, this is often not the case. The design submitted "on spec" is all

that the client is seeking. The creative work, either partial or completed, submitted by designers to prospective clients before the artists or designers secure both the work contract and equitable fees. Unethical clients or companies can use this freely-gained work as they see fit without fear of legal repercussions.

The AIGA (the professional association for design) notes unpaid / spec work[6] could be in many forms:

- Speculative or "spec" work: work done for free, hoping to get paid for it
- Competitions: work done in hopes of winning a prize
- Volunteer work as a favor or for experience, without expectation of payment
- Internships: a form of volunteer work that involves some educational gain
- Pro bono work: volunteer work done for public benefit

For students and professionals, there could be an ethical difference between the two and which constitutes what may be deemed 'unacceptable practices.' The job seeker / designer and the potential client make the decisions and accept the risks. Designers would consider unpaid spec work with no

---

[6] https://www.aiga.org/position-spec-work

compensation or hopes of winning something (prize, job) to be unacceptable.[7]

4.   Job candidates should question the requested spec work they are asked to complete, how should they communicate those inquiries to the hiring manager? The hiring manager needs to provide explicit instructions to the job applicant if they are requiring spec work as examples. There is no time to be wasting on asking questions and obtaining answers and waiting for the interviewing representative to be 'found' to obtain the answer. The company needs to have firm knowledge that the information the job applicant has is complete to avoid communications issues and wasted time on that aspect. The job candidate's time is JUST as important to them as the company's man-hours are to them.

5.   Ethically, the hiring manager should NOT provide any spec work that would need more than one hour of actual labor on the piece. If it can be proved that someone with the company had the documented skills and proof of being able to complete this type of project in one hour, and the job candidate is required to complete similar work in the same time period, it passes the test of validity and reliability for use as a testing

---

[7] Cass, J. (2009, Aug. 12). The "Pros" and Cons of Spec Work. *Just Creative.* Retrieved from https://justcreative.com/2009/08/12/the-pros-and-cons-of-spec-work/

model.

6. Theoretically, the job applicant could and
should provide enough work samples if the
job is a creative position where the ideation
and creation of a physical piece is required
for review as a job candidate. Spec work
that takes the candidate more than an hour
should be compensated for that work by the
company, enabling: 1) ownership of the
work by the creator to the (hiring) company,
2) avoiding DOL employment law issues
and liabilities.

7. The hiring manager should know from the
published job description or at least the
internal job description what is required of
the candidate and can develop and/or
design a test spec for all candidates to the
position to perform within an exact time
period. This prevents any claims of
favoritism based on EEOC legalities and
regulations.

8. The hiring manager should be clear and
specific as to when questions are allowed,
and how to contact the hiring manager (and
when they are unavailable). The company
has the equal onus of being professional to
demonstrate their positive brand message
to the potential new hire as well as the
applicant has in demonstrating their
eagerness to show their skills. Each
applicant doing spec work in applying for
the same job should be granted the exact
same information, time-line, deadline,

materials, and any other considerations to perform on an equal basis with their job competitor and to legally protect the company from any implied prejudicial treatment accusations.

9.   How much leeway do candidates have with spec work? Should they follow directions to a T, or improvise a little to show their uniqueness? Does it differ depending on the assignment? All applicants who provide spec work on as a hiring test, should be provided equal levels of instructions, deadlines, and opportunities. There is no clear-cut answer to this question, because if a mechanic applies for a job, s/he may have to demonstrate they can change oil in a car without much leeway for 'uniqueness.' Designing a dress for the wife of the President of the USA and a charity ball she will be attending would be open to huge improvisation because of the creative nature of the task.

10.   Research the company you are applying to thoroughly before going for an interview. Ask questions about any spec work required. If the spec work seems like it would entail hours or weeks of work to complete, then either 1) tell the hiring company that you will expect payment, as a 1099 contractor, for the work performed on their behalf, regardless of whether they are satisfied with the end product or not, and they can apply that 1099 income to the first paycheck if hired; or 2) tell the company of

any objections working for a company who unethically used job seekers to perform work for the company without payment. Those underhanded actions showcase and demonstrates a behavior and business practice that may be expected from them as an employee in the future. Who wants to work for bosses or a company with a lack of ethics and fairness?

AVOIDING ANSWERING 'ILLEGAL TO ASK' INTERVIEW QUESTIONS

Not all recruiters, hiring managers, or even human resources practitioners are aware of or practice 'safe interviewing' techniques. Sometimes the interviewer will ask questions from a range of the 'off-the-cuff' (oh dear, what do I ask this applicant?) or on other occasions they will ask a structured list of directly and specifically job-related questions vetted by human resources or even a legal counsel. The reason job interviews need to be structured and vetted to ask the same questions of every candidate who is interviewed for an employment position is to ensure equity and equality, regardless of who the applicant is – all related to the Equal Employment Opportunity Commission's (EEOC) regulatory compliance and standards.

While it is illegal to not hire someone based on their ethnic background and other EEOC-identified factors, it is, alternatively, not illegal to hire someone specifically *for* their ethnic background. Hiring managers may review a resume to see if the person is possibly a match to a *perceived* skill-set or qualification based on the applicant's ethnicity. The hiring manager may presumably be looking for a diversity candidate to fulfill quotas for a company's Affirmative Action Plans (AAP). They will seek resumes with names associated with African-American persons of color (or other minorities). The search may be for an ethnic minority – as a stereotype – that would be more qualified than another ethnic job applicant (e.g., an Eastern Indian for math or engineering skills; an Asian for software programming, etc.).

Interviewers and interviewees should avoid the 'tell me more about yourself" question. That question is directed to a gray area of illegally-appropriated answers to EEO-related questions. What interviewers *should* be asking is, "Tell me more about your career progression," which is a more appropriate question, directly relevant to career, the job seeker's current and past jobs, and could lead to learning more about the candidates achievements not listed on the resume. Candidates should not discuss family, kids, or religion (in which case the interviewer would need to gently remind the candidate the question should pertain to the job, not their private life).

Asking questions of a job applicant about their potential for holding bad credit and debt is not against the law and is not illegal to ask (versus EEOC questions about sex, religion, politics, country of origin, etc.) - as long as any of the questions asked in an interview are: 1) asked equally of ALL job candidates, and 2) are directly related to the applicant's ability to perform their job to minimum standards.

When the questions or assumptions develop in these EEOC-protected areas, here is how the job seeker should handle the question, and answer, or avoid the topic.

1) Age. Yes, there are millions of job seekers over 40 still in the workforce and seeking a new job in their career or looking for a change in their career path. One of the more common excuses job seekers are given, "you are overqualified," which is recruiter-speak for "I think at your age, you will be asking for a salary we can't afford to pay," and/or "If we hire you, you will keep on job searching and leave us in few months once you find the position that will pay you what you think you are worth." The Age Discrimination Act protects workers over 40 who may have the same qualifications as a younger candidate (under 40). Technically, there is no such thing as being 'overqualified' – either you are qualified to perform the minimum-required tasks and responsibilities of a job – or – you are not. As a job seeker, you may need to stress your 'wealth' of knowledge because you have been exposed to many job related problems and issues you have been able to successfully resolve.

It is vital to avoid being asked – how old are you? Or worse, after you leave the interview, someone commenting, "Did you see that last applicant? He was so old and hunched over, I was afraid he was going to fall over dead half-way through the interview!" Before the interview, it's best to 'put on your best face,' and have someone critique your 'look' for any ageism factors and perform action follow-ups to avoid the aging look against potentially younger competitors.

a)   Do you have graying hair? Get it dyed professionally while in the job-search process.

b)   Do you normally wear an old-fashion, dated suit or dress for the interview? Purchase a newer, more-modern outfit.

c)   Do you shuffle, or are you stooped over, when you walk or sit? Get a back brace that will pull your shoulders back and your spine in a straighter alignment.

d)   Do you have age- or liver-spots on your skin? Get a matching skin-tone, cover makeup to hide those.

If a job seekers is asked what age they are, the first question back to the interview is to ask what the purpose of the question is in relationship the ability to perform the job as written in the company job description posted publicly.

2)   Religion. There are jobs that may interfere with some employee's religious practices. For instance, Islam requires followers to pray five times a day. The Jewish religion may mean workers are unable to handle certain food products (pork), or may be required to start their religious observations between dusk on Fridays to sundown on Saturdays, as well as take certain days off for religious observances. Wearing a

yarmulke (head covering) to an interview will make the interviewer obviously aware of the job seeker's religion and practices as an Orthodox Jew. Wearing a hijab and/or scarf to an interview will make the interviewer instantly aware of the job seeker's religion and practices as a Muslim.

Wearing the customary accessories that identify religious practices should be taken into consideration with the research performed on the company, it's diversity practices, and their ability or willingness to work around religious practices and customs.

Interviewers cannot legally ask a job seeker, "What religion are you?" or consider that job seeker's religion in hiring considerations. If the interviewer gets to the end of the interview and asks if there is anything that you know of that could prevent you from performing the tasks and responsibilities of the job, the interviewee must notify the hiring manager of any '*religious-related restrictions*' that may cause potential interference in the completion of the minimum job responsibilities. Orthodox Jewish applicants can then indicate, "I must finish my job tasks, and leave before dark on Fridays, to be home before the sun sets for Sabbath. I can come in early on Mondays to make up for those early leave hours on Fridays during the winter months when the sun sets early during daylight savings time." A practicing Muslim may indicate, "I must wear a headscarf to cover my head, but will wear subdued colors and in a professional manner. I must take a break at 12:00 noon exactly, daily, for prayer hour, which I will do during my lunch break to avoid any inconvenience to my coworkers." Another potential issue may be, "My religion forbids me interacting with co-workers during certain activities, such as after-work functions serving alcohol. I am hoping that will not be a problem if I offer my regrets for not attending such functions?"

3)   Politics. This is a hot topic to avoid in conversations in today's business environment. Unless one works inside a political office or for a political entity, it's best to steer 100% clear of any political discussions, including using any terms, remarks about candidates, derogatory comments, or political-based jokes. Regardless of what political leanings a job candidate has – Liberal, Conservative, Socialist, or Progressive – a job candidate should never be asked about their political leanings. If an interviewing manager does ask about political interests, the job applicant should ask in return, "Is there a particular standard of politics that is required for this position?" The answer to the question will allow the job seeker to decide if the business environment is one in which they wish to work.

4)   Gender Affiliation. It is a changed world from several decades ago when it comes to acceptance for folks who are considered 'different.' Lesbian, gay, bi-sexual,

transgender, and queer (LGBTQ) job seekers are under no obligation to offer any information about their sexual preferences, any information about their medical history, nor answer any questions about their 'intentions' for dealing with (potential) workplace harassment. All work environments who hire any job seeker should provide a professional, harassment-free, and dignified workplace for the new hire to perform their job responsibilities. Most job applications ask for gender identification for EEOC and AAP, as well as health insurance purposes - but usually this is after the offer letter of employment is extended. Job applicants are under no obligation to answer any questions related to their gender or gender identification during an interview. If asked or there are questions that are probing, then the interviewee needs to be prepared to ask in response, "Give me an example of a situation in this job where my personal gender affiliation would be critical to the success of the company and its strategic goals?"

5) Country of Origin. Unless job requisition specifically asks for qualifications via language qualifications or familiarity with the culture and country, then what country the interviewee originates in has no bearing on the applicants ability to perform a job if they have the experience or job skills. In some cases, a hiring manager may wish to perform a test of language skills if the

interviewee seems to have an accent and
seems to speak with difficulty in the
language accepted by the interviewing
company (e.g., a French Canadian, where
English is their Second Language, may
need to be proficient in law or medicine
where communications are critical). The
interviewer can ask and test the English
language based on the job description
needs and requirements, but cannot ask the
interviewee what country them came from
and make a determination on their hiring
decision solely based on the country of
origination of the applicant.

6) Family Matters. It is illegal to ask female
(and male) applicants about personal family
matters, including current or future planned
number of children, anticipated family size,
if children are through natural birth or
adopted, or if the applicant is married or a
single parent. As long as the job applicant
can get to work on time, perform through
the work-shift as required, and then leave at
the end of the shift, then the company has
no business asking about the job applicant's
family. If asked about family – again – ask
about the relevance of your answer to the
job itself.

7) Citizenship. Recruiters can ask if the
candidate can 'legally' work in the USA, but
cannot ask the applicant if they are a USA
citizen. The hiring company cannot
discriminate on whether the applicant is or
is not a US citizen, either. All hiring

managers can ask is if the applicant has the legal ability to work in the country (regardless of citizenship, green-card status, or visitor's Visa). Once the employee is hired, they are required to complete an I-9 form and to provide proof of ability to work in the USA via a Social Security card, Birth Certificate, Passport, Green-Card or permanent resident identity card, etc., via the currently allowable proofs listed on the I-9 form monitored and managed by the Department of Homeland Security (DHS) and the Immigrations and Customs Enforcement Agencies (ICE). Some companies will also enter the new hire's data into the e-Verify system, which matches the documentation the new hire has provided to agency and system information and documentation. (Not all companies are required to vet new hires through this system, but all government contracting companies and newly hired Federal government employees' information are entered into the system to verify employment eligibility.)

Other topics to avoid in resumes, cover letters, or interviews that have no place in the job qualifications vetting process are:

8)   Pictures of Job Applicant. Job seekers should never add in photos of themselves on resumes – this practice opens up prejudicial treatment before they even get into an interview. The only place a job seeker should put their professional head

shot on is either on their LinkedIn profile or an actor's resume who is applying for parts based 'on their looks.'

9) Hobbies. Hobbies can potentially create the wrong impression of a job seeker. And hobbies seem to be gender-related. For example: while men may be predominantly golfers, women may be hobbyists in gourmet cooking or miniature doll-house model building. Listing hobbies may incline the hiring managers to think of the job seeker in a stereotyped role, so avoid mentioning hobbies until after hired.

10) Jokes. While humor is important, jokes can sometimes come across as crass, prejudiced, biased, or political, and there is always one person in the crowd it will usually offend. Avoid those. Smile a lot instead!

INTERVIEWS – WHAT TO
KNOW BEFORE YOU GO

An **interview** is a conversation where questions are asked, and answers are given. In common parlance, the word "interview" refers to a one-on-one conversation between an interviewer and an interviewee. (Wikipedia.com)

Noun a meeting of people face to face, especially for consultation. *synonyms:* meeting, discussion, conference, question and answer, session, examination, evaluation, interrogation; audience, talk, dialogue, exchange; talks; *informal* - rap session, confab; *formal* - confabulation, interlocution "all applicants will be called for an interview." (dictionary.com)

Verb: hold an interview with (someone). "he arrived to be interviewed by a local TV station about the level of unemployment"; *synonyms:* talk to, have a discussion with, have a dialogue with, hold a meeting with, confer with; question, put questions to, probe, interrogate, cross-examine; poll, canvass, survey, sound out, ascertain the opinions of; *informal* - grill, pump, give the third degree to; examine (dictionary.com)

In business, interviews are one of many critical recruiting tools for businesses to find a qualified person to fill a job position to perform work to minimum standards in exchange for a paycheck. For you, the job seeker, the goal is to get your foot in the door to meet with a company representative to convince that representative you are the best person they can hire to perform that job.

It is a two-way street. Some job seekers fail to understand they are also interviewing that company as an 'employer of choice.' You must both be striving towards a mutual acceptance.

1.   Be prepared mentally and professionally for a dynamic interview. You want to ensure you are comfortable with the people and the work environment and that starts with being comfortable in what you wear. Dress professionally and ensure you avoid any age indications to avoid age bias. Dress in a nice dark blue or pinstripe suit (men or women) or a business-professional dress. Use very little jewelry (best to avoid all except a wedding ring). If you have been enjoying or letting your gray hair grow out, go get it colored – you can always let it grow back out again. Ensure your shoes are polished. Get your nails professionally manicured. Women should always keep an extra pair of pantyhose in their purse in case you get a snag or run just before the interview.

2.   Research the heck out of the company and if you can suggest a 'correction' in a typo on

their website or marketing materials, then
you can demonstrate your 'eye for details.'
Although they are interviewing you for an
open position, YOU are interviewing them
for a future career and lifestyle. Don't show
up empty handed. Have a list of questions
to ask the hiring manager, interviewer, or
the headhunter. If you can bring points into
the discussion that you found out about the
company during your research, they will
know you - as the job candidate - are
serious about the position.

3.   Laugh before you start the interview (or get
online to start the interview), even if it's a
forced laugh. This will relax you, assist you
in getting the scowl or overly serious look off
your face, and imbue your personality with a
little more friendliness, as well as pep up
your own day. Smile throughout the
interview.

4.   When you walk into an interview room or
meet anyone in the company, immediately
stretch your hand out and provide a 'firm'
(not wimpy) handshake (but don't squeeze
too hard - some older folks may have
arthritis), and repeat their name back to
them (everyone loves the sound of their
name on other folks lips!).

5.   Your carry in list should be a paper copy of
your resume, a paper copy of your list of
recommendations if they ask for them, and
a typed list of questions to ask the future
employer about the problems or issues or

concerns they have and need to solve a
problem inside their company / business if
they hire you. Be prepared - carry in a small
folder (not a huge loaded briefcase) in
which you have 2-3 printed resumes and
your list of references if the hiring manager
asks for them - but don't offer that list until
asked.

6.   Ask the interviewers what 'pains' them. If
hired, what 'pain' can you as the new hire
resolve for them (an empty chair filled or
business, technical, or people issues they
need someone with skills to fix).

7.   Be prepared to answer the following topics
in an interview:
- How you can demonstrate an ability to
perform the job – 'tell the interviewer how
you performed this job in your current or
past employment
- Provide examples of work performance (if
not previous employer's proprietary work)
or tell about their achievements (e.g., as a
salesperson, weekly, monthly, or annual
revenue, sales numbers, number of new
contracts obtained in what time period,
value of those contracts, average sale,
etc.)?
- Finest accomplishments on past projects or
program goals? Received recognition from
employer for those achievements?
- Process used to resolve issues, concerns,
or problems with peers, coworkers,
supervising managers, clients, or

customers?

- **W**hen / how did the job candidate obtain skills sets, or that level of experience in the main tasks and responsibilities of the job requirements?

- **W**ho / where did job candidate get direct training for specific skills sets – mentors, formal schooling, on-the-job training; how much was supervised training?

- **W**here did they get their career-specific training – technical training programs? formal degree or certification programs? Special trade school? Seminars?

- **W**hat do they want to be when they grow up? (sets the interview with a little humor and allows the interviewee to go outside the box and provide more insight into their own mindset and personality)

- **F**inally - the interviewee may be presented with an existing 'problem.' Be prepared to provide ideas or suggestions that could potentially resolve the problem in a fair and equitable manner and in favor of the company.

8. Use positive body language; look folks in the eyes when speaking; sit up straight, but lean in slightly to indicate you are interested in the interviewing manager and what they have to say. Sit in a comfortable position, but not slouching or leaning backwards away from the interviewer (if at a table, put both arms up on the table; if in a seated position, lean in towards the interviewer).

9.	Smile naturally; try to avoid 'smirky' or strained smiles - folks can detect those and start to feel uncomfortable. You need to be in a happy mood to project a natural smile - listen to some comedy on the car radio or podcast before you walk into an interview and the endorphins from laughing will keep you in a great mood.

10.	When you leave, note to the interviewing representative(s), 'It was a pleasure meeting you, (say their name)!" This makes them feel they were important to your day (and they may be important to your future career!) Write a thank you note in advance - you don't need to write the name of the person on the inside of the note - just a 'thanks so much for meeting with me to consider me for this position' general note. Once you leave the building with the business card of the person in hand, write the address on the outside of the stamped envelope and mail it directly from the closest mailbox. This impresses folks that you took the time to write the note and mail it versus sending a quick email (which they may ignore or never see).

COMPENSATION

BENEFITS & COMPENSATION
QUESTIONS AND CONSIDERATIONS

Most companies offer a HR-related or
recruiting website that offers a list of most (if not all)
of the company benefits for which employees would
be eligible once hired (or after a probationary
period). There is more to compensation than a
weekly or monthly paycheck. Consider all the
options when job shopping – especially if there are
two competing offers for a new job from two
companies.

1)   When searching for a new job, be careful
        you are comparing apples to apples and
        oranges to oranges for compensation when
        reviewing job offers. Don't jump to a new
        job for a small salary increase unless –
        again, look at the benefits – the
        compensation package outside the
        paycheck is at an exponential or part of a
        larger overall salary package. You may get
        another 25-50 cents per hour, but may also
        get more health and dental insurance
        benefits, and other company perks the last
        company didn't offer. When you add up the
        cost of the compensation, plus your new
        salary you may find you receive an
        additional $40-$80 in your paycheck, but
        also another $1,000 in health and welfare

benefits (value) monthly.

2)   Don't put 'absolutes' in front of the recruiters
        during interviews ("I can't work for less than
        a $XX,XXX salary). They may be hunting for
        a willing candidate to take a lower salary in
        exchange for a huge potential in the long-
        run such as on-the-job training for a position
        without candidate experience; or the perks
        in the job outweighs the take home
        paycheck (company pays 100% for all
        health insurance benefits for the employee
        plus all the family members). The total
        salary package for health and welfare
        (including dental and eyecare) benefits, plus
        additional quarterly or annual bonuses, and
        participation in a company match 401(k)
        plan may be the equivalent of an additional
        $12K-$30K annually.

3)   Salary may be secondary to earnings value,
        because there may be more intrinsic value
        over the long-term employment with one
        company versus a higher-salary at the
        second company. If the health and welfare
        benefits pay the entire monthly premium for
        the family, but the hourly wages are $2-4 an
        hour less, the employee may still be 'ahead'
        financially because paying for part or all of
        the benefits at the higher-paying (per hour)
        company may end up with less in the
        employee's pocket. (Note: the cost of
        health care plans for a large family with
        several dependents, could range between
        $500-$600 for a minimum coverage plan to
        as much as $3,000 monthly for a 'Cadillac

plan' so ask what the COBRA cost would be for that health care plan for a comparative market valuation.) The cost of tuition reimbursement offered to employees to gain educational degrees to increase job skills and enhance the skill sets and knowledge open the job seeker up for broader career possibilities in the future is also a huge bonus.

4) Human resources managers and the executive team in a company spend a lot of time and effort designing and compiling and negotiating with vendors for health and welfare benefits to attract strong job candidates, as well as to retain current employees. When reviewing benefits health plans, companies determine the best ROI for the company's overhead costs, as well as the maximum amount of premium co-pay the employees can 'tolerate' before they decide to move to another company who pays more towards the benefits. Business compensation plans can range between paying a portion of an employee's monthly costs or up to 100% for both the employee and their family members.

5) When the recruiter calls to inquire (or emails), ask - diplomatically and tactfully - what the "minimum salary range" is for the position; you don't want to waste your time or the recruiter's time, if the salary minimum is more than 10% below what you would accept for any position (for instance, you want a job that pays $70K (USD), and the

recruiter has quoted the salary minimum is $55K. There is a pretty good chance they would not be able to stretch the salary range for this position to the $70K plus benefits and other compensation. If the salary alone is not at the level you are comfortable with, but the compensation may make up for the difference ask about a market valuation of the company compensation and 'perks' (gym membership, tuition reimbursement, guaranteed annual bonuses, and anything else the company offers all employees). The value of the comps and perks at one company may outweigh the combination of salary and compensation from another competitive company job offer.

6) Often overlooked are severance packages – especially for high-level executives in the C-suite who have huge responsibilities for making the company grow, protecting the legal interest, as well as research and identify acquisitions and procurements to increase the company's asset. Because these executives are usually in these high-level positions, on average between 3-5 years. they often negotiate a severance package before they accept the position. This will include XX weeks of pay (to compensation for potentially six to 16 months between positions); 18 months of paid COBRA / health benefits, and/or even a placement package for seeking and finding a new position

7) Ask about a Paid Time Off (PTO) leave policy and/or flex-time if the employee has a personal doc appointment or family emergency; in other words, is there another employee on staff that can fill-in for emergencies (not that there will be many or any, but this could lesson any guilt if the employee needs to call out of work). An hourly employee may take off from work and only be docked for the actual hours not worked. Salary employees may be able to take off a few hours, but not be deducted any hours (the assumption is they normally would work more than the 40 hours weekly on average, so a few hours off would 'balance' out).

8) Is the company large enough where there are opportunities to take on more work to prove capabilities so there is potential for advancement in the ranks? When hiring into any company, the goal is work up higher in the ranks and earn promotions that provide more salary and compensation or perks. A used car salesperson dreams of moving up to new car sales, and new car salesperson dreams of moving up to a sales manager position. Small companies may not have that type of opportunity, whereas larger companies who are growing quickly, may have far more opportunities for promotional growth or responsibilities growth.

9) Does the company have tuition reimbursement for increasing the worker's

skills, e.g., computer classes (Excel, Project, Word), community college classes (towards degree programs), or other learning opportunities? Gaining more skills, learning new methods, adding more technology knowledge, and/or gaining a new educational degree will add more value to the worker in the long run, for the current employer, as well as the for moving to new career positions in the market. Does the company have cross-training programs so the worker can learn new skills and take on projects others don't want or have no time to do? This provides new opportunities for learning and expanding knowledge about the company and its products and services, but also diversifies the employees experience, making them more valuable (as well as sought after by poaching companies).

10) Sometimes the company offering you a position may be average for the offered salary range and compensation … but … the name of the company may have a certain status that will get you hired faster in the future *because* you worked at that company. An example of this type of 'brand' companies would be Apple, Microsoft, Google, and Facebook if you are in the information technology world. The competition for working at these companies is fierce, and these companies only take the best and brightest in internships and new hires for even the lowest-ranking jobs. Some job seekers work hard to get

accepted at these companies because they know the compensation packages are great, even if they are working 60-80 hours a week. In the long run, if they leave those companies, having worked there puts a higher-ranking experience status on their resume to gain employment in other IT-related companies.

SALARY NEGOTIATIONS

Know your value by researching the market rate thoroughly for your job description. Ensure you have also considered education and years of experience and are comparing apples to apples and oranges to oranges. Prepare your research and be prepared to share your data with the hiring manager or supervisor. If management knows what the competition is offering and believe you may be thinking about moving, they may review the research to review if thorough and legitimate. There are many salary search tools online – including the US government's Bureau of Labor Statistics website, the Glassdoor website, and/or Salary.com to name a few.

1.   Establish a spreadsheet of levels of compensation related to years of experience, education, skills and training, as well as any job-related requirements (e.g., a security clearance or uniquely specific degree: a Bachelor's Degree in Computer Science versus Information Technology). The factors to be considered for job salary negotiations are: geographic location, years of experience within the industry (or field), education level, skills, licenses and certifications, and in some cases leadership experience (number of years) and career level will be considered. Once you identify

the job title and description, research the ranges of those salaries (with the other factors noted above included) from at least three sources, then look at the lowest and highest salaries, and aim for the middle (average). If you have more years of experience and education than the average minimum requirements, you can bump up the salary level.

The going rate for an active security clearance in government contracting and federal jobs also can increase the salary proportionately. For example, for each level of clearance (Confidential, Secret, Top Secret, TS/SCI, etc.), add another ~$10-15K to the salary base, so if you have a current TS/SCI that could mean another $30-$45K in compensation (clearly negotiable).

2.   The Cost Of Living Adjustment (COLA) will also affect salary levels and ranges for the same job description in two different geographic areas. A job seeker seeking work in San Diego, CA, New York City, NY, Washington, D.C., or Honolulu, HI, where living expenses are exorbitant, will need to ask for 25-35% more in salary adjustments. If the job seeker is looking for the same job in Richmond, VA, Topeka, KS, or Asheville, NC the COLA would be more in common with the national average for that salary. There are other locations in the country where the salary and compensation would be below the national average.

3.   Talk to recruiters and headhunters (job fairs are great conversation starters). Ask them what the 'going rate' is for XYZ positions in geographic areas – regardless of the employer. Sometimes they can provide a 'safe range,' but in other cases they may not be able to discuss proprietary salary ranges. Sometimes a raise or a huge salary isn't the cash increase in a weekly paycheck, but additional values via perks or bonuses that increase the total compensation package offered by an employer. Examples include: tuition reimbursement, professional training or certifications, mentoring and coaching (internal or external), childcare, health and fitness (gym memberships), flexible work schedules, and/or paid parking or transportation (subway) fee reimbursement.

4.   Ask for a specific salary – not 'around $75,000,' but $75,250; research indicates this gets the hiring manager's more focused attention and increases the willingness to agree to that higher range. Ensure the requested salary is 'more' than you are willing to accept, so if the hiring company negotiates just a little lower, it still may be higher than your expectations, and you both win.

5.   Be sure to time the request for salary raises at a good time within employment tenure (perhaps after a huge contract win). Bring your personal work-related accomplishments and achievements to the

table that supports the increase in your compensation. Use a brag sheet to list the reasons you deserve the raise (or the new job) at this salary level. (This list should be updated monthly to add to the performance evaluation to bolster annual pay raise, also.)

6. Be prepared with well-rehearsed conversation starters and rebuttals. "I'm really excited to work here. M experience will bring an enormous value to your company workforce and strategic goals. I appreciate the offer of $68,000, but I was expecting the $82,000 range based on my experience, education, drive, and performance. Can we look at a salary of $75,000 for this position?" "Oh, you seem surprised at that amount – what actually is in your budget for this position?"

7. An article in Psychology Today indicated a research study concluded if you ask for a raise on a Thursday, you have a little bit higher percentage of success. Likewise, meeting with potential hiring managers on Thursdays means they are not under the Monday pressure to deal with issues and agendas on that back to workday, nor distracted by last-minute work on Fridays that need to be accomplished before they take off for the weekend.

8. Ask for the raise or higher salary with confidence. Act like a wimp and they won't take you seriously. Don't talk about your 'personal' needs – that sounds like begging.

Focus on achievements and future goals.
Go to the bathroom before you meet with
the supervisor or hiring manager, look in the
mirror, smile, stand up straight, give yourself
a pep talk, and then walk with confidence
into the interview or meeting with your boss.

9.   You will get resistance. Be prepared to 'walk
away' from a job you are seriously
interested in. Ask if the salary is at all
negotiable. If you are willing to walk away
from a salary, that indicates you know your
value to the hiring manager. That is the
worst case scenario. Be prepared for 'no'
from a current supervising manager if
asking for a raise. Don't threaten the power
that can make the decision if you don't get
what you want. If the answer is 'no, now,'
then ask when the salary can be discussed
in the future (if asking for a raise with the
current employer) and set up a calendar
date to meet again.

10.   Ask when the first performance evaluation
occurs, and would the budget be available
to get the new hire to the desired salary.
What is the average salary increase is for
the employees within the company or on
that level of compensation? What annual
bonuses are issued and what is the
average? Ask about future promotions and
salary increases. In some instances, a
company may not be able to provide the
salary range requested, but really want to
hire the job seeker. Human resources or
the department manager (or even the C-

suite executive) may be able to creatively come up with alternative solutions. One example would be to offer a hiring bonus or bonus for compensation for a specific project completion after 90 days, six months, or the completion of a portion of the project within a documentable time-related schedule.

LESSONS LEARNED

JOB SEARCH LESSONS-LEARNED FOR
GOVERNMENT CONTRACTING POSITIONS

A client of the author shared their 9-month job search within the federal government contracting industry in 2014. During the Obama Administration, these truths were pretty self-evident. While the Trump Administration has increased spending in the military arena, the goal is also to pull back on government oversight and regulations, discouraging spending (and hiring) in many agencies that are less vital overall. The author's client provided some interesting observations and 'lessons learned.' If you are seeking employment in the federal contracting industry, remember these points.

It is always easier to find a job – especially within your industry – if you already have a job. If you reach the point you are desperate in finding the job with the right salary – take what you can get 'now.' Then commit to working your job search like a part-time job after your regular job. With luck, the federal government contracting employment market will open up as the political climate changes. Keep plugging away, don't let yourself get sucked into the wrong direction because you are reaching the end of your rope.

1. Government contract numbers have been dramatically reduced in the last few years (2014-2019). Government contracting officers (GCOs) state some work will not be achieved, 'wish-lists' for upgraded equipment or services are on the back burner, or services totally cut. Reduction of work impacts the market, vendors, and profit margins. This isn't the same marketplace of 15-20 years ago during the first and second Gulf Wars when just about anyone could get a government contract and vendors were hiring breathing bodies left and right to perform the work on the contracts..

2. Cutbacks are compelling GCOs to 'milk' the situation in a buyer's market. There are many reports of 'after bid' changes (mods). Vendors aren't aware this is illegal and don't report mods to the oversight agency for fear of losing a contract. The small contractors eat the losses, often thousands from future contract work, as well as development costs for the bid. This seems to be consistent among Service Disabled Veteran Owned (SDVO) businesses (according to source). This means jobs are tenuous, short-lived, and job seekers may be back out on the street when a mod or contract was changed, and funding was reduced.

3. Contractors are forced to rescind contingency-on-contract-award, offer letters because of a contract mod (or the vendor pushes the start date into the future). This

forces seekers to look elsewhere for immediate employment. Job seekers should not put all their eggs in one basket. Accept all contingency-on-contract-award, offer letters – then wait for the first company to contact you for firm funding and the start date.

4. In the past (pre-2015), contracts were bid in five-year increments, with five-year options. The government has found it practical to start rebidding contracts annually. It is rare to find a contract with additional option years now. Job seekers in government contracting may find themselves 'job-hopping' when they move between companies, following a contract, or suddenly scrambling for a new job. Recruiters in the government contracting industry will overlook the 'short job tenures' – knowing it may not be the job seeker's fault that they had less than two years with the last three employers – because it's the nature of the beast in government contracting. (Some job seekers will actually note 'contract defunded' as a reason they left their last position on their resumes.)

5. Government contracting officers are required to find the best ROI for investment and award the contract to the lowest bidder with the highest value. They should accept a middle-bid and aim for a company providing 'added value' to the contract deliverables. Instead, GCOs award the 'lowest priced, technically acceptable'

(LPTA) bid. Larger companies (able to sustain financial losses) underbid contracts to get in the door (to seek added contracts). This leaves smaller companies unable to compete. This means job seekers may need to focus on the larger government contracting companies for their target employers versus the small 'new boy on the block' vendor. Companies who are 8(a) companies who may have just received a large five-year contract are a good target to search for jobs – those contracts will likely remain in place because of the 8(a) company status.

6.   Economics, newer contracting norms, and current 'contracting mods 'practices have forced workers to take 25-65% cuts in salaries and impacted competitive market salaries for job seekers' experience. If a seeker earned a salary between $90K-$120K years ago (pre-2015), they may only find jobs in the $45-60K salary range today. Job seekers may have to decide to take a lower salary. While the economy has improved since 2016, and the market is now a 'job seeker's market' for hiring due to many companies' inability to find qualified workers, job seekers need to do as much salary research as possible before they 'settle' for a lower salary.

7.   Job seekers tell the truth about past salaries. Tell recruiters, "I am willing to negotiate a reasonable salary." If a seeker was making $180K in a war zone (or

outside the continental United States;
OCONUS), the job seeker may only be able
to make $80K here in the states (inside the
continental United States; CONUS). Be
reasonable in salary requests.

8. Job seekers can also consider looking in a
similar industry. If past experience is in
logistics for military materiel, then look in the
maritime or inter-modal transportation and
shipping industry. Mature seekers need to
consider salary concessions for an entry-
level position to get into a new industry. The
employer doesn't care about 20 years of
experience if they can pay another
candidate $20K less with the minimum
qualifications.

9. A federal statute exists against age bias, but
mature seekers should their years of
experience are competing with 'just as
qualified' freshly transitioning veterans.
When considering salary, ask – are there
other qualified seekers willing to take less?
If the answer is yes, then the more mature
(in age) job seekers should focus on what
value added you can provide and is the
value added worth the salary price to
employers.

In the federal government hiring system,
veterans get 'points' that increase their
status in the queue of qualified candidates
for a position. If all else is equitable
(educational degrees, years of similar
experience, skill sets, etc.), then the veteran

will be considered 'higher' qualified based on their military service experience. To compete, job seekers have to have 'more' qualified and documentable assets and/or capabilities to 'beat' the points system for qualified veterans also applying for the position.

10.   When submitting resumes, ensure military-ese is transparent, as well as translated. Don't copy military performance evaluations into the resume. Rewrite those military-speak wording and language into language that the corporate world will understand. Reduce passive language (picked to do something versus 'did something') and cliché terms (in support of = what did you actually do?).

Even in the military there are accomplishments that can metricized similarly to the corporate world of achievements. Show capabilities with measurable and documentable metrics (performed XYZ, achieved ABC, resulting in increase of $XXX in revenue or XXX reduced man-hours).

If you work in the government contracting field with any tasking related to Human Resources, you NEED this guidebook to assist you in your job responsibilities:
Human Resource Professionals in Government Contracting Guidebook: http://amzn.to/2t3GMga

LOOK FOR THE CHAPTER SERIES
IN E-BOOKS ON AMAZON

- How To Change Careers
- Resignation - Giving Notice
- Education, Training, And Certifications To Enhance Your Job Capabilities To Land That Next Job
- Job Seeker Business Portfolios
- Must Have Job Skills
- How To Get Job Experience
- Equating Volunteering To Work Experience On Your Resume
- Avoiding Age Bias In The Job Search
- Creating Job Alerts
- First Steps After Losing A Job
- How To Determine The Best Salary For The Job
- How To Look For A Job On The Down Low
- Job Fair Advantages
- Job Overqualification And The Law And Job Seekers
- Job Search Steps And Resources
- Passive Job Search Activities And Preparation
- Reading And Interpreting Job Descriptions
- Researching Your Future Employer
- Researching Your Next 'Employer Of Choice'
- Resume Farming For Job Seekers
- Reviewing The Job Announcement

- Scam Job Announcements
- Using LinkedIn To Turn On A Job Search
- Obtaining References
- Leadership Wording In Resumes
- Degrees Vs On The Job Training – Resume Description
- Listing Technical Skills In A Resume
- What Not To Include In A Resume
- Resume Gaps – Addressing The Workforce Absence
- Resume Keywords & Language
- Making A Resume Automatic Tracking System Friendly
- How Far Back And How Much Job History
- How To Write A Cover Letter
- How And Why To Avoid Lying On Your Resume
- Formatting A Professional Resume
- Avoiding Filler And Passive Words In Your Resume By Substituting Action Verbs
- Metrics To Build Capability Believability
- Beating The ATS - Getting Past The Firewall
- Keep Your Resume Updated And Dynamic
- Types Of Resumes = Bio, Resume, CV = What Is The Difference?
- Elements Of A Perfect Cover Letter
- Creating Your First Resume - Elements To Include
- Why Recruiters Will Not Call You Back
- Converting Objective Statements To Years Of Experience Listing
- Filler (Killer) Words In Interviews
- Background Checks For Job Searches
- Speculation Work & Skills Testing

- Avoiding Answering Illegal To Ask Interview Questions
- Interview Preparation
- Benefits & Compensation Questions And Considerations
- Salary Negotiations
- Job Search Lessons-Learned For Government Contracting Positions

ABOUT THE AUTHOR

Dawn D. Boyer, Ph.D. completed her Doctor of Philosophy in Education (Occupational & Technical Studies, with a concentration in Training & Development in Human Resources) from Old Dominion University in Norfolk, VA in 2013. Her dissertation is entitled, 'Competencies of Human Resources Practitioners within the Government Contracting Industry,' which identified unique KSAs for Human Resources Managers working for federal level government contracting companies. This groundbreaking research was the impetus upon her textbook guide for Human Resources Professionals in Government Contracting, completed in 2017 and for sale on Amazon. This textbook was the cornerstone for the culmination of her 25+ years of work in the Human Resources and Recruiting field, including working for private sector and government contracting employers.

Dr. Boyer's current business offers job seekers Search Engine Optimized (SEO) resumes for increased visibility to recruiters – getting the candidates past the recruiting 'firewall' and connected for interviews for faster hires and job placement. Her tech-based knowledge of how ATS software systems work allows her to structure resumes for recruiters' Boolean search queries. Her SEO coding within resumes is so unique, no other resume writers offer this service. She also assists business owners develop their brand and marketing plans within social media marketing, planning, and management and as a mentor through the Small Business Administration's Senior Corps of Retired Executives (now simply referred to as SCORE).

She has been an entrepreneur and business owner for 25+ years, currently in her consulting firm, D. Boyer Consulting, near Richmond, VA, and servicing clients inside the United States and internationally. (At one point, more than half her clientele were in Afghanistan!). Her background experience is 24+ years in the Human Resources field, of which 11 years are within the federal defense contracting industry.

Dr. Boyer's experience in federal (defense) contracting as a Human Resources Director or Senior Manager has provided her insight, experience, practice, and capabilities to perform within this industry, as well as instruct others to abilities needed in middle-management or executive human resource roles. She assists (50 authors as of this publication date) academics and writers publish their works or manuscripts as a third-party publisher – DBC Publishing.

She is the author of 800+ books (as of December 2019) on the topics of business and job searches, career guides, genealogy, student study guides, Human Resources in Government Contracting Guidebook (textbook), over 200 family lineage (genealogy) books, adult education (andragogy), women and gender studies, business practices, memoirs, motivational quotes (2,000+ / 3,000+ series), 'Interview with an Artist' series, and over 110 illustrated adult coloring books.

HIRE THE AUTHOR FOR
PUBLISHING YOUR WORK

Interested in publishing your own academic essays,
projects, poetry, memoirs, or personal story?

Have you been compiling data in Family History
software and want to publish your family history or
lineage for sale online or gifts to your family?

Contact the author for publishing project estimates,
consulting, and assistance.

She may be reached
via her business website

D. Boyer Consulting
http: //DBoyerConsulting.com

or by email:
Dawn.Boyer@DBoyerConsulting.com

CONNECT WITH THE AUTHOR

Dr. Boyer is active on social media and invites readers to connect to her on social media. Follow her on LinkedIn to catch her weekly job search tip posts.

**Join her 13,600+
connections on LinkedIn**

www.linkedin.com/in/DawnBoyer

Dr. Boyer's books are listed on her Amazon author's page at:

www.amazon.com/author/dawnboyer.

ABOUT THE BOOK

This tip book on job searches is so valuable, it's as useful to the first job search after school as well it is for the more mature worker looking for that last job before retirement. No one should be a professional job seeker (constantly looking to switch jobs every 1-2 years). But, you do need to search for a job 'professionally.' This book helps make that happen.

This book is a compilation of 52 of the author's e-books on each topic related to job hunting, resume writing, searching for that new job, or switching careers. Dr. Boyers' quick tips in each chapter are easy to read, understand, and put into practice from that moment one decides to seek a new career position … to the handshake after an interview welcoming the qualified candidate onboard with the company.

Each chapter consists of 10 bulleted points in a concise and basic summary, with vital 'need-to-know' information about what to do, what to avoid, how to do something right, and advice on special ways to write a resume or act during an interview.

After reading this book, the reader should have an arsenal of 520 useful, practical, and powerful tips to use to ensure their job search is successful.